Daniel Moore

The Divine Authority of the Pentateuch Vindicated

Daniel Moore

The Divine Authority of the Pentateuch Vindicated

ISBN/EAN: 9783337778606

Printed in Europe, USA, Canada, Australia, Japan

Cover: Foto ©Lupo / pixelio.de

More available books at **www.hansebooks.com**

THE DIVINE AUTHORITY OF THE PENTATEUCH VINDICATED.

BY

DANIEL MOORE, M.A.

INCUMBENT OF CAMDEN CHURCH, CAMBERWELL,
AND TUESDAY MORNING LECTURER AT ST. MARGARET'S, LOTHBURY:

AUTHOR OF "THOUGHTS ON PREACHING," ETC.

LONDON:
BELL AND DALDY, 186 FLEET STREET.
1863.

PREFACE.

THE appearance of the present publication, in defence of an integral portion of our Sacred Writings, is mainly due to the pertinacity of error, in selecting for its renewed attacks, whether open or insidious, the credibility of the Mosaic record. Baffled, disarmed, put to confusion again and again, infidelity still holds fast by the conviction that this is the more vulnerable heel of the Christian system; saying to all who would go forth to do battle against the Scriptures, " Fight neither with small nor great, save only with this Book of the Law."

The latest specimen of the versatility of modern error, in adapting its methods of attack to the more sceptical appetencies of the times, has attached an unhappy notoriety to the name of the Bishop of Natal, —a prelate, who has taken advantage of his high position in the Church, and of his previous reputation in another line of study, to aim the more deadly blow against the ancient Scriptures. The feelings called forth by his book, whether those of apprehension for the mischief it might do, or those of indignation and astonishment at its ill-concealed impiety, may be considered, by this time, to have pretty well subsided. Appeal was made by the Bishop to the manly intelligence of the British nation, and the response has been given. By its most competent and accredited organs, the verdict of the public has been declared, both upon the author and his book. It pronounces a sentence upon the one of an unhonoured and speedy oblivion. It convicts the other of the sin of religious unfaithfulness, and the signal folly of having made a great mistake.

All this, however, furnishes the stronger reason why the occasion itself should be turned to some useful account. No time is better for looking to the state of our defences than after a repulsed attack. The citadel has withstood the shock nobly; and at its base, in piled confusion, lie the spent and harmless missiles of the foe. But a fuller acquaintance with the real extent of our strength may not be without its effect on both sides: on ours, by making us more prepared to guard against any future assaults; on that of the adversary, by so convincing him of the impregnable nature of the Christian evidence, that he will deem it the wiser course not to multiply assaults, from which nothing but discomfiture is likely to be gained.

In the belief that such a review of the GENERAL

EVIDENCE for the truth of the Old Testament histories would be useful at the present time, the ensuing chapters have been prepared. The persuasion was strong, in the Author's mind, that any force which may belong to modern objections against the Pentateuch, might be traced, in great measure, to the very imperfect acquaintance, among Christians generally, with the strength of cumulative evidence to be adduced on the positive and historic side. And our opponents have not been slow to take advantage of this ignorance. The sound principle, laid down by Bishop Butler and other great thinkers, that positive evidence can be overthrown only by evidence of its own or a like kind, has been altogether set at nought in modern controversy. The whole case of Revelation has been made to hinge upon certain antecedent conditions of likelihood. History, with its facts; miracle, with its proofs; prophecy, with its fulfilments,—are not to be heard in the courts of our "higher criticism." *That* only is considered to be religion which agrees with certain *à priori* conceptions of the human mind, and all is denounced as conjecture or baseless myth besides.

We have aimed, in these pages, to be more careful in fixing our principles, as well as to be more honest if, not more logical, in following them out. The line of reasoning pursued will be sufficiently apparent from the headings and outlines of the several chapters,

Well-worn and familiar as many of the arguments may appear to the practised student in theology, and with claims to originality, it may be, of the slenderest kind, yet to many of the intelligent and thoughtful laity, it is hoped, the book will not be wholly wanting in freshness, and may be found to present some aspects of the evidence for Revelation, which the current literature of the day has hitherto but imperfectly supplied.

Nor is the Author without hope that such a publication may be of some service to his younger brethren in the ministry. Possessed of many notes on the general subject of Christian evidence,—some on this very Pentateuchal history, collected during the period of student-life,—he felt it might be in his power to supply a want, not unfrequently felt by those who have but few books and but little time to read,—namely, a presentment of the main argument for the authenticity of our Old Testament Scriptures in a tangible and compendious form. That his book may mark out for Biblical students a line of useful reading, and stimulate them to seek access to larger works, is both his object and his earnest hope. His own obligations to these treasures of our sacred literature will be more or less apparent throughout the work; and, as a rule, have been specifically acknowledged. But the accessible sources of information on the credibility and Divine authenticity of the Mosaic record extend far beyond the citations here made, and to a few of these the student may not be sorry to have his attention directed. Thus, on the subject of the EXTERNAL Evidence, in addition to the chapters devoted to its consideration in the works of Leland, Lardner, and Bishop Tomline, it may be proper to specify such works as the *Origines Sacræ* of Bishop Stillingfleet; the *Connection of the Old and New Testament* of Dean Prideaux; the treatise of *Josephus against Apion*; the *Horæ Mosaicæ* of Mr. Faber; the recent *Bampton Lecture* of Mr. Rawlinson, together with the modern continental works of Hengstenberg and Havernick.

On the INTERNAL Evidences, enough will be found in the valuable work of Dean Graves on *The Pentateuch*; the late Professor Blunt's *Undesigned Coincidences*; Bishop Marsh's *Authenticity of the Five Books of Moses*; and the section on this subject contained in the well-known *Introduction* of the Rev. T. H. Horne. The ingenious work of Bishop Warburton also, apart from the peculiar views of the writer, will be found to contain, on this branch of the evidence, much striking and original argument.

On the history and transmission of the sacred record the student will consult with profit Bishop Gray's *Key to the Old Testament*; Dr. Brett's "Dissertation on the Ancient Versions of the Bible," published in the third volume of *Watson's Theological*

Tracts; Stackhouse's *History of the Bible;* the *Lectures on Biblical Criticism,* by Mr. Davidson; and the *Critical History and Defence of the Old Testament Canon,* by Professor M. Stuart.

At the close of the volume will be found an Appendix, dealing, in as compressed and succinct a form as possible, with the specific objections of Bishop Colenso. Writers of this class nearly all fall into the same mistake. They entirely overlook the peculiarities of Eastern character; seem unable to regard the history from the stand-point of Hebrew or Asiatic life;· forget, in fact, that *the Bible is an Oriental book.* A learned modern Jew has thus expressed himself in reference to the Bishop's work : " The Doctor is evidently deficient in the power of divesting himself for the time of his modern Western notions and mode of viewing things, and adapting himself to the Eastern mind and fashion, such as they were at the period and in the country of the writer of the Pentateuch. The Doctor's mind is clearly deficient in poetical apprehension. Long study of mathematics and the severe logic of exact science, to which the course of his thoughts has become habituated, have fixed his mind on the strict letter and logical sequence of ideas, and have, in this respect, narrowed it. Accustomed to employ no terms, except those of which he was prepared to give a clear definition, such as is approved of in science, he applies the same standard to persons, to whom such habits of thought and trains of ideas were strangers."[1]

It was the Author's primary wish to have written upon the subject of the Pentateuch, without any reference to this recent collection of short-lived and superficial cavils. But the leading portion of the work, now offered to the public, was delivered in the form of sermons to the writer's ordinary congregation. And as the unhappy notoriety of the Bishop's objections made it impossible to omit all notice of them from the pulpit, so the acceptableness, to his hearers, of the explanations offered made it inexpedient to exclude these brief refutations from the volume.

Whether, in relation to modern controversies or not, however, the subject itself has an undying interest. The adversary has by no means overrated its importance, whether to the Church of Christ, or to the world at large. Not its importance to the world; for the Pentateuch is the foundation of all morals, all literature, all legislation, all history. The Decalogue of Moses is the code of the world's jurisprudence. The Sabbath of Moses is the sabbath of the world's rest. The Messiah of Moses is the central object of the world's hope; and the Genesis of Moses gives the

[1] *Colenso's Objections Examined:* Dr. A. Benisch, Intro. p. xi.

only reasonable account of the origin of the world's existence. Neither in its importance to the Church has this ancient work been over-estimated. For it is the pillar and ground of the truth; the shrine of the primeval revelations; the outline of God's first thoughts and final purposes to our race; in short, to quote the words of one, whom rationalists are not slow to honour, " all the history, prophecy, proverbial wisdom of Israel, has its root and being in the law of Moses. Deuteronomy is the Deuterosis (repetition) of the law; and all the other parts of Old Testament Scripture is the Deuterosis of Deuteronomy. Though David was a greater master of lyric song, and Isaiah of the prophetic word, than Moses, yet, without the law of Moses, there had been neither a David, nor an Isaiah. And we abide by the undeniable fact, that the Law, however it may have arisen, is as necessarily presupposed by the whole of the post-Mosaic history and literature, as for a tree is the sustaining and nourishing root." [1]

The Author is quite aware that, in relation both to the external and the internal evidence in favour of the Pentateuch, much more might be adduced, and, indeed, ought to have been adduced, if a complete view of the subject had been in contemplation. Thus,

[1] Delitzsch, *Comment über Gen.* p. 12.

a more extended examination would have shewn that each one of the five books could boast its separate array of proofs, over and above those which belonged to them in their aggregate and collective form. But the proof of this would have required a volume, much larger than either the writer had time to prepare, or than, on such a subject, he thinks the public would care to read. He has, therefore, confined himself to a summary: full enough he hopes for the Biblical student, to direct him in a course of larger reading,— suggestive enough to general readers, to enable them, at least for all the purposes of their own practical comfort and conviction, to think out the subject for themselves.

D. M.

Camberwell, April 20, 1863.

CONTENTS.

SECTION I.

PRELIMINARY OBSERVATIONS ON THE FORMS OF MODERN SCEPTICISM.

Intellectual activity of the age — Religious subjects not excepted. — The Church wounded by her friends. — Considerations in mitigation of public uneasiness on this account. — I. Scepticism had been long working in the popular mind. — Essays and Reviews. — The sceptical element in modern literature. — II. Modern Scepticism the reproduction of the infidelity of a former age. — Progress of sceptical opinion — in England, — in France, — in Germany. — III. Prevailing tone of Continental criticism. — Directed especially against the Mosaic record. — Reasons for the selection of this part of revelation. — The science of historic criticism. — Unfairness of modern attacks upon revelation . 1

SECTION II.

EXTERNAL TESTIMONY TO THE CREDIBILITY OF THE MOSAIC HISTORY.

Preliminary inquiry. — To what class of composition does the Pentateuch belong ? — Every book to be judged of by its avowed design. — Revelation designed for our salvation. — I. External testimonies to the facts of the Mosaic History. — Connexion of Jewish History with that of the principal nations of the earth. — Corroborations of the Mosaic account from the earliest documentary sources. — Testimonies of Berosus and Manetho. — Testimonies from Grecian and Roman authors, — Strabo, Justin, Tacitus. — II. Coincidence of the Mosaic records with the ancient mythologies.—Instanced in the different accounts of the Creation, the Fall, and the Deluge.—Legends of the Chaldeans, Egyptians, Persians,—our own Scythian forefathers. — III. Evidence from outward and visible commemorations of important events in Jewish history.— Leslie's four verifying tests.—The process explained—applied to the case of the destruction of the firstborn, or the departure out of Egypt.—IV. Corroborative testimony of Josephus.—His qualifications as a trustworthy historian.—Summary of the argument from external testimony 14

SECTION III.

TESTIMONIES TO CREDIBILITY AFFORDED BY THE BOOKS THEMSELVES.

Division of evidence into external and internal.—I. Literary characteristics of the Mosaic record—Archaisms of expression—peculiar language of the Pentateuch. II. Local and historical knowledge of the writer — Acquaintance with Egyptian life and habits— References to extinct Canaanitish races. III. Minuteness of detail in the narrative—instanced in marches, and encampments. —The genealogical records of the Pentateuch. IV. Personal character of the Author of the Pentateuch—i. He was a thoroughly competent man—ii. An utterly unselfish man—iii. An honest and impartial man. V. Verisimilitude of the narrative—i. Seen in its illustrations of Hebrew life and character.—ii. In undesigned coincidences. VI. Moses the bearer of a Divine legation—i. His pure system of Theology — ii. The success of his enterprise— iii. The Hebrew commonwealth placed under an extraordinary providence 37

SECTION IV.

THE SECURITIES FOR THE GENUINENESS AND SAFE TRANSMISSION OF THE BOOKS.

Importance of uncorruptness in the documents. I. History of the preservation of the sacred writings—in the Ark—in the Temple —Collection and collation of copies by Ezra after the Captivity— the Samaritan Pentateuch—change in the Hebrew character—

destruction of the copies by Antiochus Epiphanes.—The new edition of Judas Maccabeus—its probable loss at the Siege of Jerusalem.—The Septuagint translation. II. The history of the documents traced by a retrogressive method to the time of the Captivity—to the time of the division of the kingdoms—to the time of Joshua. III. The official custody of the documents— the generally diffused knowledge of its contents.—The Targums. —The traditional veneration for the writings of the people themselves 64

SECTION V.

THE PENTATEUCH A REVELATION FROM GOD.

Three degrees of truth in a document. I. The highest form of truth assumed in the writings themselves.—Moses claims to be the oracle of GOD. II. The books always accepted as Divine by the Jews—seen in the titles given to them—confirmed by the authors of the Apocrypha—so regarded by later Jewish writers. III. The Divine authority of the books always assumed in the New Testament.—The testimony of Apostles and Evangelists.—The testimony of the LORD Jesus Christ Himself.—How the force of this testimony has been evaded. IV. The Divine authority of the Pentateuch allowed in every age of the Christian Church—by the early Fathers—from the time of the Reformation downwards 85

SECTION VI.

THE INSPIRED AUTOGRAPH AND THE HUMAN COPY.

All Scripture given by inspiration of God—I. What is inspiration— definitions of Lee and Gaussen—no authoritative definition—in- spiration of different kinds—danger of theories of inspiration.— II. Inspiration claimed for the inspired autographs only—Trans- lations of the Scriptures—various readings—their unimportance —probability of minor interpolations—the Elohistic and Jeho- vistic titles of the Divine Being.—IV. The possible use by the sacred writers of uninspired sources of information—always under the direction of the Holy Ghost—The perfect security for a divinely authenticated revelation 104

SECTION VII.

AUXILIARY EVIDENCES.

I. MIRACLE—intuitive force of the argument from miracle—constantly appealed to in Revelation itself—miracle a special object of Infidel attack—assumption that a miracle is impossible—unfairness of sceptical controversy in relation to miracles—miracles possible, and the true evidence of a Divine mission.— II. PROPHECY—prophecy an evidence for the later ages of the world—Mosaic prophecies—The curse on Canaan—predictions with regard to the Arab tribes—admission of Gibbon—The Messianic prophecies—prophecies relating to the Jews themselves—their present condition—The Jew a witness to all time.— III. THE CONNECTION OF THE DISPENSATIONS—the adaptative character of the Levitical and Christian dispensations—Force of the argument from adaptation—The argument of the Epistle to the Hebrews—The Gospel the germination or development of the Law 129

SECTION VIII.

MODERN OBJECTIONS — FORCE OF THE ARGUMENT FROM ADMITTED DIFFICULTIES.

I. Special repudiation of the book of Genesis—alleged difference of authorship of the first eleven chapters—Genesis the foundation of all the other Mosaic books—frequent quotations from the earlier chapters, both from the later books of the Old Testament and in the books of the New. II. Alleged disagreement of Scripture with the facts and discoveries of science—Objections of Geologists—Objections founded on alleged facts of history or antiquities—common source of these apparent disagreements. III. The argument from admitted difficulties—Difficulties often referable to the brief and condensed form of the narrative—to the remote antiquity of the time with which it deals—to our limited knowledge of the original language—difficulties subservient to the interests of revelation itself 160

SECTION IX.

RECAPITULATION — CONCLUSION.

The general course of the argument — The difficulties which beset philosophical infidelity — The loss of the Mosaic record would leave a void in universal history — Duty of being prepared for future attacks — The spirit in which the subject should be approached 184

APPENDIX:

OR, REMARKS ON SOME RECENT OBJECTIONS, PARTICULARLY THOSE OF BISHOP COLENSO.

Introduction — First objection. The beating of the Slave — Second objection. The Family of Judah — Third objection. The Size of the Court of the Tabernacle — Fourth objection. Moses and Joshua addressing all Israel — Fifth objection. The Extent of the Camp compared with the Priest's Duties — Sixth objection. The Number of the People compared with the Poll-Tax. Seventh objection. The Israelites dwelling in Tents — Eighth objection. The Israelites Armed — Ninth objection. The Institution of the Passover — Tenth objection. The March out of Egypt — Eleventh objection. The Sheep and Cattle of the Israelites in the Desert — Twelfth objection. The Number of the Israelites, and the Extent of Canaan — Thirteenth objection. The Number of the First-born and Adults — Fourteenth objection. The Sojourning of the Israelites in Egypt — Fifteenth objection. The Exodus in the Fourth Generation — Sixteenth objection. The Number of the Israelites at the Exodus — Seventeenth objection. The Danites and Levites at the time of the Exodus — Eighteenth objection. The Number of the Priests and their Duties — Nineteenth objection. The Priests and the Celebration of the Passover — Twentieth objection. The War on Midian — Sum of the series of objections — Earnest appeal to Bishop Colenso — awful responsibility attaching to sceptical publications — Conclusion.

                                              So I fared,
Dragging all precepts, judgments, maxims, creeds,
Like culprits to the bar ; calling the mind
Suspiciously to establish in plain day
Her titles and her honours ; now believing,
Now disbelieving ; endlessly perplexed
With impulse, motive, right and wrong, the ground
Of obligation, what the rule and whence
The sanction : till demanding formal proof
And seeking it in everything, I lost
All feeling of conviction ; and, in fine,
Sick, wearied out with contrarieties,
Yielded up moral questions in despair."
                                    WORDSWORTH.

" Every man may be allowed to say that he will not believe without sufficient evidence; but none can, without great presumption, pretend to stipulate for any particular kind of proof, and refuse to attend to any other, if that which he may think he should like best should not be set before him. This is, indeed, the very spirit of infidelity."—BISHOP HORSLEY.

THE DIVINE AUTHORITY OF THE PENTATEUCH.

SECTION I.

PRELIMINARY OBSERVATIONS ON THE FORMS OF MODERN SCEPTICISM.

" And though all the winds of doctrine were let loose to play upon the earth, so Truth be on the field, we do injuriously, by licensing and prohibiting, to misdoubt her strength. Let her and Falsehood grapple: who ever knew Truth put to the worse in a fair encounter? Her confuting is the best and surest suppression."—MILTON.

WE live in an age of great intellectual activity; and that, in relation to every department of human thought. Against the intrusion of this spirit Religion has no reserved rights. If exercised fairly, she desires to have none. She challenges investigation; dares the manly argument to the encounter; fears not "this rocking of the battlements," knowing that her foundations can never be moved. All error is short-lived. It will have its day, and live through its day. But truth is immortal. It partakes of the eternity of its Author, and must outlive all its foes.

Moreover, that active and searching spirit, which some are disposed to condemn, is due, in great measure, to the general advancement of society, in all departments of knowledge; to the progress of science; to the diffusion of cheap literature; to the extent of our commercial and political relations; and to that widened spread of education, which, during the last half century especially, religious men have been the foremost to promote.

Still, in the manifestations of this sceptical or inquiring spirit, some things have taken place for which we were not quite prepared. The attacks upon the truth have come from a new and unexpected quarter. Religion has been wounded in the house of her friends. Of many modern assailants of Revelation, the Church may complain truly, that they are not open enemies that have lifted up the heel against her, but men who were brought up in her bosom; who did eat at her table; who drew, from her altars, both life and the means to live. "She nursed the pinion that impelled the steel."

Such things, occurring in the history of the Church of Christ, could not fail to discourage some, and to alarm many more. People doubted, and inquired one of another, "whereunto this would grow." To see men of mark for their ability, and scholarship, and goodness, and outward devotedness to the cause of Christ, falling away from the faith; to observe, among the teachers and guides of our youth, the repudiation of all reverence for ancient truth, as if, in its traditional and accepted forms, Christianity were a thing of the past; to find that by men, occupying high official positions, the dear truth of ages was being degraded to the rank of a peradventure, and not unfrequently to something lower than this; in a word, to find that by means of books, and sermons, and lectures,—some from professors' chairs, and now one even from a Bishop's throne,—men were scattering broadcast the seeds of unbelieving thought,—no man forbidding them,—all this was enough to fill devout minds with much uneasiness, and may at least excuse those who allowed themselves in some transient misgivings for the safety of the Ark of God.

Some considerations to be offered in this section will perhaps help to show that, in relation to these recent sceptical efforts, there is very little cause for religious alarm, and not very much occasion for surprise.

I. FIRST, we deem it of some importance to note that the more recent efforts of scepticism are but the outward expression of thoughts which had been *working in many minds* A LONG TIME BEFORE.

About three years ago, appeared the notorious volume, entitled *Essays and Reviews*. A combination of accidental circumstances attracted towards this book a measure of public notice, which, we may believe, surprised none more than the authors themselves. As a literary effort, it was slight; as a specimen of academic scholarship, it was unworthy; as an agency for effecting a revolution in the theology of the nation, it was inadequate, ill-considered, and, in many respects, entirely behind the age. Yet the book created a panic in some circles. The foundations of revealed truth were supposed by many to be giving way. And at the sight of seven men, bound together by nothing but a vow to initiate a new movement for "the free-handling" of the Word of God, "the isle was frighted from its propriety." From all this we may be said to have pretty well recovered. But "one woe is past; and, behold, there come two woes more hereafter." Ought we to have been unprepared for this? Clearly not. Emanating from such sources, these sceptical productions are ominous signs of the times, no doubt. But they are not the primary cause of the evil. This lies deeper, more concealed, is more subtle in its working, and more widely spread. Thoughts, like those by which all devout minds have been recently shocked, have, in loose and unsystematized form, been floating in men's minds for some years past,—the impalpable phantoms of a new and yet to be adjusted faith, to which they might give understanding, but at present no tongue.

Many of these flitting forms of scepticism,—the shreds and patches of old misbeliefs,—had first presented themselves to the religious imagination through the medium of our popular literature. This great source of the national intelligence had become impregnated with the poison widely and deeply. We may not go so far as a writer in the *Westminster Review*, who says, that the whole mental food of the day,—science, history, morals, poetry, fiction, and essay,—is prepared by men who have long ceased to have any faith in revelation. But we fear it would not be difficult to name certain writers of eminence, in most of these departments, whose pages bear traces of a Christianity much too lightly esteemed, and exhibit the smouldering embers of an out-dying faith in anything which professes to be the declared truth of God. At all events, in relation to the particular forms of pernicious teaching we have now to complain of, we know that we had them in our secular literature, long before the time, when, aided by the usurped authority of gown and bands,—rochet and lawn,—they were put forth with all the pretensions and sanction of a theology. Bunsen could not write upon "Archæology" without asking us, in effect, to put our Bibles under a bushel; nor Buckle, upon "Civilization," without making assumptions which would cast God out of His own world. Professor Stephen will not give his eloquent "Essays" to the world, without surmises which strike at the root of our cardinal Christian verities; while Darwin is prepared to make all nature a God to herself, in order that he may propound a new theory on the "Origin of Species."

From works of this class the transfusion of the sceptical element to secular literature of a lighter and cheaper kind, was easy and natural. The plague had begun. All classes had caught the distemper. The poor at their clubs, the young in their debates, the rich at their convivial tables, university students in their common-rooms, were all heard insinuating hesitative doubts as to the Divine facts of Revelation,—doubts, and often something more. The public mind was evidently ripening for a comprehensive scheme of unbelief. All that was wanting was something to give it authority, status, weight. Infidelity, as such, would never find favour with the English nation. Better that it have its hierarchy,—ministers to serve at its stripped and dismantled altars, and articles for its pantheistic creed.

Modern sceptical writings are the result of this state of things, as well as an instalment of something yet to come. But great as the evil of it may be, is it so great as that of a deep underground misbelief, working its silent way beneath our homes, our schools, our very churches,—felt to be shaking the fabric of the faith, but never suffering itself to be seen? If the seeds of a pernicious poison have found their way into the religious heart of any considerable section of the community, ought we not to rejoice that something has happened to bring the symptoms to the surface? It is only of late that the stalking form of Infidelity has come in such "a questionable shape," that, like Hamlet, we could speak to it. It has enfolded itself in a cloud of words; or it has lain in ambush between two chapters of an innocent and attractive book; or it has disguised itself under the veil of a little playful irony; or it has let loose its Parthian arrow from the string, and fled. But now it stands forth. And, therefore, "be its intents wicked or charitable," they shall be avowed and met. Incensed, as we had been, at the masked and stealthy assaults which have continually been made upon Revelation, our wish had almost taken the form of Job's wish : " Oh ! that mine adversary had written a book ! " And the wish has been answered.

II. We observe, SECONDLY, as tending to alleviate any fears on account of this outbreak of modern scepticism, that the objections which have been put forth are for the most part OF THE OLDEST AND MOST FAMILIAR KIND.

Objections have been started, in the history of the Church, which, while they remained unanswered, were fairly calculated to inspire uneasiness. They had, for the time, the recommendation of novelty; and the opponent seemed to have got upon unbroken ground. Such, for example, was the alleged discovery of Eastern records, running back many ages beyond any probable date which could be assigned for Noah's flood ; or the supposed contradiction to the Mosaic history, said to be found on certain monumental remains in Egypt; or, we may add, the impression produced, on their first announcement, of the generally accepted deductions of geological science, as being incompatible with the Scripture account of the creation. True, the fears raised by these apparently adverse testimonies have since become entirely dissipated. One after another the objections died away before the light of advancing information, or a sounder scholarship, or a higher science. But still, until it was satisfactorily proved, either that the facts of science had been misapplied or the actual teaching of Scripture had been misunderstood, the very novelty of the objections gave them force. It seemed as if Revelation were being exposed to a new form of hostile encounter, and that new weapons would have to be sought in order to the resistance of its attacks.

We have not this fault to find with our neo-scepticism, at all events. If we except its outward form and accessories, its greater parade of scholarship, its air of scientific candour, its more minute dissection of details,— it offers little in the way of objection to our sacred records, with which the Christian world has not been, in the main, familiar more than a century ago. We have Paine without his coarseness; Hume, observant of the dignity of an academic chair; Bolingbroke, restrained within the limits of civil and decorous speech. But the points selected for attack remain the same,— miracle, inspiration, prophecy, historic truth, and the reality of any preternatural communication from God to man. And the genesis, or geographical course, of infidel opinion, during the last century and a half, as traced out by an able modern writer,[1] is very note-worthy. Beginning with

[1] *Rationalism and Deistic Infidelity*, pp. 10–20. By Dr. M'Caul, 1861.

the English Deists of the seventeenth and eighteenth centuries, it was taken up and nursed by Voltaire, D'Alembert, and their fellow-labourers in France; from them it was incorporated into the rationalistic systems of Germany; and out of those systems another scepticism — which is not another — has been vamped and furbished up for English use again. A strange phase of international commerce, but not the less true. We first send out the raw material of our country's infidelity; and afterwards, when it has been worked up by German hands into more scientific form, we take our native produce back.

III. THIRDLY, as against any surprise which might be felt at the effects of modern scepticism, we observe that the old artifice of infidelity, of " attacking Christianity through the sides of Judaism," has been greatly encouraged by THE PREVAILING TONE OF CONTINENTAL CRITICISM, especially as directed against the facts recorded in the Books of Moses.

This ancient collection of writings, as every one knows, has been the battle-field for controversy in all ages, almost from the days of the Apostles until now. We can hardly wonder at this. There were points of attack on this side of the evidence for Revelation, where the adversary would have us at some advantage. For, in the first place, the books must be their own evidence. Their historic domain was for the most part unique. Whether, to affirm or to deny their statements, no other records could be appealed to, professing to give an account of creation and its primeval facts; neither, apart from these writings, have we any contemporaneous literature, illustrative of the infancy and childhood of mankind. Itself the basis and rudiment of all history, the Pentateuch has rather to *give* light. It can be only in a secondary sense that it has any light to receive.

And this suggests another reason why it was likely that the sceptic would select for his attack the Mosaic record. The book lay at the foundation of our revealed system. He saw that he had only to make a wide and effective breach there, and the entire fabric would be shaken. True, an opponent will sometimes assure us " he meaneth not so." It has been a fashion of modern rationalism to pretend that the Mosaic institutes are only a sort of decayed and superfluous outbuilding; and to urge, that if every vestige of them were swept away, the grand structure of Christianity would remain in all its solidity and all its strength. But we have not so learned Christ. The whole body of Revelation is a perfect unity, an organised and cohering whole of Divine truth, " fitly joined together and compacted by that which every joint supplieth;" insomuch, that not only Moses cannot say to the prophets, "I have no need of you;" but even the Divine Founder of Christianity will not allow Himself to say of Moses, "I have no need of thee;" saying as He does to the Jews, "For had ye believed Moses, ye would have believed me: for he wrote of me."

But what has been the characteristic feature of these modern attacks upon our sacred records? Why, without neglecting the opportunity of disinterring many a long-buried, and, as we had supposed, long-silenced objection, scepticism has introduced a piece of new cloth into the old garment, by alleging generally, against the earlier Bible narratives, that they are *unhistoric;* are the legendary and unreal creations of the world's minority; that, though possibly having some slender basis of traditional fact, as a rule, they can only be regarded as belonging to the department of poetic myth.

The course of modern reading and thought, particularly on the Continent, greatly favoured this form of sceptical attack. A new science had, within the last century, sprung up among literary men,—not before it was needed, perhaps, and certainly capable of many useful and important applications. We allude, as will be supposed, to the science of "Historical criticism,"—the agreement, among exact and unprejudiced thinkers, as to certain canons of literary interpretation, which should enable us, in reading the professed annals of a country, to part off the respective territories of fact and fiction; should help us to eliminate the fabulous element from some of our school-book histories: in a word, should teach us to separate the legendary period, which is probably the early normal stage of all nations, from that at which authentic records may be looked for, and true history begins.

For consolidation and reduction to something of a scientific system, the new science was no doubt greatly indebted to Niebuhr; though, to his honour be it spoken, he never applied the principles of it in attempts to mythicise the Divine facts of Revelation.[1] This unenvied distinction he left for his followers — to be earned by Bunsen and his Oxford sponsors, in the denial of historic credibility to the narratives of the Old Testament; by Strauss, and a host of imitators, who are wont to relegate to a limbo of dream and rhapsody the most cherished and sacred realities of the Gospel.

No doubt, however, can exist but that, by the wider and more general cultivation of the principles of historic criticism, the cue was given for a new and more specious attack upon Revelation. The Bible was a written document, and it must be subjected to the ordeal of documentary tests and laws; its authenticity sifted; its reasonableness examined; its congruousness with fact, with probability, with other known truth, left to be tried as we should try that of any other book.

---

[1] See a noble testimony to Niebuhr's views on this subject in Mansel's *Bampton Lectures*, pp. 321-2. "In my opinion," he says, "he is not a Protestant Christian who does not receive the historical facts of Christ's early life, in their literal acceptation, with all their miracles as equally authentic with any event recorded in history."

Have its friends anything to urge against this? Nothing whatever; so only that the principles of investigation be fairly applied: that is, so applied as not to override those other and older laws of literary criticism, which were in use among scholars, before the term "historic science" had been heard of. But herein, as we venture to think, consists the utter unreasonableness of modern infidelity, in its dealings with Holy Scripture. It raises difficulties; it starts objections; it hunts out apparent discrepancies, and then proceeds to argue upon these adverse appearances as if there were no positive evidence on the other side. Now, as Bishop Butler teaches, "probabilities to us are the guide of life." They must be our guides in the search after truth also. And therefore, when, in this search, the contest lies between two sets of probabilities—the one arising from *testimony*, on the sufficiency of which we can pronounce with confidence, and the other arising from *surmises*, which, on account of our limited information, we cannot prove to have any foundation at all—it is the part of argumentative honesty to exhibit these conflicting probabilities together. Modern scepticism never does this. Its reasoning is always one-sided. We have not, as in all fairness we ought to have, so much conjecture weighed against so much testimony; but we have the whole weight of infidel objection balanced against an empty scale. The object of our succeeding chapters will be to weigh the claims of Revelation in a more righteous balance.

SECTION II.

EXTERNAL TESTIMONY TO THE CREDIBILITY OF THE MOSAIC HISTORY.

"The truth of our religion, like the truth of common matters, is to be judged of by all the evidence taken together. And unless the whole series of things which may be alleged in this argument, and every particular thing in it, can reasonably be supposed to have been by accident (for here the stress of the argument for Christianity lies), then is the truth of it proved."— BISHOP BUTLER.

IN entering upon the task, proposed at the close of the last section, our first duty will be to look at the evidence for the credibility of the Pentateuch as viewed from its historic side; in other words, to call attention to the strength, and variety, and fulness of those external testimonies, by which we vindicate the authenticity of the record, and prove its sufficiency for all the purposes for which it was given to mankind.

This last attribute of the document, however, will force upon us a preliminary inquiry. What kind of composition is the Pentateuch, or what, upon its own shewing, does it profess to be?

In an investigation like the present, this question will be seen to be of vital moment. We take it to be an accepted law of literary criticism, that every book should be judged of according to the class of literature to which it avowedly belongs, or the specific object for which it was written. Take an example. If you put a professed history into my hands,—a story of the fortunes of a particular nation, and supposed to be the production of one mind,—I judge of it by the rules of historic writing. I expect to find in it methodical arrangement, an orderly sequence of events, chronological consistency, adequate appliances specified for everything which might be startling in the relation, and no particulars kept back which might be essential to a thorough understanding of the facts. Does the Bible profess to be a book of this sort? Nothing of the kind. It is a collection of different tractates; composed at different periods; penned by many different hands; and, in subservience to its own primal design, intended often for different specific ends. Hence the great difference of character and style in the writings: —according, as in the Mosaic books, they contain fragmentary glimpses of the past, going up to prehistoric times; or compilations from public or family records, needful for the settlement of tribal immunities and rights; or codes of legislation, wholly or in part, to endure for all time; or taking the subsequent writings, according as they deal with prophecy, with biography, with morals, with sacred song, with whatever might furnish materials of faith and hope, of devotion and piety, to all who were looking forward to the coming of the world's Redeemer.

It follows, therefore, that a book thus composed cannot be judged of according to the precise laws of a regular history; and, consequently, that no exception could be justly taken to it, even if it were proved to be deficient in that statistical accuracy, or descriptive fulness, or logical distribution of materials, or philosophical precision of thought and expression, which the demands of historic writing require. As to Moses, so far from regarding him chiefly as the historian, though he is the oldest of historians, our conventional forms of speech commonly refer to him as the lawgiver. Yet he neither enters into all the reasons of those laws, as a Montesquieu might do, nor consolidates them into a systematic code, such as the Pandects of Justinian; but he scatters them up and down the surface of an irregular and broken treatise, making them, in evident subordination to his paramount design, at one time to give place to the resumed thread of his narrative, and at another to some affecting expostulation with the people, on account of their ingratitude to the Most High.

And, on this understood disregard by the author, of all technical or scientific plan, do we claim that the Mosaic writings should be received. We accept, in this view, the challenge that has been made to us, to deal with the Bible as we would deal with any other book. We neither expect metaphysics from Chaucer, nor poetry from Coke, nor information on physical science from Froissart. Each had his design, and by the harmony of his composition with the principles of that design, the work of each has to be judged. Apply the same rule to the Scriptures. Judge of each several book, according to its avowed purpose and intention. And not giving much heed to the fact, whether some statistics be rightly computed here, or some event be dislocated from its proper order there, inquire whether the whole collection of writings, as they stand, fulfils their manifest object, which is, to illustrate the Divine government as seen in the progress of the Jewish nation, and to reveal, in the person of the expected Messiah, a scheme of redemption for mankind. The leading subject of the Bible, we must ever remember, is our salvation. With this the book of Genesis opens, in the promise of a victorious seed to the first mother of our race. With this the book of Revelations closes, in the words,—" And the Spirit and the Bride say Come, And let him that heareth say, Come. And let him that is athirst come. And whosoever will, let him take the water of life freely."

The point determined, to what class of literary composition the Pentateuch shall be considered to belong, we may proceed to the point more immediately before us,—the amount and kind of external testimony to be cited in favour of the veracity of the Mosaic history.

All antiquity, Jewish and Heathen, is in favour of the fact, that the Hebrew nation was favoured with a Revelation from God; that the Jewish religion, in its more settled and extensive form, was originally introduced by Moses; and that it continued in Canaan for about 1500 years before it gave place to Christianity. If history and documental evidence can be believed in anything, it may be believed in this. The Divine legislation of Moses, being the most remarkable fact in that dispensation,—the bond of national separateness, and itself incorporated into the whole structure and habits of Jewish life,—has been brought before us with every possible variety of attestation that the subject admits of. The Jews are their own witnesses, and possess a world-wide historical renown;—having been mixed up with the transactions of the most celebrated nations of the earth, with the Egyptians, the Phœnicians, the Chaldeans, the Persians, the Grecians, the Romans, with every nation who might see in them a tempting prize for their political ambition, or to whose friendly aid they might themselves apply to obtain deliverance from the invader's power. In this way, the Jewish annals may be said to have points of contact with universal history. The great lawgiver himself is the hero-property of all time; and an acquaintance with the chief occurrences of his history is a knowledge that pervades the world.

We proceed to some proofs of this; and, first,—

I. To the testimonies, in corroboration of the

Mosaic record, derived FROM THE EARLIEST DOCUMENTARY SOURCES.

The exact period at which the art of writing became first known in the world cannot be determined. Time was when De Wette, and others of the rationalistic school, deemed that a proof conclusive against the received authorship of the Pentateuch was to be found in the fact, that the art of writing was not known to the Hebrews until the time of the Judges. The ground has been abandoned; and, even by the originators themselves, the objection based upon it withdrawn.[1] All probability is in favour of the Jews being well acquainted with the art of writing when they quitted Egypt. Moses was "learned in all the wisdom of the Egyptians;" and among them, not only have we the evidence of hieroglyphical inscriptions upon stone, as early as B.C. 2450, but also of writings upon papyrus, both in the hieroglyphic and the hieratic characters, coincident with the commonly assumed date of the Mosaic record.[2] From the Chaldæans, also, it is probable that the Jews would derive some knowledge of an alphabetic system, the art being known to that people before the migration of Abraham.

The bearing of this fact, of a limited acquaintance with the art of writing, on our present inquiry, is of

---

[1] See Gesenius' *Hebrew Grammar*, Excursus I., p. 290. English Translation, together with other authorities cited in Rawlinson's *Bampton Lecture*, p. 327.

[2] See this point discussed at length in Rawlinson's *Bampton Lecture*, sect. ii. p. 42.

course to show how little direct corroboration of the Mosaic record we are to look for, from contemporaneous, or even closely subsequent authorities. However near to Mosaic times may have been the documentary sources from which their information was obtained, the two writers, who alone are worthy to be quoted, as illustrating the history of this period, namely Berosus and Manetho, did not live until about the fourth century before the Christian era. These writers, however, fragmentary as their compositions are, it is generally allowed, are to be had in all respect. Niebuhr himself has endorsed their general historic trustworthiness; whilst, connected as they were, respectively, with the two countries most closely associated with the Pentateuchal history, Chaldæa and Egypt, and each having access to all the documentary or monumental records of his countrymen, their brief and scattered statements have a reputation for general truthfulness and fidelity, which has been denied to later and more laborious compilers. Of Manetho in particular, it has been proved, since the art of hieroglyphic interpretation has been discovered, that he drew his information from original sources, the general authenticity of which is vindicated by agreements of the most minute and satisfactory kind.[1]

Now the general testimony of these two writers,— representatives of the two earliest seats of civilization

---

[1] See an able article on Egypt in *The Biblical Dictionary*, by Mr. Stuart Poole.

in the world,— the one giving us the fruit of his researches among the most ancient Chaldæan records, the other decyphering for us the monumental remains of Egypt, is not only conclusive as to the authenticity of the Mosaic record, but, allowing for the Oriental tendency to fable, and, on some points, for a wish to conceal or distort facts not creditable to the author's own nation, is conclusive also as to the general truth of its historic facts. In illustration of this, an example from each writer may be cited; and that in relation to his own country. The following is the simple account, assumed to be drawn directly from Berosus or the sources which he used, of the building of the Tower of Babel. " At this time the ancient race of men were so puffed up with their strength and tallness of stature, that they began to despise and contemn the gods: and laboured to erect that very lofty tower, which is now called Babel, intending thereby to scale heaven. But when the building approached the sky, behold the gods called in the aid of the winds; and, by their help, overturned the tower and cast it to the ground. The name of the ruin is still called Babel, because until this time all men had used the same speech, but now there was sent upon them a confusion of many and diverse tongues."

The other example is from Manetho; and the instance selected is that of the Exodus. It is untrue in

[1] See the fragments of Abydenus in Muller's *Frag. Hist. Gr.* vol. iv. p. 282, quoted by Rawlinson, *Bampton Lect.* p. 67.

some particulars, most probably the invention of the Egyptian annalist to apologize for his own nation,—as for instance, that the Hebrews were a leprous and impious people, who, under the conduct of a priest of Heliopolis, called Moses, made war upon Egypt, and took possession of the country until they were defeated and driven out by the Egyptian king,—but the conclusion of the account is very striking: "Being defeated, the king made a composition with the people that they should leave Egypt and go without any harm being done to them whithersoever they would: and that after this composition was made, they went away with their whole families and effects, not fewer in number than 240,000, and took their journey from Egypt through the wilderness for Syria: but that, as they were in fear of the Assyrians, who had then dominion over Asia, they built a city in that country which is now called Judæa, and that large enough to contain this great number of men, and called it Jerusalem."[1]

Other testimonies, besides those of Berosus and Manetho, but like those in being derived from the earliest documentary sources, may be cited as abundantly confirmatory of the general persuasion existing in those early times, that Moses was the leader of the Jews when they departed from Egypt, and was the founder of the laws which go by his name. As we come down nearer to the Christian era, testimonies to the same effect may be multiplied

---

[1] Josephus against Apion, book i. vol. iv. 338.

indefinitely. Strabo, who flourished in the century before Christ, gives an account of the laws of Moses as forbidding images, and limiting Divine worship to one invisible Being. Justin, a Roman historian, tells us that Moses being driven from Egypt, led a band of exiles and encamped at Mount Sinai, and there consecrated the seventh day a sacred solemnity. Tacitus says, Moses gave a new form of worship to the Jews, and a system of religious ceremonies, the reverse of everything known to any other age or country. He notices also the journeyings of the people in the wilderness, and the relief under a great thirst. Juvenal mentions Moses, as the author of a volume, which was preserved with great care among the Jews; and in which the worship of images, and the eating of swine's flesh, were forbidden; and in which circumcision and the observance of the Sabbath are enjoined. Longinus quotes the expression in Genesis, "And God said, Let there be light, and there was light," as a specimen of the true sublime: and the Orphic verses, which are very ancient, commend the worship enjoined "by him who was drawn out of the water, and who received two tables of stone from the hand of God."[1] These and many other testimonies might be cited, all conclusive to this one fact, at all events, that the existence of Moses as a lawgiver, and the reality of his book as a

---

[1] For a fuller collection of these testimonies see Bishop Newton's *Dissertation on Moses and his Writings*. Works, vol. i. pp. 22-40.

history, must have been accepted and acknowledged by ancient nations, as undoubtingly as by the Jews themselves.

II. We invite attention to another form of external evidence; namely the COINCIDENCES WITH THE LEADING FACTS OF THE MOSAIC HISTORY, WHICH ARE FOUND IN THE MOST ANCIENT MYTHOLOGIES.

The Pentateuch is an abridgement of the physical, social, and moral history of mankind, during its earliest stages. Almost all nations have such abridgements. It seems to be a very instinct with us to desire to know something of the beginning and early progress of our race; to be supplied with some adequate rationale of our being's origin and purpose; and, if possible, to be furnished with some adequate explanation of those elements of conflict and disturbance, which cause that, whether in the world of nature, in civil communities, or in the heart of man, things never continue in one stay. All the mythologies of the ancient world are but the expression of this irrepressible thirst for information on topics, connected with our moral state and history. Whether invented, borrowed, corrupted, or handed down from one generation to another, they all testify to the fact, that mankind need a Revelation, and that they will cleave to the semblance of one, if the reality be not given.

The striking feature, however, of these mythologies to which we have now to call attention, is that the semblance and the reality have so much in common; touch upon the same inquiries, deal with the same difficulties, offer solutions of the same conflicting phenomena; and all this by means of legends, which, however disfigured and distorted, discover their common family resemblance,—their derivation from the same parent stock.

Let us proceed to illustrate this statement. I take the cosmogonies; and whether I adopt the system of the Chaldæans, learned in all the lore of the stars; or that of the Egyptians, resting on its foundation of absolute atheism; or that of the Persians, with their six distinct creations of the world; or that of the Chinese, with their allegory of the mundane egg; or even that of our own Gothic ancestors, overlaid with its thick crust of wild and incoherent fictions;—yet, what do I find but an inception of all things, more or less analogous to the exordium of the Mosaic record; with darkness and water as the rudimental conditions of the physical universe; and even, in some of the accounts, with a reference to six different periods of time as being required for the work of creation?

Or, I take that subject, one of the deepest and most thrilling which can exercise human thought, the original innocence and subsequent fall of man. And I consult the records of the Golden Age of Hesiod; or I look into the legends of our Scythian forefathers; or I read how the four rivers divide off into four streams, in the Indian paradise; or I take the fable of the golden apples in the garden of the Hesperides; and in all these, I cannot fail to see dim and shadowy intimations of the fact, that, as man came forth from his Maker's hands, he was holy, and innocent, and happy. But I read on; and everywhere, scattered up and down the pages of these mythological histories, I find allusion to some demoniacal power which drew man away from his allegiance, and introduced misery into the world; the very serpent form of the tempter being in some instances preserved; whilst the rudiments of a sacrificial system, found in every part of the heathen world, seem to testify at once to the deep sense in man of his far gone depravity, as well as to his hope, through faith in a propitiation, of seeing the anger of God taken away.

More conclusive and all but universal, as if in anticipation of what the impertinent sciolism of later ages would find to urge against such a revelation, is the consent of all pagan antiquity to the fact, that, in consequence of the growing wickedness of mankind, the world was once destroyed by a deluge. Here, instead of making selections from any given mythological systems, we may better throw out a defiant challenge to the opponent, to name a single traditional religious system, of any note in the world, from which is excluded all reference to the earth, as having been once covered by the waters of a flood. Ancient or modern, barbarous or civilized, the voice of the nations is consentaneous. From monumental remains in

Egypt, which antedate all secular history, down to the most recently reported traditions brought home to us from the Sandwich Islands; from the rude legend of the Druids, making the lakes and the sea to swell, till they should serve as a lustration to purify a polluted globe, to the classical fable of Deucalion, waiting in his ship on Mount Parnassus until the subsiding of the waters,—the same inference is forced upon us that the Mosaic narrative is true: some of the legends having preserved with singular accuracy the number of persons who were saved, and others retaining, with slight variations, the touching incident of the raven and the dove.[1]

Of course, in the citation of these mythological testimonies, no proof is sought to be made out that the compilers of such early records must have derived their information from the Pentateuch. This might be the case, in some of the bordering nations, but in the case of others, as of the Goths, or Hindoos, or Chinese, all indebtedness to the original Jewish sources must be, in the highest degree, unlikely, if not impossible. The cause, therefore, of these singular traditional agreements, among men of all climes, and all ages, must be looked for in certain transmitted mutilations of the facts themselves; in certain relics of original truth, derived primarily from Noah, and

[1] For more of these mythological testimonies see Faber's *Horæ Mosaicæ*, vol. i. book i. chaps. 1–4; and Curwithen's *Bampton Lecture*, disc. 1–4; or Bryant's *Ancient Mythology*.

through the Gentile lines of his three sons, however changed or corrupted in their transit, carried to all parts of the earth. Such a supposition, it is submitted, should not detract from the worth of these testimonies, in favour of the Mosaic record, as the primitive and divinely accredited repository of the facts to which they refer. The case stands thus. A multitude of religious systems, belonging to widely scattered peoples, agree in relating the same facts. Of these systems, one will be allowed, at least, to have in it a fair show of reason and consistency; whilst all the rest are disfigured either by palpable falsehood, or gross absurdity. Now, of course the mixture of absurdity, in the *false* systems, must vitiate their own claim to credibility, but by no means precludes them, as far as they agree with it, from authenticating a system, which, on other grounds, has been shown to be consistent and true. The benefit of each upon the other is reciprocal, though not alike. The Pentateuch throws light upon the inconsistencies of paganism; paganism offers its indirect contingent of proof that the Pentateuch is true.

III. A THIRD form of external evidence we would advert to is that which arises from a variety of OUTWARD AND VISIBLE COMMEMORATIONS, illustrative of the Pentateuchal history, and based upon the universal acknowledgment of the Jewish people, that the facts to which they refer are true.

In the illustration of this part of our argument, we have only to follow out, and apply the method of reasoning, adopted by the celebrated Leslie, in order to establish the credibility of any alleged fact. He specifies, it will be remembered, four verifying conditions; arguing, that any fact, in which all these conditions meet, may safely be accepted as true. These conditions are, first, that the fact be publicly witnessed; secondly, that it be of a kind of which men's senses could be competent and certain judges; thirdly, that monuments be set up, or outward actions performed, in memory of the facts thus publicly wrought; and lastly, that such monuments or outward actions had their beginning at the very time when the alleged fact occurred, and were continued without interruption afterwards.[1]

The force of these rules, it will be perceived, is that, whereas, according to the first and second marks, the facts are required to be so public and palpable as to make any deception about their reality impossible, and therefore that no false account could be palmed upon a nation *at the time;*—the conditions, introduced into the third and fourth marks, make it equally impossible that any imposture would find acceptance *afterwards;* seeing that appeal is supposed to be made to existing monuments or actions, and if these were not to be found, all faith in the alleged fact must be withheld at once.

[1] Leslie's *Short Method with the Deists*, p. 16. 3rd Edition.

The form of verifying process here recommended is particularly applicable to the case of the Mosaic record. The facts there recorded are not those of an ordinary secular history—the annexing of territory, the conclusion of treaties, the extension of commerce or of arts — they are, for the most part, Divine facts; facts bound up with the religious life and hopes of the Jewish nation, and having on them the signature and seal of a befriending and interposing God. Hence public institutions and outward actions were constantly performed among the Jews, in memory of these events; such actions and observances dating their inauguration from the time when the commemorated event occurred, and declared to have been instituted to the very end that the memory of such event might be kept alive.

Instances in illustration of the kinds of commemoration referred to will occur readily,—as in the giving of a new name to a place which had been the scene of some special deliverance, or the setting up of some stone or altar upon the spot to be regarded ever afterwards with religious reverence. In like manner were memorials of other notable events, in the national history, laid up with sacred care in the Tabernacle. Such were the two tables of stone, in remembrance of the giving of the Law at Sinai; and the vessel of manna, in memory of the miraculous food of the wilderness; and Aaron's rod that budded, to keep the people in mind of their ungrateful rebellion; and the censers of Korah and his company, formed into large plates, for covering the altar, to be a perpetual monument of the Divine displeasure against sin.

Let us, for a moment, see how these verifying critical tests may be brought to bear on some of the leading facts of the Mosaic history,—such, for example, as the destruction of the first-born, or the departure out of Egypt. Here the facts were public enough, for they were witnessed by two millions of people: palpable enough, for what delusion could impose on the senses of so great a multitude?—commemorated enough, by continuing ordinances or memorials, seeing that, on the face of the narrative, references are made to such institutions, as to something which the people knew to be in existence then, and even to have been in existence as long as they or their fathers could remember. On this shewing, and in reference to the particular events referred to, let us ask ourselves, How could a man,—at any period after the event, no matter when—say to an assembled nation, on settling down in a new country, " Observe now that ordinance of the Passover, which your fathers have kept ever since their deliverance out of the land of Egypt," if the people must have been obliged to reply, " Our fathers never have practised such an ordinance, neither did we ever hear of this Passover at all?" Or, again, how could the writer of a book, speaking of the stones which were set up in Gilgal to commemorate the passing through the Jordan, add the words, " And they are there unto this day," if every man and woman, who first heard the statement must have known that no such stones were in existence, or, if they were, that they originated in some different cause? The supposition is felt at once to be impossible. We have a monument in the heart of our metropolis. It commemorates a great fire. And we know how a poet of the last century, in describing it, says,—

> "As some tall bully lifts its head and lies,"—

but will the satirist of some ten centuries hence, if the Monument should stand as long, ever raise a doubt of the fact that there was a great fire in London in the year 1666?

IV. LASTLY, among forms of testimony to the general credibility of the Mosaic history, we cannot refuse to assign an important place to the writings of the GREAT HISTORIAN OF THE HEBREW NATION — the laborious and accomplished JOSEPHUS.

On all accounts, this writer is entitled to the highest consideration. The age in which he lived makes him, in many respects, an independent witness to the truth of the ancient revelation. His high family connexions, and even reputed descent from the Asmonean princes, gave him access to all the documentary treasures of his nation. His literary attainments are the astonishment of Jerome, and command the critical suffrages of Scaliger; whilst of such high reputation were his histories deemed by the Emperor Vespasian, that his great work was ordered to be deposited in the library at Rome, and a statue was erected in honour of its author.

The "Jewish Antiquities," which extend to twenty books, bring down the history from the beginning of the world to the twelfth year of Nero, when the Jews rebelled against the Romans. His two books against Apion, a grammarian of Alexandria, who had grossly misrepresented the Jews, are not only interesting for their many incidental corroborations of Scripture in relation to Jewish history, but have the further value of preserving some fragments of ancient historians, whose works, though lost to us now, were confidently appealed to by Josephus then, as corroborative of the facts of the Mosaic narrative, as well as of the estimation in which the great lawgiver was held.

Such was the writer, who has done so much to render the Hebrew nation conspicuous in the eyes of the world, and who has furnished so full an outline of Bible history that, had the Old Testament been completely destroyed, we might, from his writings alone, have recovered a large portion of its leading facts. Nor can we read, without interest, his terrible description of the calamities which attended the siege of Jerusalem, confirming, with apparent unconsciousness, the words both of Moses and of Christ, and declaring that "neither did any other city ever suffer such miseries, or any age breed a generation more fruitful in wickedness."

We deem the testimony of Josephus, therefore,

both to the Pentateuch as a record, and to Moses as its author, to be of exceeding validity in relation to the modern controversies, partly as showing that the Hebrew Scriptures were, in the main, what we regard them now, and partly as authenticating the claims of the Jewish faith and polity to a foremost place among the recognized religious systems of antiquity. Not only do his writings, in many important instances, express and embody the leading opinions of the Jewish Church and people, both of his own and former times, but in an age, sure to examine and sift such claims to the utmost, he brought out the history and the writings of the Jewish lawgiver to the full view of the civilized world — challenged assent to them as the acknowledged and accredited annals of a great people, whose fortunes were imperishably intertwined with those of all the greatest nations in the earth — exhibiting the exploits of Moses in his great undertaking, not only as the basis of their peculiar Hebrew polity, but as the corner-stone of a great edifice of religious truth, from which should go forth laws to endure for all time, and light to inform and teach the world. Yet, in any material particulars, none were found to gainsay the testimony of Josephus eighteen hundred years ago; neither have any gainsaid it since. Qualified as he was, pre-eminently, to be the exponent of Jewish thought and feeling, at the dawn of the Christian era, his writings form a connecting bond between sacred and heathen testimony, which gives coherence and strength to both.

Between Moses and Jesus of Nazareth the chain of Jewish belief has no missing link. The Hebrew polity is a Divine system, of which the Pentateuch is the central fact.

But, on grounds of external testimony, we shall not pursue our argument further. We claim to have adduced, in support of the credibility of the Mosaic record, the consenting testimony of all history, all time, all races, and all tongues. We have gone back, for our proofs, to the earliest documentary sources it is possible to consult. We have inquired of men who represent the most cultivated ages of Greek and Roman literature. We have brought together vestiges of coincident fact and statement, culled out of the mythologies of all nations; and we have appealed to those institutions and observances, which, for ages after their setting up, were regarded with sacred awe by the Jewish people; and which, whether as an ordinance of worship, or a pillar of stone, or a sculptured emblem laid up in the ark of God, were always regarded as associated with certain Divine transactions, and designed to elicit from all who looked upon them the grateful acknowledgment, "O God, we have heard with our ears, and our fathers have declared unto us, the noble works that Thou didst in their days and in the old time before them."

Such an amount of consentaneous testimony, it may be said, is not sufficient, according to the principles of our inexorable historic criticism. But if so, it is well that we should know what those principles, in their practical application, are. They are principles which make document a nullity, authorship a fable, testimony a lie; which leave us without any certain canon of literary authenticity to guide us, and in effect overturn all history.

SECTION III.

TESTIMONIES TO CREDIBILITY AFFORDED BY THE BOOKS THEMSELVES.

" The Divine knowledge is indeed too excellent for man, and could not otherwise be imparted to him than in scraps, and fragments. But these are then only understood when the human mind, by just and dextrous combinations, is able to restore them, in some imperfect degree, to the shadow and the semblance, at least, of that simplicity and unity, in which all truth originally exists in the self-furnished intellect of God."—BISHOP HORSLEY.

" This verse marks that, and both do make a motion
    Unto a third that ten leaves off doth lie."—GEORGE HERBERT.

WE commonly divide the evidences for the authenticity and truth of a written document into external and internal. By external evidence, we mean that which is derived to us from the history, so far as we can trace it, of the document itself; from corroborative testimonies which may be gathered from other sources; and from any institutions, observances, memorials, of facts, which, while agreeing with the statements of the document under consideration, are still existing in ths world. By internal evidence, we mean that which comes of a minute inspection and examination of the document itself; the form of its cypher, the style of its composition, the unity and consistency of its several parts, and the harmony of its subject-matter with its understood or avowed design.

This classification cannot always be rigorously adhered to, because there must always be, about the vicinity of its border-line, arguments, which may be registered either under one kind of evidence or the other. Keeping to the convention, however, as far as we can, we purpose, in the present chapter, to consider the evidences for the credibility of the Pentateuch which are to be gathered out of the books themselves.

The line of argument, in this case, differs from that we have hitherto pursued. For we first make certain assumptions, in regard to the record, and then shew that its contents are such as we should expect to find them, if the assumptions so made were true. Thus, we assume Moses to be the writer of certain books, believed to have been composed more than 3000 years ago; assume, in respect to four of them, that he was eye-witness of the principal facts which he relates; assume, that he had a Divine commission to inaugurate a civil and religious polity for the guidance of his nation; and assume further, that in the acceptance and adoption of such polity by the Jews, we have the political birth of a great nation, the foundation of all that is distinctive and peculiar in Hebrew life. Do the contents of the books harmonize with these suppositions? is the next question. In other words, are we able to adduce marks of antiquity in the books, proofs of intelligence and probity in the writer, evidences of consistent design in the structure of the composition, and phenomena of life, and conduct, and character on the part of the nation, all of which are explicable enough on our assumed suppositions, but which would be a mystery and a paradox on any other? We think the books do furnish these marks.

I. We offer a proof, first, from the more marked LITERARY CHARACTERISTICS of the Mosaic record.

The style is just that, which, assuming Moses to have been the writer, and the time of the exodus to have been its date, all scholars allow they should expect such a composition to exhibit. Its phrases, its images, its descriptions, its abrupt transitions, are all strongly marked by a cast of archaic simplicity;—full of that rude vigour, and unchastened boldness of thought, which characterize the infancy of language, and the unsystematized forms of primeval speech. Still more is this appearance of a remote authorship evidenced by the many antiquated and obsolete verbalisms, to be found in the record; obsolete, that is, in the time when other sacred books were written, as in the days of David and Solomon. The Hebrew language, as we have seen, never existed in its purity after the time of the captivity. Up to that time, however, it probably underwent fewer changes than that of most other nations, owing to the little intercourse, which, both by their religion, their prejudices, and their laws, the Jews allowed themselves to have with foreigners. Notwithstanding this, learned men are at no loss to discover differences in the Hebrew style of the different compositions written between the times of Moses and Malachi. The Hebrew of the Pentateuch is not exactly that of the Psalms; whilst that of the Psalms differs more widely from that of Ezra and Hosea.

In relation to the Pentateuch, however, the striking difference from all later writings consists in the use of these peculiar archaisms; expressions being found in the Mosaic record, which are found in none of the later writings; whilst, conversely, many expressions in the later writings, are represented by a different equivalent in the Pentateuch. Nor is this all. Among these obsolete verbalisms, are some which are clearly of Egyptian origin; words which were never likely to have been used by a native of Palestine; and bearing strong presumptive evidence of being the language of one born and educated in Egypt.[1]

The almost universal agreement on this subject among modern scholars has not been, we are told, without its effect on the rationalists of Germany. The argument that the Hebrew of the Pentateuch is of a form much too perfect for the age of Moses, is one advanced with less confidence than formerly; the

[1] Bishop Marsh refers as a striking example of this to the two texts, Gen. xli. 2, and Isa. xix. 7, in the former of which we have a word which is pure Egyptian, and in the latter its equivalent in pure Hebrew, both being rendered in the Septuagint ἄχι or ἄχει. See *Authenticity of the Five Books of Moses*, p. 14.

admission being made instead, that a considerable number of archaisms do exist in the books, but that they were incorporated into them from genuine documents of the Mosaic period, while the author himself belonged to a much later age.[1] The probability of this strained hypothesis we shall not stay to discuss: being quite content to have hostile testimonies to the fact, that vestiges of an archaic literature are to be traced in the Pentateuchal writings, such as, if Moses were indeed the author, all scholars would expect to find.

II. We observe next, as falling in with our assumption of their reputed authorship, the *amount of* LOCAL AND HISTORICAL KNOWLEDGE, discovered in these books.

The acquaintance displayed by the writer, with the history, geography, usages, natural products of Egypt on the one hand, with the names, condition, and local peculiarities of long extinct Canaanitish races on the other, is such as could have belonged only to one who was contemporaneous with the events he refers to, and who had been a resident among the scenes he describes. Thus, the scene of a considerable portion of the transactions is laid in Egypt; among a people whose early beginnings are shrouded in mystery, in legend, in a historic darkness which may be felt. To feel after truth, among the rubbish of their own fabulous and

[1] *Aids to Faith*, Essay vi. p. 239.

incoherent annals, is to grope for the wall like the blind. Yet on the manners, usages, institutions, laws of this ancient nation, the writer of the Mosaic books touches with all the easy and familiar naturalness of one, who knew the people as well as they knew themselves. This is what no writer of a later age was likely to have ventured upon. The intercourse between Egypt and Judæa, whether for commercial or political purposes, did not rise to any height, till a period much later than that which rationalists commonly assign to the composition of the Pentateuch; even if information, obtained by such means, would have supplied all those minute,—for a forger perilously minute,—details of Egyptian habits and Egyptian life, which, if not true, the first uncovered tablet of that monument-loving people might falsify or disprove.

But these tablets have given forth another testimony. The last and latest results of archæological discovery bear witness, in the judgment of Hengstenberg, to an amount of exact acquaintance with Egyptian history and antiquities, on the part of the author of the Pentateuch, such as only a person, born and bred in Egypt, was likely to have possessed, or only a forger of transcendant genius could have been enabled to display.[1]

Nor less particular and minute is our author, in his references to the early Canaanitish communities,—

[1] See *Ægypten und Mose*, translated by Mr. R. D. C. Robbins, reprinted in Clarke's *Biblical Cabinet*, New Series (Edinburgh, 1845). See also *The English Cyclopædia*, p. 387.

to peoples, who without residual trace or vestige, have been swept by the rod of the Divine indignation from the earth. Many of these had disappeared even before the time of the Judges. Yet, in this record, they have a local habitation and a name; the cities they built, the border countries they joined, the successive appellations they were known by, the conquering nations by whose hand they fell, all being set down with statistical particularity. Still more remarkable is the topographical exactness discovered in the Pentateuch,—the truthful fidelity of its descriptions to all that modern travel has brought to light, of the general features of the Sinaitic peninsula. Of late years, the lands of Scripture have been explored by travellers, both English and continental, singularly equipped with powers of observation, and capabilities for following out any proofs of historic search; and yet, from Ritter to Laborde, from Robinson to Stanley, the consentaneous testimony meets us, that whether the country be viewed through the medium of the Bible, or the Bible be read in the light of what may now be seen in the country, "the Holy Land is the best commentary on the Holy History;" and that, for the wondrous harmony which is found to subsist between them, the only solution to be offered is that he by whom the history was penned, was in a condition to say, " We speak that we do know, and testify that we have seen."

III. We note a further proof of the perfect truthfulness of the record, in its EXCEEDING PARTICULARITY on points of public, social, and domestic detail.

The book is either a veritable composition, written by Moses within forty years from the exodus, or it is the work of an impostor. But an impostor does not gratuitously multiply the facilities for his own detection. He will set down what may be needful to give coherence and plausibility to his fabrication, but nothing more. Are there any signs of such cautious reticence on the part of the author of the Pentateuch? None whatever; but of the very reverse. The book abounds with incidental notices, very natural for an eye-witness and veracious chronicler to record, but very difficult for any fabricator to contrive, and almost sure to lead to his detection if he should be bold enough to make the attempt. Of this kind are the particulars,—given, first in the order of their occurrence, and afterwards in a summary,—of the various Jewish marches and encampments; the little incidents by which some of them were distinguished, and the names given in consequence, to the places where they occurred.[1] With these transactions the people addressed are assumed to be familiar,—to have had a personal share in them as well as the writer himself. Would not a writer of the age of Samuel,—the age fixed by modern scepticism as

---

[1] See for more detailed mention of these, Graves on *The Pentateuch*, pt. i. sect. ii. Faber's *Horæ Mosaicæ*, sect. ii. ch. iv.

the most probable for the composition of the Pentateuch,—have been careful to leave out such particulars?

More pertinently still, do these remarks apply to the *genealogies* contained in the Pentateuch. These documents, at whatever time we suppose them to have commenced, became the accepted rule of all the civil and ecclesiastical affairs of the nation. There was no appeal from them. The order of precedence among the tribes, the limits within which marriage might be contracted, the conditions of succeeding to a family inheritance, the right of admission to sacred offices and employments, the honour of being of the same family with the expected Messiah, might all be made to turn upon the faithful keeping of these national registers. Two examples, taken, one from the ecclesiastical, and the other from the civil institutions of the nation, will show the paramount authority accorded, by common consent, to those documents. On the return from the captivity, and the recommencement, by Ezra, of a sacred service, certain men put themselves forward as candidates for the priesthood. But a search into the genealogies, preserved during the whole time of the captivity, was fatal to their claims. "These sought their register among those that were reckoned by genealogy, but they were not found: therefore were they as polluted put from the priesthood."[1]

The other example is taken from the history of

[1] Ezra, ii. 62.

Jeremiah. The prophet buys a field from his cousin, on the express ground that the right of inheritance, and consequently that the right of redemption, was his. The usual forms being gone through for completing a purchase, the evidence of the purchase, formally signed and sealed, was consigned to the especial custody of Baruch, to be kept in an earthen vessel for many days. And then the reason is given. Carried away, as Judah will soon be, bitter days are in store for her. " Houses, and fields, and vineyards, shall be possessed again in this land."[1] Here the ground of confidence in the restoration of the property is, that whenever the predicted time of prosperity should come, an appeal to the genealogical records of the nation would vindicate the claim of the prophet's descendants to the property, as secured by the law of Moses, according to the first partition of the land among the tribes.

From these instances it will appear that not only are the genealogies of the Pentateuch bound up with the civil and ecclesiastical institutions of the Jewish nation, but that they constituted a part of the original deed of settlement, by which the people became established in the land. The question may fairly be asked, Whence, but from authentic documents of the time, could a compiler obtain such materials? Or if, *after* the time, any fabricator should invent them, how could he obtain for them any acceptance or authority?

---

[1] Jer. xxxii. 15. See whole chapter.

IV. The argument from internal evidence is further strengthened by what the book discloses of THE CHARACTER OF ITS REPUTED AUTHOR.

i. First, as a witness to the facts he had to describe, Moses was a *thoroughly competent man.*

No one, in reading the Mosaic books, would say of the author of them that he was an *ignorant* man, deficient in knowledge of his subject; or a *weak* man, likely to be imposed upon by false representations; or an *enthusiastic* man, easily carried away by the force of a heated imagination. On the contrary, he is everywhere calm, judicious, self-possessed, thoughtful. Especially, in trying emergencies, do we see the singular force of his character. It is then he evinces that steady fixedness of purpose—that strength of moral determination, which no tumults of the people could shake, and no blandishments of a court had ever been able to turn aside. And on a par with these moral qualities were his high mental endowments. Of these his writings give proof. His laws are quoted by all nations as a monument of matchless wisdom. His ethics rest on a basis of the most pure and sublime morality. Philosophers stand amazed at the far-seeing exactitude of his scientific statements; and even rhetoricians are willing to sit at his feet, to learn lessons of the lofty and the bold in style. As against all suspicion of fanaticism, or ignorance, or mental or moral weakness, therefore, we may say, fearlessly, that no man, more than Moses, was ever fitted to undertake a Divine legation. He was not only learned in all the wisdom of the Egyptians, but he excelled in every nation's best. He was the man for a great people to make a hero of, and to worship. And the Jews did worship him—would have worshipped him even in death, if it had been possible; "but no man knoweth of his sepulchre unto this day."

ii. Again, in regard of any views of personal advantage or aggrandizement, Moses was *an utterly unselfish man.*

If there had been a particle of ambition in him, he would have remained in Egypt. On account of his relations with the court, the most commanding positions were open to him there; and he possessed those high administrative qualities which, as in the case of Joseph, would soon have made him necessary to the interests both of Pharaoh and the kingdom. But the opportunities were all disregarded and thrown away. A good man, Moses could not endure the vices of Pharaoh's court. A humane man, he could not bear to look on the distresses of his brethren. Every prospect of worldly advancement, therefore, shall be renounced, in order that he, a prince in rank, may cast in his lot with a community of slaves. The very name of the son of Pharaoh's daughter he repudiated;— "choosing rather to suffer affliction with the people of God than to enjoy the pleasures of sin for a season; esteeming the reproach of Christ greater riches than the treasures in Egypt."

But there might be ambition still, it may be said. Was it nothing to be "king in Jeshurun"—to be the chief over the heads of the people and all their assembled tribes? Little could Moses foresee of such preeminence, and very slow was he to take any steps towards it, if he did. First, forty years are spent—forty of life's best years—in the inglorious obscurity of shepherd-life. Called, at the end of that time, to undertake the liberation of his countrymen, he discovers an unwillingness to enter upon the task, so resolved and reiterated, as even to provoke the Divine reproof; whilst, after success on success, and miracle on miracle, had proclaimed him, beyond controversy, to be the bearer of a mission from God, he never attempts to take the least advantage of his position. He sets up no throne of temporal monarchy for himself; seeks no places of profit and emolument for his family; but leaves his sons to take up their position indistinguishably with obscure Levites, and then nominates, as his successor in the commonwealth, his servant Joshua,—a man belonging to another tribe. Surely a writer of this character might be expected to speak the truth, if it were only on the ground that, having no self-seeking ends to compass, no reason can be imagined why he should speak anything else.

iii. Once more, we hold that Moses is entitled to our confidence, on the ground that, as a narrator of facts, he is *a scrupulously honest and impartial man.*

The contrast between Josephus and Moses in the

matter of style,—the one turgid, diffuse, and always straining after rhetorical effect, the other unconsciously producing that effect by his easy, dignified, and unaffected naturalness—has been often noted. The difference is observable also, in comparing the narrative impartiality and candour of the two writers. Josephus is evidently very tender of the reputation of Moses,—conceals or palliates his failings to the utmost. Moses, on the contrary, keeps back nothing; both his own faults and those of the people are set down, without palliation and without disguise. Indeed, whether affecting himself, or those most dear to him, there is nothing too humiliating for him to record. The unhallowed marriage of his parents, the idolatry of Aaron his brother, the penal leprosy of Miriam his sister, the profaneness of Nadab and Abihu his nephews, the curse of Jacob pronounced on his tribe, the perpetual murmurings and backslidings of the people, and the sentence of God pronounced upon himself for his rash and unadvised speech,—all these things are set down with the utmost plainness, and with the full knowledge, by the writer, that they and the history would go down to all time together,—a reproach and dishonour both to his own and his country's name.

On what principle, it may surely be asked, is the veracity of such a writer to be discredited? Or what new thing is that, in human motive,—in the motives of a literary impostor especially,—which, with the unlimited choice of all fictitious materials before him, should lead him to give the preference to those which were to disgrace his family, offend his countrymen, and condemn himself?

V. Again, we find an evidence for the credibility of the Pentateuch in the VERISIMILITUDE OF ITS NARRATIVE DESCRIPTIONS, as well as in the apparently ACCIDENTAL COINCIDENCES discoverable between one part of the writings and another.

i. Observe this in relation to some *marked points of Hebrew life and character*.

In distinguishing the more salient features of character in different nations, an able and thoughtful modern writer has remarked, that, just as the instinct of Greece was a regard for symmetry of form and thought, or that of Rome was a passion for command and power, so the race-endowment of the Jewish people was the *love of order;* an instinctive regard to fitnesses and adjustments;—habits of systematization being a very necessity to them, and all the arrangements both of ecclesiastical and secular life being framed according to line and rule.[1]

The form in which this alleged quality of the national mind discovers itself, is in the spirit of a closely compacted clanship, making the people, on any emergency, ready at once for concerted action; in the faculty of administrative management, as seen in the

[1] See *Considerations on the Pentateuch*, by Isaac Taylor, pp. 34–50.

orderly distribution of offices and employments,—work found for every man, and fit men chosen for the work; in the love of external symmetry and detail,—extending to the ordering of a march, the disposition of an encampment, the exact measurement of all Tabernacle fittings,—so many on this side, and so many on that.

With this clue to the national character, let us take the Mosaic record in our hands, and see if it be not full of the very particulars which the documents of such a people might be expected to contain;—namely, of enumerations, and inventories, and catalogues, musterrolls of tribes, and recitals, even to tediousness, of things lawful to touch, or taste, or handle;—details, absolutely needful for a people such as the history shews the Hebrew race to be, but almost the last things which a forger would be at the trouble to invent.

Nor is this all. As the writer already referred to has shown, we have, in this peculiar quality of the Jewish mind, an explanation of very many of the difficulties advanced with so much confidence by a modern rationalist. Things are represented as being accomplished by the Israelites, such as the preparations for the Exodus, the observance of the Passover, the adherence to an elaborate Tabernacle ritual, which, on account of the systematized organization required for them, are declared to be "demonstrably impossible." The impossibility, however, will be found to exist only in the objector's own mind, and the narrowness of his acquaintance with the strongly marked characteristics of the Hebrew race. A more accurate knowledge of these would have taught him that the habit of organization was, to the Jews, a second nature: and on the front of the Tabernacle, as well as on the banners of the marching tribes, he might almost have seen the apostolic superscription written, "Let every thing be done decently and in order."[1]

ii. See a yet more striking testimony to the consistency and coherence of the narrative, in examples of what are commonly called *undesigned coincidences*.

The force of this kind of evidence will be readily acknowledged. It consists in the bringing together, from different parts of an author's writings, instances of minute consistency and agreement, which, as being too subtle and unapparent for an ordinary reader to notice, it is not likely that any fabricator would be at the pains to contrive. Every student of Christian evidence is aware with what success this test of truth has been applied, by Paley, to the New Testament, shewing what refined and delicate shades of agreement may be traced between the Acts of the Apostles and the

---

[1] Two interesting examples of this feature of Jewish character, and quoted by Mr. Taylor, are drawn from the history of our blessed Lord. One is in the miracle of feeding the five thousand, where we read: "And he commanded them to make all sit down by companies upon the green grass. And they sat down in ranks, by hundreds, and by fifties." (Mark, vi. 39, 40.) The other—an illustration, to be quoted with all reverence,—is from the account of the resurrection: "And seeth the linen clothes lie, and the napkin, that was about his head, not lying with the linen clothes, but wrapped together in a place by itself." (John, xx. 6, 7.)

Pauline Epistles. By some able writers of more recent date, the same plan has been applied, and with results equally satisfactory, to the different parts of the Mosaic writings.[1] The instances are difficult to give, without a lengthened detail of particulars. We must be content with one or two, not perhaps the most striking, but as admitting most easily of compression.

Thus, an instance is found in the account of the marriage of Isaac to the grand-daughter of Nahor. Now Nahor, being Abraham's brother, the more natural alliance to have been looked for would have been between Isaac and the *daughter*, and not with one belonging to a generation later. But a close inspection of the history suggests a remembrance of the fact that Isaac was the son of Sarah's old age; and therefore that he would be coeval with his uncle's grandchildren, and not with one of his children, to whom it would have been the first thought of a forger to have married him, or else to have taken credit to himself for minute truthfulness in having avoided the mistake.

Another instance is well worked out by Professor Blunt, in what he calls "the consistent insignificance of Bethuel," in the whole matter of Isaac's marriage. He was alive, and matters of deepest import to him had to be arranged. Yet he never appears, and no reason is assigned why everything is left to be man-

[1] Professor Blunt's *Undesigned Coincidences*, part i., and Graves *On the Pentateuch*, part i. sect. iii.

aged by the mother and brother. Make the supposition, never hinted at in the narrative, that, from old age or other cause, Bethuel was incapable of attending to family matters, and you have an explanation, very consistent with the artlessness of truth, but involving a liability to exception, which a forger would not be likely to incur.

But a more striking example still is to be found in the book of Numbers. On the day when Moses set up the Tabernacle, and anointed and sanctified it, the princes of the tribes made an offering of six wagons and twelve oxen; which Moses, in assigning to the service of the Levites, thus divided: "*Two* wagons and *four* oxen he gave unto the sons of Gershon, according to their service; and *four* wagons and *eight* oxen he gave unto the sons of Merari, according unto their service."[1] Now wherefore this unequal division? Why twice as many wagons and oxen to Merari as to Gershon? No reason is given; but if we turn to a former chapter, we find the casual mention of a circumstance, out of which we can make a reason; namely, that, to the sons of Gershon, it was appointed to carry the cords, and the curtains, and the hangings, and all the *lighter* parts of the Tabernacle, and for which therefore *two* wagons might be sufficient, whilst to the sons of Merari, it was assigned to convey all the wood-work, and *heavier* parts of the structure,—a service for which we may suppose *four* wagons would

[1] Num. vii. 7, 8.

be required.[1] Will any presume to say that this is the coincidence of contrivance? a cunningly elaborated agreement between the contents of two separated chapters, purposely left of the writer for the critical acumen of after ages to discover? Or shall not the more rational inference be allowed, that, in such a consentient harmony of narrative, we have the artless simplicity of Divine fact? the truth of nature, the consistency of one, who had neither the humours of others to study, nor any purpose of his own to serve?

VI. Lastly, among internal evidences of credibility, we note the PERVASIVE CONSISTENCY of the entire record with the claims of Moses to be considered the bearer of a DIVINE LEGATION.

These claims are the key-note to the whole history. They lie at the foundation of that otherwise unaccountable submission yielded, by a great nation, to the authority of one man. The improbability that he should receive such submission had been anticipated by Moses at the outset. "And Moses said unto God, Behold, when I come unto the children of Israel, and shall say unto them, The God of your fathers hath sent me unto you; and they shall say to me, What is his name? what shall I say unto them? And God said unto Moses, I AM THAT I AM; and He said, Thus

---

[1] Num. iv. 25. The account will be found given with greater fullness in Blunt's *Undesigned Coincidences*, part i. p. 80, and also in Graves *On the Pentateuch*, part i. sect. iii.

shalt thou say unto the children of Israel, I AM hath sent me unto you."[1]

Such high pretensions, it will be acknowledged, could be sustained only by marks of superhuman wisdom and agency, in everything pertaining to the legation itself. And they are so.

i. Thus they are sustained by that *pure system of theology and morals,* which the Mosaic writings everywhere reveal and enforce.

Whence was it, we are entitled to ask, that among the Hebrew tribes so much wisdom prevailed, when the veil of the covering spread so widely over the face of the neighbour nations? Why was this Goshen all light, when a darkness, that might be felt, overshadowed all the heathen world besides? How came they by those transcendant and sublime views of God and His government,—His unity, His perfections, and His grace,—the promise of a Messiah, and the prospect of a life to come, unless it were by the express teaching of God, through the medium of His favoured servant Moses? Look at Egypt, with its gods many and its lords many. Look at the Chaldæans, with their cruel rites, and human or inhuman sacrifices. Look at Tyre, and Carthage, and the Phenician states around them, and mark their deep and dark descent in all that regards morals and religion; and then inquire, how it came to pass, that a nation of escaped slaves should have originated such lofty thoughts of God,

[1] Exod. iii. 13, 14.

such spiritual views of worship, such an exalted standard of morals,— in a word, should have been able to set patterns of heroic greatness, both in service and suffering, to which even under a better dispensation, mankind still look back with consolation and delight? How, we ask, is this contrast in respect to religious truth, between the Jews and other nations,—nations far beyond them in general civilization and enlightenment,—to be accounted for, but on the supposition, that the great Hebrew legislator stood in the nearest alliance with God, receiving from Him those sacred emanations of light, and truth, and heavenly grace, which have made his theology Divine, and his name immortal? This is the interpretation of the mystery, supplied by the book itself, and it is the only one which harmonizes with the facts.

ii. The claim by Moses to have received a Divine commission, when undertaking the deliverance of his people, is still further confirmed by the *marvellous success of the enterprize itself.*

The exodus from Egypt was one of those remarkable events to which the annals of history present no parallel. Here was a people, originally invited to settle in Egypt, but afterwards reduced by their proud oppressors to a state of abject bondage:—the Egyptians not being willing to lose the value of their services as useful labourers, and yet jealous of their growing political ascendancy, as an independent community. How this oppressed population were to be rescued by the energy of one man, himself an outlaw, and a fugitive, and a poor shepherd feeding another man's flock, in the distant solitudes of Midian,—is a problem which only one principle will solve. The Hebrews had no thought of a general rising against their tyrannical rulers. They had neither the heart for such an undertaking, nor the means for carrying it into effect. Still less could the idea of organizing so bold a movement have originated with Moses. He had made an attempt, once, to befriend his nation, and that under the most favourable circumstances, and had failed. If the people refused his mediation when he came before them as the adopted son of Pharaoh's daughter, how were they likely to range themselves under his banner, when he appeared as the exiled shepherd of the priest of Midian?

Plainly, therefore, nothing short of Divine power could have originated the design, or accomplished the prodigious result. When the first displays of preternatural agency began, Moses had formed no plan of conduct, either for himself or his people. He seems to have lived, day by day, on Divine guidance and direction. As the time of deliverance drew nigh, and the orders were given to be ready for departure on a particular day, such hasty preparations would be made as the circumstances would admit of,—but, in the way of organized preparations upon a large scale, whether of arms for an engagement with the pursuing hosts of the Egyptians, or of bribes and presents for conciliating the predatory tribes of the desert, or of provisions and stores for all the hardships and perils they must expect to meet with in the course of their journey,—nothing was arranged, and nothing could be. Sufficient for the day must be the wants thereof, and the Lord must provide. And, for forty years afterwards, it was the same. The entire narrative exhibits a series of miraculous interpositions, from the night that Israel left Egypt, till they came to the brink of the Jordan. Admit this, and all is clear. Deny this, and the whole account is as broken, as incongruous, as "unhistoric," as the most inveterate rationalist could desire it to be. How is it possible, we can well suppose a modern objector to say, that this mighty exodus, with all its after successes, could be accomplished, at such short notice, and with such demonstrably inadequate resources? Or what sane man would have undertaken the expedition, under such circumstances? To which we should reply, that the ground of the objection makes so much the more for the credibility of the history,—gives it its air of verisimilitude and consistent fact. If everything had happened, in conformity with the laws of human means and human agency, the embassy of Moses would have had nothing to distinguish it from a human embassy. But the narrator sets out with the declaration that this embassy was DIVINE; and, therefore, it does but vindicate its own consistency, when it makes Moses to believe that, by constant providential succours, God *would* authenticate His servant's work, and when it makes the result to shew that He *did.*

iii. Once more, in furtherance of these Divine claims of Moses, we urge the uniform assumption, in his writings, that the whole affairs of the Hebrew commonwealth were placed under *an extraordinary providence.*

The idea of a theocracy was a new thing in the earth;—in the history of polities, *is* a thing by itself to this day. It was not that the Lord was Israel's God for purposes of worship only; He was the TEMPORAL KING of the Hebrew nation. By Him princes ruled, and magistrates decreed justice, and Levites presided over religious affairs, and the heads of thousands, and of hundreds, and of fifties, maintained order among the people—all, the lowest, as much as the highest, holding their patent of authority direct from God.[1] Hence their power to enforce the peculiar laws and ordinances of the Mosaic constitution—laws which no human legislature would have ventured to impose, and to which, apart from a belief in their Divine origin, no people would have been willing to submit. The enactment that all property should revert to the original owner every fiftieth year; the requirement that all contracts for personal servitude should terminate at

[1] The theocracy of Moses was not a government of priests, as opposed to kings : it was a government by God Himself, as opposed to the government of priests by kings. Stanley's Lectures on the *Jewish Church.* Preface.

the end of seven years; the command to observe every seventh year as "a year of rest to the land"—a year in which there should be neither sowing nor reaping; were all regulations, involving such an arbitrary interference with free commerce and social rights, that obedience to them could only have been obtained by the universal persuasion of the people, that Divine wisdom had dictated the policy, and that Divine power and goodness would be employed to preserve all, who obeyed the injunctions, from any accruing harm or loss.

At all events, in relation to the hypothesis of a human authorship of the Mosaic institutes, it would be difficult to say which is the more improbable, that a legislator should invent a code, which presupposed the necessity of Divine interference for its effectual carrying out, or that, while clogged with this necessity, any people could be found to accept such a code. Yet such is the case we have to deal with. The entire Mosaic constitution rests upon the expectation of a constantly interposing Providence, and, it is manifest, would have lost all its hold upon the confidence of the people, if that expectation had not been as constantly fulfilled. With the avowal of a Divine commission had the great legislator commenced his undertaking; the proof that he was acting under it must be apparent to the end. And apparent it was. In every page of the record the words shine through, "I AM hath sent me unto you."

Such are a few arguments for the credibility of the Pentateuch, supplied by the writings themselves. Not less convincing, in themselves, than those advanced in the former sections, it seems almost obvious to say of them, as the apostle says of prophesying, that they are signs "not for them which believe not, but for them which believe." For these last, however, such testimonies should have an especial value. Gathered out of the document itself, they require no extraneous aids. Springing out of a reverent collation of one Scripture with another, their number may be indefinitely and continually increased. Whilst, supplying as each fresh corroborative example does, a new and independent testimony of its own, a conviction of the general veracity of the sacred writings takes possession of the mind, such as any merely speculative objections are not likely to disturb. It is no easy matter to break the force of an established and foregone belief. Critical difficulties and exceptions we shall feel may serve to prove our limited knowledge on many subjects connected with the Mosaic books, but, in the face of such preponderating evidence, can be of no logical avail to prove either that their author is not trustworthy, or that his record is not true.

SECTION IV.

THE SECURITIES FOR THE GENUINENESS AND SAFE TRANSMISSION OF THE BOOKS.

> " Authority,
> And this as perfect as its kind can be,
> Rolls down to us the sacred history,
> Which from the universal Church received,
> Is tried, and after, for itself believed."—DRYDEN.

THE general scope of the arguments advanced in the two preceding chapters was to establish the historic credibility of the Pentateuch; to take it out of the province of poetry and mythus; to vindicate its claims to literary genuineness, on the same principles as we are content to allow those of the Histories of Herodotus, or the Commentaries of Julius Cæsar. But, between these secular compositions and the writings of Moses, there is one important difference. Herodotus and Cæsar may have had their histories corrupted, to any conceivable extent, without the world being any the worse for it. Their books are a *caput mortuum* of dead facts, which, now, at least, can affect no one human interest. But the ascertained uncorruptness of the Mosaic record is vital to man's moral happiness. The contents of it are the basis of all doctrine, all precept, all law. Its facts are undying facts, and the truth of them is the life of the world.

Nothing can be more important, therefore, than the inquiry which next meets us, Are we sure that we have in our hands, at this day, the true book of the Law of Moses? Can we say, with all confidence, that the collection of writings, called by that name, whether found in the Jewish synagogue, in the Christian church, or in the Mahomedan mosque, is, in all its essential features, identical with that which was in the hands of the children of Israel before they crossed the Jordan?

I. Our first answer to this question will be given in a sketch of *the* HISTORY AND CUSTODY *of the document itself from the time of its first composition.*

The materials for the early history must come, of course, from the Sacred Volume itself. The document was completed at the close of the wilderness wanderings, and it thus records its first destination: "And it came to pass, when Moses had made an end of writing the words of this Law in a book, until they were finished, that Moses commanded the Levites, which bare the ark of the covenant of the Lord, saying, Take this book of the Law, and put it in the side of the ark of the covenant of the Lord your God, that it may be there for a witness against thee."[1] Here we have the

[1] Deut. xxxi. 24–26.

first recognition of the Scriptures as a sacred deposit. The Jews were hereby constituted librarians for the world. To them, in trust, were "committed the oracles of God."

The books remained in the ark, not only during the remainder of the journeyings of Israel, but for some time after, at Jerusalem,—the collection being added to, from time to time, by such historical and prophetical writings, as, having on them the impress of Divine authority, were composed between the times of Joshua and David. On the completion of the Temple of Solomon, it was ordered that the entire body of sacred writings, as they then existed, should be removed to a place of safe keeping, provided for them in that holy receptacle. In the Temple, and enriched successively by the compositions of the several prophets who flourished between Josiah and Zephaniah, the precious deposit was preserved, until the time of the invasion of Nebuchadnezzar. By him the Temple was rifled and burnt, and whether the autographs of the law and the prophets were destroyed with it, or were carried to Babylon, is not certain. That copies should be in the hands of some of the captives,—the priesthood, and elders, and princes of Israel,—seems more than probable; and, indeed, by Daniel, in this sad time of exile, we find the law of Moses expressly quoted. Still, for the most part, it is acknowledged that the more irreligious portion of the people relapsed into utter ignorance of these Scriptures, during the time they were at Babylon. As they had not heart to "sing the songs of Zion in a strange land," so neither had they any mind to study her precepts, or to meditate on her promises. Hence the first work of Ezra, after the rebuilding of the Temple, according to the prevalent opinion and tradition of the Jews, was the diligent collection and collation of all existing copies, with a view to an authoritative settlement of the canon, and the renewed deposit of all books, allowed to be Divine, in the archives of the new edifice. Ezra, being himself an inspired man, must be considered to have been guided by a Divine influence in the selection of his materials, enabling him to reject all spurious writings, and, in fact, to make his copy as perfect as that which is supposed, rightly or wrongly, to have perished by the hands of Nebuchadnezzar.

As perfect, but perhaps not in point of textual minuteness, identically the same. For, at this stage in the history of the sacred text it is that we meet with that first change in the written Hebrew character, which, though of no moment in the case of Ezra's copy (because, as we shall have occasion to notice presently, there was an independent manuscript, written in the older character, to compare it with), undoubtedly opened the door for a multiplicity of various readings, and thus became a fruitful source of textual dispute. The occasion of the change arose in this way. During the seventy years' captivity, the younger Jews, for the most part, had not only lost their original language as the medium of speech, but even for writing purposes had allowed the old Hebrew, or Samaritan character, as it is called, to be replaced by one of Assyrian origin. Whether from a desire to accommodate himself to this altered written usage of the nation, or whether, as some think, from the wish to have nothing,—not even a literature,—in common with the Samaritans;[1] certain it is, that, in preparing his new edition of the Scriptures, Ezra departed from the character in use before the captivity, and adopted one of Chaldean form, a character designated ever afterwards by the Samaritans as "the writing of Ezra," and, with the exception of the points, answering to the square letter now in use.

Accurate, however, and divinely authenticated, as we are permitted to believe this copy of Ezra was, it too, with all the subsequent additions and final completion in the times of Malachi, was doomed to be lost. Antiochus Epiphanes, the greatest enemy the Jews ever had, entertained a special antipathy to their religion. He obtained possession of all the copies of the Hebrew Scriptures that were to be found, not in private houses only, but, as is inferred from the account given in the Apocrypha, of the sacred original of Ezra itself. For, says the writer of the book of the Maccabees, "he entered proudly into the sanctuary,"

---

[1] See Dr. Brett's *Dissertation on the Ancient Versions of the Bible*, Bp. Watson's *Theol. Tracts*, vol. iii. p. 6, and Davidson's *Biblical Criticism*, c. iii. p. 21. 1852.

and when his people " had rent in pieces the books of the law which they found, they burnt them with fire."[1] But, in the meantime, synagogues had increased: and synagogue copies were transcribed with greater care than any others. And, therefore, no sooner had " Judas Maccabeus recovered the city and the Temple, the Lord guiding them,"[2] than, from one or more of these synagogue copies, most probably from the one in possession of his father Mattathias, he ordered a most accurate transcript to be made with a view to its being deposited in the Temple. This document, it is believed by some, met with no better fate than its predecessors,—having been lost at the siege of Jerusalem in the first Christian century. True, from a passage in Josephus, it has been inferred that the Maccabean or Temple copy was recovered on his special request to Titus; but the possibility is at least to be admitted, that it may have perished in the siege, or have been irrecoverably carried away by the Romans, as part of the Temple spoil.

But be this as it may, there had been happily secured again, in the providence of God, an independent security for the integrity of His written word, in the preparation, 300 years before, of the translation of the Scriptures into Greek by the Septuagint. Much controversy has arisen in regard to the circumstances under which this celebrated version was compiled; and, at this distance of time, it may not be easy, in the

[1] 1 Maccabees, i. 21, 56.   [2] 2 Maccabees, ii. ; x. 1.

accounts of the transaction handed down to us, to separate the fabulous element from the real. Thus far, perhaps, the accounts may be taken as history. About the year 277 B.C., Ptolemy Philadelphus, king of Egypt, was desirous to found a library of unsurpassed extent and value at Alexandria. In such a collection, he was told by his librarian, the law of the Jews ought to have a place; but as the Hebrew character was unknown to the Egyptians, the object could only be accomplished by ordering a translation to be made. With this view, the king wrote to the high-priest of the Jews to send him the book, with a number of qualified interpreters to superintend its translation. The request was complied with, and seventy-two persons, or six persons from each of the twelve Jewish tribes, men of great learning and piety, were conducted to a place, appointed by the librarian as favourable for learned retirement, and there, as some say in seventy-two days, they completed a work destined to live to all time.

Other parts of the narrative, resting though they do on the authority of Philo and Josephus,—as, for instance, that the seventy scribes were shut up in separate cells, in the isle of Pharos; that they were forbidden to hold any communication with each other; that when they came to compare their versions together every word was found to agree; and that, in commemoration of such a miracle, the Jews both of Greece and Egypt repaired annually to the isle of Pharos, and held a religious festival on the shore,—we may, with all due reverence for the version, be somewhat slow to accept. They are referred to, chiefly as showing the sacred estimation in which this version was held by the Jews themselves,—a circumstance still further proved by the fact, not only that this version was publicly read in the synagogues of Judea, in the first Christian century, but also that He who was Himself " the truth," and who knew what His nation would accept as the truth, most commonly, in referring to the Old Testament Scriptures, made use of the Septuagint as the medium of His citations.

From the time of our Lord and His Apostles, however, the feeling of the Jews towards this their once honoured version changed. It was enough, for their rejection of it, that it should have had the approval of the Nazarene. One of the early effects, therefore, of the dispersion which followed on the destruction of Jerusalem by the Romans, was the establishment of schools for the cultivation of sacred literature. Each succeeding century saw an order of learned men spring up, who gave themselves, with incredible industry, to the critical perfecting of the sacred writings,—their labours terminating in the final settlement of the Masoretic text, and so preparing for that grand invention of the art of printing in the fifteenth century, whereby it should come to be said of the Hebrew Scriptures, as of those heavens to whose authorship they first bore their testimony, "Their line is gone out through all the earth, and their words to the end of the world."[1]

II. We have thus traced the history of the Mosaic documents, in their downward course, from the ancient manuscript to the modern printed page; from their safe keeping in the ark of the covenant, to a consecrated place in the Jewish or Christian sanctuary. In order to a proof of the essential uncorruptness and identity of the record, however, a *reverse* method of investigation to that we have been pursuing, is commonly adopted by our theological writers; and a retrogressive view of the history of the Jewish people, step by step, is taken, in order to shew that at no one period of their national vicissitudes, since the day they crossed the Jordan, could a document like the Pentateuch have been palmed upon them, or even its essential features changed. Let us glance at the proofs of this.

Now the identity of the record for a period of 2300 years back,— that is, to the time of the return of the Jews from the Babylonish captivity,—we establish easily. The Septuagint version was composed 277 years before Christ, and, from the universal prevalency of the Greek language, would be known, more or less, to the learned of all nations. Besides which, during the greater part

---

[1] Ps. xix. 4. For an account of the origin, age, and critical labours of the Masoretic doctors, see Horne's *Introd.* vol. ii. part i. c. 2, p. 87, and Davidson's *Treatise on Biblical Criticism*, chap. viii. and ix.

of this first period, the books have been read and explained in Jewish synagogues every Sabbath day,—translations made of them, copies multiplied, quotations cited, Sadducee and Pharisee, Christian and Mahomedan, alike acknowledging their undoubted authenticity.

But how do we bridge over the next retrogressive period, the period of the captivity itself,—that disastrous portion of Jewish history, during which the very language of the people must almost have died out, through their constant intermixture with the Chaldæans, the Persians, and the people of the East,—insomuch that when Ezra read in their ears the words of the Law, it became needful that one should stand up and interpret,[1]—giving the Hebrew words in the Chaldee vernacular? How know we that the books did not get changed or corrupted then? Or how can we be sure that the entire collection was not a forgery made up by Ezra himself? The latter supposition is negatived by the fact that the people themselves asked to have the law read to them, as a book, with which they had long been familiar, and which they expressly designate as "the Book of the Law of Moses, which the Lord had commanded Israel."[2]

Nor is it less easy to overthrow the other supposition of any material change in the contents of the books themselves. Allusion has been made to an older

[1] Neh. viii. 8.
[2] See Ezra, iii. 2, 4; viii. 6, 14, 25; Neh. viii. ix. x.

Hebrew copy of the Pentateuch with which *we* can compare the version of Ezra, though a Jew would not. This copy is that of the Samaritans,—a bitter and hostile offshoot from the ancient people, who, during the captivity had preserved a Pentateuch of their own. And this version, if exception be made for the celebrated text in Deuteronomy, where the Samaritan copy reads Mount Gerizim, and the Jewish Mount Ebal,[1]— a difference which national prejudice may sufficiently account for in either case,—is, in all material particulars, identical with that which Ezra the scribe recited in the ears of the people in the street that was before the water-gate. The testimony is of the highest value. The scribe, we are sure, for the accuracy of his record, would never have been indebted to the Samaritan; the Samaritan, if that record had been wanting in accuracy, would have been but too glad to have exposed the untrustworthiness of the scribe. The whole matter, therefore, was plainly of Divine ordering; in order that the proof might be at hand for all time, that, during the dreary interval of the captivity, God had not left His word without a witness, and that even from among those who could not be called its friends.

The same form of argument, based upon the national jealousies between Israel and Judah, tides us over another retrogressive period. For each of the two kingdoms had its separate copy during the period of

[1] Deut. xxvii. 12, 13.

their separation. And since the Jew would not, at that time, have accepted a copy from the Israelite, nor the Israelite from the Jew, it follows that the document must have been their common property, before the disruption took place, an event which we commonly fix about the year 975 before the Christian era.

As we draw nearer in our ascent up the stream of time to the date at which the Pentateuch is reputed to have had its beginning, our proofs of a prior existence multiply. But the necessity of quoting them is superseded by the consideration of one fact alone. From the time of the disruption of the kingdoms, back to the time of the entrance of the Israelites into Palestine, the authority of the Mosaic books is so closely interwoven with the religious, political, social, and domestic life of the Jews, that the originating of such a record, or even any material falsification of its contents, would be utterly impossible. It would be no easy thing, argues Bishop Stillingfleet, to forge a Magna Charta, and induce a whole nation to accept its provisions as binding. Yet, more than a Magna Charta was the Pentateuch to the Jews. It formed the basis of every civil and religious regulation. It defined territory; it fixed property; it settled family rights; it ruled the laws of inheritance; it regulated the successions to the priesthood; it framed statutes for the government of the household; and, on pain of excommunication from the privileges of the commonwealth, enjoined the strict observance of a somewhat burdensome and costly ritual.

And the Divine obligation of every part of this Mosaic constitution is acknowledged by each one of the sacred writers, in succession, from the time of Solomon backwards to that of Joshua. In all expostulations or reasonings with the people, the ultimate appeal is to the Law of the Lord. The quoted words of Moses suffice to seal all truth, and end all strife:— Psalmist, Prophet, Warrior, Judge — the heads of tribes and the people of the land — all doing homage to the great Legislator, even to the very day when the first leader of the armies of Israel gathered the elders of his people "under the oak which is by the sanctuary at Shechem," charging them, in the name of him whom many of them had seen, — his eye not waxed dim, nor his natural force abated, — saying, "Be ye therefore very courageous to keep and to do all that is written in the book of the Law of Moses, that ye turn not aside therefrom to the right hand or to the left." [1]

Such proofs, in relation to the authenticity of a written document, it must be allowed, throw upon the opponents a grave burden. They are phenomena to be accounted for: and if the hypothesis by which we account for them be disallowed, the objector is bound to furnish us with a more convincing explanation of

[1] Josh. xxiii. 6.

his own. Take the authorship of the books, for instance. A whole nation's testimony, together with that of the writer himself, is not to be cast aside lightly. But if Moses did not write the Pentateuch, who did? Or, take again the possibility that the entire record should be a fictitious composition. Then a time must be specified when the forgery was first received; say, near to the age of Moses, or some considerable time afterwards. But it is a record of passing occurrences; and, if published *near* the time, the men of the age would at once have exposed the imposture: whilst, if it should be alleged that it was not published till a *long time after* the Mosaic period, we urge, in disproof of such a position, that two bitterly antagonistic races had each their independent copy of this book, both acknowledging it to be ancient, and both believing it to be true.

III. The proofs thus urged we think might be accepted as conclusive to the genuineness of the Mosaic writings in the form in which they have come down to us; but as against the possibility of mutilation or essential damage to their integrity, one or two subsidiary considerations may be offered.

i. Thus we may advert to the security afforded by the *official custody of the documents*.

Locally, as we have seen, they were watched with jealous sacredness. Neither in the ark, nor in the honoured receptacle provided in the Temple, could any one approach to injure the precious deposit. But this was not the only security. A particular tribe of the people, set apart from all the rest, was consecrated among other things for this especial purpose of keeping watch over the sacred books;— the maintenance of their own tribal and communal prerogatives, moreover, depending upon the nation's confidence that the writings were preserved intact,— in a state of perfect and indefeasible correctness. From the time of the captivity to the close of the Old Testament canon, the securities of official guardianship were still further strengthened, in the establishment by Ezra of the Great Synagogue, or national council,— a body of men, who, among other duties, were commissioned to supervise all questions relating to the canonical authority of the sacred books; and who left after them that order of synagogal interpreters, which became an established institution in Israel for nearly a thousand years.[1]

ii. Another security against textual corruption is to be found in the extensively diffused *knowledge of the contents of the Pentateuch through every class of the community.*

From the time the books were completed, their contents were systematically made public to the whole

---

[1] The name given to the class of persons here referred to, as instituted by Ezra and the Great Synagogue, was that of "Meturgeman." For an account of their office and duties see Dr. Etheridge's *Targums on the Pentateuch*, p. 5.

nation. It was a part of the express injunctions of the great Lawgiver, that, at certain stated periods, the Law should be recited in the hearing of the assembled people.[1] Anticipating the time when they should have a king over them, an injunction was given that the monarch should write, for himself, a copy of this law in a book, out of that which is before the priests, the Levites, and to read therein all the days of his life.[2] The priests also were commanded to teach the children of Israel all the statutes which the Lord had spoken by the hand of Moses,[3] and parents were charged not only to make themselves familiar with its contents, but also to teach it diligently to their children,[4]—the same solemn inhibition being annexed in all cases, under the severest penalties, against any addition being made to this Law, or suffering any part to be taken away.[5]

In this way the whole nation virtually became, in common with the priests and Levites themselves, the conservators of the purity of the books. Every class of the community was obliged to have its copy. The priests must have one, because out of it they had to instruct the people. Heads of families must have one, because they were commanded to read it to their children. The magistrates must have one, because, by its contents, they were necessarily guided in their daily

---

[1] Deut. xxxi. 9–13.   [2] Deut. xvii. 18, 19.
[3] Lev. x. 11.   [4] Deut. vi. 7.
[5] Deut. xii. 32.

administration of the law. How, with so many checks, could material error find admission into the writings; or, on the supposition of wilful falsification, how could a forger obtain such multitudinous consenters to his fraud?

iii. A further security for the unaltered integrity of the writings is to be found in *the different Aramaic paraphrases, or " Targums,"* as they are called, some of which are known to have been in use before the Christian era, and to have had the sanction of ecclesiastical authority.

The origin of these Targums is to be referred to the official interpreters already spoken of. At the return from the Captivity, and indeed for some time before, the Hebrew language, as it exists in the Bible, had ceased, as we have seen, to be the vernacular of the Jewish people. Accordingly, when the reader in the synagogue read the lessons for the day from the Hebrew originals, not only did the interpreter render the Scriptures, verse by verse, into the popular dialect, but authorized expositions of them first delivered in Hebrew, were rendered in the same way. At first, these translated paraphrases were confined to oral discourses; but the importance of them to a right understanding of the Scriptures, by the people at large, soon led to their being preserved in a written form. Of this description of Biblical literature some of the earlier specimens are lost. But two of those on the Pentateuch—known as the Targums of Onkelos, and Jonathan Ben Uzziel—have been preserved, and are remarkable for their fidelity to the received Hebrew originals.

Nor does the value of the Targum testimony end here. Allusion has been made to the Samaritans, as having an independent version of the Pentateuch. It is a great corroboration of our argument that they had their independent Targum too,—a document remarkable for its literal adherence to the Hebrew text, and certainly in use long before Christian times.[1] Can demonstration be stronger than this to shew that, as with the text, so with the paraphrases of these hostile and never-intermingling races, the source of general agreement is to be looked for, in the derivation of their writings from some common manuscript,—a manuscript, which must have had its existence before their feuds began? Surely " in the mouth of two or three witnesses shall every word be established."

iv. The last security we shall advert to for the textual completeness of the sacred writings, and especially of the Pentateuch, is the *traditional veneration for them of the people themselves*, as for a trust, which, to the minutest word or letter, they must be ready to lay down their lives to preserve.

This deep-seated national feeling has its appropriate expression in those words of Josephus,—" How firmly we have given credit to these books of our nation is evident by what we do: for during so many

---
[1] Etheridge *on the Targums*, p. 5.

ages, as have already passed, no one has been so bold as either to add anything to them, to take anything from them, or to make any change in them; but it is become natural to all Jews, immediately and from their very birth, to esteem these books to contain Divine doctrines, and to persist in them, and, if occasion be, willingly to die for them." [1]

To the same feeling of intense and jealous veneration, are to be referred those elaborately useless computations of the Masoretic doctors, which, on the supposition that an inspired mystery was veiled under the minutest literal arrangements of the Mosaic record, led them to calculate which is the middle letter of the Pentateuch, which is the middle clause of each book, and how many times the same letter of the alphabet occurs. In transcribing from a well-authenticated copy, they would make a scruple of changing the situation of a letter, however evidently misplaced, supposing that some mystery had occasioned the alteration.

The traditional sentiment we have spoken of, however, finds its culminating point, in the account which has been preserved, in the Talmud, of certain directions which were to be observed by the scribes, whilst preparing a roll for the use of the synagogue. First, the parchment must be of a particular skin, the ink of a special preparation, the lines of uniform width apart; and if three words only were written, without a line, the manuscript was thrown aside, as unfit for use.

[1] Against Apion, *Works*, vol. iv. 337.

The scribe must sit, while he is copying, in his full official dress. He must retire for a special act of purifying, every time he comes to the name of God. If a king or great man should speak to him, while he is writing, he is not to take his eyes off the roll. Stroke for stroke, must he keep to his authentic copy, forbidden to put down even a " yod " from memory ; whilst, should there be discovered, on the revise, as many as four mistakes in one column,—even such a thing as one word touching another, or a deficient or redundant letter,—the labour of thirty days was lost, and the manuscript commanded to be destroyed. It is further to be noted, that few of these synagogue rolls ever fell into the hands of Christians, or of strangers. When they became worn out, and unfit for further use, in order that no desecration might befall them, they were ordered to be buried in the earth.[1]

Irksome, puerile, childishly superstitious, as some of these regulations may seem, they may at least serve to shew that it was no easy thing to introduce any foreign or fictitious element into the sacred writings; and, so far, they may be allowed to supplement our former proofs, that such as the Mosaic books were, when they were first laid up in the Ark of the Covenant, such are those books as we have them now. The preservation of the record at all, through all the

---

[1] For a full account of these minute precautions see Davidson's *Treatise on Biblical Criticism*, ch. xxiii. p. 323.

revolutions and vicissitudes experienced by the Jewish people, is of itself a unique fact in documentary history. It could not be accounted for by any vigilance of human custody. Levites might keep watch by the Ark, and priests stand day and night in the Temple. A pious king might rejoice on finding a copy of the Law amid sanctuary ruins, and a learned scribe, in the collation of scattered versions, might shew all good fidelity; but the true solution of the fact, that a record should have survived, in all its literal and uninjured integrity, for the space of three thousand three hundred years, is best given in that saying reported of the Jews to this day, that "of the letters and syllables of the Law God had more care than of the stars of heaven."

SECTION V.

THE PENTATEUCH A REVELATION FROM GOD.

" For whatsoever we know we have it by the hands and ministry of men, which lead us along like children, from a letter to a syllable, from a syllable to a word, from a word to a line. .... But God himself was their instructor, He himself taught them, partly by dreams and visions in the night, partly by revelations in the day, taking them aside from amongst their brethren, and talking with them as a man would talk with his neighbour in the way. Thus they became acquainted with the secret and hidden counsels of God."
— HOOKER.

WE may speak of three degrees of truth as belonging to a written document. It may be "poetically" true; or it may be "historically" true; or it may be "absolutely and infallibly" true.. As an example of a book which is only "poetically" true, we might take *Milton's Paradise Lost*, or *Bunyan's Pilgrim's Progress;* because, in each of these works, while certain Divine facts are assumed as the basis of the story, the writer draws upon his imagination for the rest. As an example of a book "historically" true, *The Antiquities of the Jews* by Josephus might be selected, or *The Divine Legation of Moses* by Bishop Warburton; because, to the extent of their ability, and, with such materials as were at their command, it was the avowed purpose of these authors to give forth a faithful picture of the transactions they were professing to record. Of writings of the third class, the *absolutely and infallibly* true, we have one example only; never have had, and never can have more than one; namely, the book of Revelation; the autograph of holy and inspired men; the collection of writings, penned by heaven-taught scribes in order to lead back a wandering world to holiness, to happiness, and to God.

Our arguments hitherto have gone to except the books of Moses from the *first* class of writings we have spoken of, and, at all events, to vindicate for them a title to be admitted into the *second;* in other words, to take down the Pentateuch from the shelf of mere poetic legends, and to assert a claim for it to be accepted as a genuine and authentic narrative. It is still required of us to shew that the proper place for the record is on the highest ledge of truth that a document can attain to,—namely, that which is reserved for a Divine Revelation; for a composition, written under the inspiring influence and direction of the Most High God.

I. This high distinction we claim for the Mosaic books, first, on the EXPRESS TESTIMONY OF THE WRITINGS THEMSELVES.

The right to adduce this testimony may, by some, be disputed. The Divine original of the books, it may be urged, is the thing to be proved, what argumentative fairness can there be in bringing forward, on such a subject, the declarations of the books themselves? To this we answer, that if, by the same rules as we should try the credibility of any other document, we have proved the general veracity of the writings, nothing can be more fair than to receive their evidence on this point also. Illogical it would be, no doubt, to urge, first, the self-claimed inspiration of the writers; and, on that ground alone, to foreclose the right of examination into the truth of the books. But the general truth of the writings being established on sufficient testimony, then, as a part of that truth, we have a right to accept, for whatever an honest statement is worth, any account which the sacred penmen may give of the assistance vouchsafed to them in their own work.

In the case of the books before us, Moses has been proved to be a universally accredited writer; an honest and an impartial writer; a thoroughly competent and fearless writer; on what principle, we ask, is he to be disbelieved, when he says something, not for his own aggrandizement or advantage, but solely in vindication of the authority of his mission,— a mission undertaken with the utmost possible reluctance, and entailing upon him little but vexation, and disappointment, and thankless pains?

How far, then, does Moses, a man of truth, and integrity, and self-forgetting simplicity, lead us to believe that he penned his narrative, under a Divine influence, and a Divine dictation? His books embrace a wide range of subject,—history, prophecy, legislation, song,—does he, in any one of these departments, appear as a person who writes solely upon his own knowledge and authority? Let us take some examples. A part of his work was to chronicle events. Was he at such times left to his own unguided discretion? Read the preface to the account of the wilderness wanderings: "These are the journeys of the children of Israel, which went forth out of the land of Egypt with their armies under the hand of Moses and Aaron. And Moses wrote their goings out according to their journeys by the commandment of the Lord."[1]

Sometimes he receives direct commission as a prophet, to foretell things to come, and again inspiration is implied: "I will raise them up a prophet from among their brethren like unto thee, and will put my words into his mouth;"[2] expressions, nearly the same as those addressed to Moses, when first entering on his office.[3] Chiefly, however, Moses is regarded as a Lawgiver. How far, in this capacity, does he seem to be left to his natural prudence and sagacity? Not for one jot or tittle of that written code. Thus, at the close of some commanded ceremonial observances, the words come in, "And the Lord said unto Moses, Write thou these words: for after the tenor of these words I have made a covenant

---

[1] Numb. xxxiii. 1, 2. [2] Deut. xviii. 18. [3] Comp. Exod. ix. 10-15.

with thee and with Israel:"[1] whilst of the two tables of the testimony the language used is yet more remarkable : "And the tables were the work of God, and the writing was the writing of God graven upon the tables."[2] Whilst, once more, if any should think, that, in his poetic moods, Moses was left to the spontaneous outflow of his own imaginings, the words, in regard to his own Divine hymn, meet us, " And the Lord said unto Moses, ... Write ye this song for you, and teach it the children of Israel, that this song may be a witness for me against the children of Israel... Moses therefore wrote this song the same day."

To these may be added other testimonies. Thus there is the constantly recurring expression "the word of the Lord,"—a phrase which, whether it be, as the Targums and some of the most eminent commentators hold, a synonyme for the manifested Logos or not, must imply the presence of a Divine element in the thing spoken. And it comes in on all occasions. It was "the word of the Lord" which came unto Abraham, in a vision. It was according to "the word of the Lord," that Moses tabulated the families of Levi. By "the word of the Lord" was settled the dispute raised by the daughters of Zelophehad; and, according to their reverence for "the word of the Lord," were the servants of Pharaoh delivered from Egypt's wasting plagues. Indeed, of the one hundred and three chapters which constitute the books of Exodus, Leviticus,

[1] Exod. xxxiv. 27.   [2] Exod. xxxii. 16.   [3] Deut. xxxi. 21, 22.

and Numbers, *fifty-two* have for their first verse, with scarcely a verbal variation, "And the Lord spake unto Moses saying."

The testimony to a Divine inspiration on the part of the writer himself then, is conclusive. Throughout the entire composition, Moses is not, and does not wish to appear, in any other light than that of God's secretary, God's chief speaker, God's impersonated and embodied word. His position is nowhere more clearly defined, than in the words addressed to him, on first receiving his commission. He had pleaded, in justification of his backwardness, "O my Lord, I am not eloquent, but I am of slow speech and of slow tongue. And the Lord said unto him, Who hath made man's mouth? or who maketh the dumb or deaf, or the seeing or the blind? Have not I the Lord? Now therefore go, and I will be thy mouth, and teach thee what thou shalt say."[1]

II. We advance as a second proof of the revealed character of the Mosaic writings, the fact that, from the time of their publication until now, they have always been accepted as of Divine authority by THE PEOPLE TO WHOM THEY WERE ADDRESSED.

The fact itself might have been allowed to rest on the accounts, already given, of the scrupulous care with which the Jews have ever watched over their sacred writings. Their veneration culminates, however,

[1] Exod. iv. 10.

in the care of the books of Moses. From the time this precious trust was first laid up in the Ark, the persuasion never left the people that the utterances of their great Lawgiver were Divine utterances,—words passed from the mouth of God to the mouth of man. The first words we read after the account of his death, place his prophetic mission on a footing of unapproached pre-eminence;—"There arose not a prophet since in Israel like unto Moses whom the Lord knew face to face;"[1] whilst in the fore-front of the instructions given to his successor is a command that he charge the people "to do according to all the law which Moses my servant commanded thee."[2] If we admit that this may have been written after his death, the words still set forth the declared judgment of the Jewish church, that Moses stood in the first rank of those inspired men who held communion with God.

And, in keeping with this view of the Divine original and authority of the law, are the references made to it by almost every succeeding writer, down to the close of the Old Testament canon. Titles are given to it which part it off from every human composition. It is "The Book;" or "the Book of the Law;" or "the Law and the testimony;" or "the Law of the God of heaven." Divine sanctions are attributed to it, as to something which it was of the very essence of sin to transgress. "They have forsaken my Law which is set before them," it is said in Jeremiah.[3] "The priests

[1] Deut. xxxiv. 10.   [2] Josh. i. 7.   [3] Jer. ix. 13.

have done violence to my Law," it is written in Ezekiel.[1] Haggai says, "Ask now the priests concerning my Law;"[2] while, in Malachi, we have the command given to Israel, to "remember the Law of Moses, given in Horeb, with the statutes and judgments."[3] Indeed, in proof that the feeling of sacred awe for the writings, as being God's own words, continued with unabated intensity down to the time of the return from the captivity, it is enough to cite the words of Ezra, when reproving the people for their breach of the law of Moses, in the matter of contracting marriages with strangers; in which he tells us, "There were assembled unto me every one that trembled at the words of the God of Israel."[4] It seemed as if the reading of their heaven-sent law was the first solicitude of the people, on their return to their own land. "They gathered themselves together as one man," says the sacred historian, "into the street that was before the water-gate: and they spake unto Ezra the scribe to bring the book of the Law of Moses which the Lord had commanded to Israel."[5]

We pass on to testimonies to the same point from uninspired Jewish authorities. Among these the opinions of the authors of the Apocrypha are entitled to respectful notice.

Abounding as some of these writings do in legendary and fictitious matter, and utterly destitute as they

---

[1] Ezek. xxii. 26.   [2] Hag. ii. 11.   [3] Mal. iv. 4.
[4] Ezra, ix. 4.   [5] Neh. viii. 1.

are of Divine authority in matters of doctrine, yet their place, in the history of the Jews and Jewish literature, as coming in after the age of the prophets had passed away, must always give them an interest to the Christian student, and, on subjects about which there could be no motive for a misstatement, a right to be considered as fair exponents of the national mind. Well, by these authors we are told "the holy Law was made and given by God."[1] It is "the book of the covenant of the Most High God," its "light uncorrupt," and "its decrees eternal."[2] Moses himself they call a "holy prophet," and one of their prayers runs, "O Lord our God . . . . as Thou spakest by Thy servant Moses, in the day when Thou didst command him to write Thy Law."[3]

These writings bring us down nearly to Christian times, when the account already given, of what the Jews have ever thought of their Law, may be well supplemented by the testimony of Josephus and Philo, men who were contemporaries with the apostles, and who, as will appear, were not less zealous than Paul himself was for the Divine authorship of the Law. From Josephus, in addition to a passage already quoted, where he calls their twenty-two books Divine, we may cite another extract, in which the claim to inspired authority is put forth in direct and explicit form. He observes, speaking of the Scriptures, "It is not in the power of every one to draw up such records; nor does

[1] 2 Macc. vi. 23.   [2] Ecclus. xxiv. 23; xvii. 12.   [3] Baruch, ii. 28.

any contradiction exist in them, because the privilege of writing them belongs to prophets alone. They alone were acquainted with the facts of earliest date, which they have learned by direct inspiration from God." [1]

Nor less striking are the words of Philo. Speaking of Moses, he says, " He was that purest mind which received at once the gift of legislation and prophecy, with divinely-inspired wisdom." [2] Again, "He was breathed upon with heavenly love." [3] Whilst still more remarkable, on account of the striking accordance of the sentiment contained in it with the words of one greater than Philo, is the passage:—" The words of Moses alone, steadfast and unshaken, stamped as it were with the seal of nature itself, remain fixed since the day they were written until now; and our hope is that for all future time they will abide immortal, as long as sun and moon, and the universal heaven and the world, endure." [4] Could the learned Jew have spoken more plainly, if he had heard those words spoken in the sermon on the mount, "Verily, I say unto you, till heaven and earth pass, one jot or one tittle shall in no wise pass from the Law till all be fulfilled."[5]

III. The last words quoted may well suggest to us our next proof of the Divine authority of the books of

[1] Against Apion, i. 7.   [2] See Lee on *Inspiration*, Lect. ii. 50.
[3] Ibid.
[4] De Vita Mosis, t. ii. p. 136, see Professor Lee on *Inspiration*, Lect. ii. p. 62.   [5] Matt. v. 18.

Moses, in the testimony borne to them by our LORD JESUS CHRIST, AND THE WRITERS OF THE NEW TESTAMENT.

The testimony of apostles and evangelists hardly admits of quotation, because it spreads over the whole volume. The Law is the basis of all New Testament teaching. The voice of Moses is quoted by its authors interchangeably with the voice of God. Peter, in the Temple; Stephen, before the Sanhedrim; Paul, in the synagogue at Antioch; John, in the rapt ecstasies of Patmos,—what is the testimony of any or all of these, but that their own message and that of Moses is one? Every writer in the New Testament, in substance, is found to adopt those words of Paul before Agrippa, " I continue unto this day, witnessing both to small and great, saying none other things than those which the prophets and Moses did say should come." [1]

We pass on to testimony, therefore, most conclusive of all, in relation to the permanent authority and Divine infallibility of the books of Moses, namely, the testimony of the Great Teacher Himself. We are now on holy ground. We are presuming to inquire how He, " in whom dwelt all the fullness of the Godhead bodily;" He "in whom are hidden all the treasures of wisdom and knowledge;" He who was "Light of Light," even as He was "God of God," thought fit to deliver Himself on the claims of His servant Moses. And to a doubter of those claims, while still retaining

[1] Acts, xxvi. 22.

the name of Christian, the answers returned must be confounding. Again and again does the Holy One pledge Himself to His great predecessor's veracity. The testimony of Moses is declared to be as worthy of credit as His own:—"For had ye believed Moses ye would have believed me: for he wrote of me."[1] The mission of Moses is shown to be as Divinely accredited as His own:—"And as touching the dead that they rise, have ye not read in the book of Moses how in the bush God spake unto him, saying, I am the God of Abraham, and of Isaac, and of Jacob?"[2] Nay, more; the words of Moses are declared to be as imperishable as His own, the identical form of expression being used with regard to both, that before either could fail of accomplishment, heaven and earth should pass away.[3]

In like manner does the Saviour testify to the several contents of the Pentateuch. To the "precepts" of Moses He appeals, as the eternal rule of moral conduct: "It is written, Man shall not live by bread alone, but by every word that proceedeth out of the mouth of God."[4] To the "prophecies" of Moses does He refer, as foreshewing the eternal purpose of God with regard to Himself: "These are the words which I spake unto you while I was yet with you: that all things must be fulfilled which were written in the Law of Moses, and in the prophets, and in the Psalms,

[1] John, v. 46. [2] Mark, xii. 26.
[3] Comp. St. Luke, xvi. 17, with Matt. xxiv. [4] Matt. iv. 4.

concerning me."[1] To the "histories" of Moses does He direct attention, as supplying monitory examples of what shall come upon the careless and disobedient:— " Like as it was in the days of Lot;" "As it was in the days of Noe;" "Remember Lot's wife."[2] To the " ordinances" of Moses does He set His seal—honouring the Sabbath, observing the Passover, and submitting, in His own sacred person, to the initiatory sacrament of the Jewish Church. Nay, to the awakening power of the exhortations of Moses does He bear witness, as being of more Divinely-convincing force than would be the word of a messenger, come fresh from the spirit-world:—" If they hear not Moses and the prophets neither will they be persuaded though one rose from the dead."[1]

Testimonies, so unambiguous, from the lips of Him " who spake as never man spake," would seem to foreclose all further gainsaying. But they are not suffered so to do. A phase of Nestorianism has reappeared among us. And, with regard to our Divine Lord, the possibility has been supposed of such a submerging, such an intermission, nay rather, such an entire abnegation of all the functions of Godhead,— and that even in relation to the very objects of His mission to our world,—that, only by the most strained theological courtesy, could the title of Divine, on such a view, be conceded to Him at all. The passage from a recent book is very painful to be obliged to quote,

[1] Luke, xxiv. 44. [2] Luke, xvii. 26-32. [3] Luke, xvi. 31.

but we could not otherwise expose the almost transparent fallacy it contains. It runs thus: " It is perfectly consistent with the most entire and sincere belief in our Lord's Divinity to hold, as many do, that when He vouchsafed to become a man, He took our nature fully, and voluntarily entered into all the conditions of humanity: and, among others, into that which makes our growth in all ordinary knowledge gradual and partial." And then, having previously taken it for granted that the Jews themselves were all under a delusion about the Mosaic narrative, in believing it to be a record of facts when it was not, this writer goes on to ask, "At what period, then, of our Lord's life is it to be supposed, that He had granted to Him, supernaturally, full and accurate information on these points, so that He should be expected to speak about the Pentateuch in other terms than any other devout Jew of that day would have employed?"[1]

Now, in relation to the first part of this statement, if care be taken to limit the expressions to the childhood and youth of our Lord, we have not so much to object. The expression of St. Luke that "Jesus increased in wisdom and stature" does, undoubtedly, leave room for the inference, that, just as the sacred body of the Saviour shewed new accretions of height, from year to year, so the mind, at the same intervals, would evince new accretions of intelligence, and wisdom, and power. We could hardly admit the perfect-

[1] Bishop Colenso on the *Pentateuch*, p. 31.

ness of His humanity were it otherwise. The Eternal Word, having bowed to the discipline and limitations of our nature, could not be expected to claim exemption from the law of its mental growth,—content to hold His Omniscience in abeyance for a season, that He might learn as finite creatures learn. Not that, in any undeveloped mental state of the Saviour, we could allow a bare approach to fallibility. The intelligence which, at twelve years of age, astonished all who heard Him in the Temple, might not come up to that prodigious height of wisdom, which, in later years, spake only to silence and confound: but that He should have erred, because the multitude of His nation erred, was as impossible at one period as at the other. The full development of thought might be more perfect than the germ, but was not more Divinely true.

But besides this, it seems obvious to observe, that with these undeveloped mental states of the Saviour, in infancy or childhood, the present argument can have nothing to do. The testimonies of the Holy One to the Divine authority of Moses belong to a time after He was thirty years of age; after the spirit of wisdom had descended upon Him in all His measureless and omniscient plenitude; after the waters of the Jordan had been afraid, and the Mount of Transfiguration had trembled, because, above them had been heard the voice of the infinite God, saying, " This is my beloved Son, in whom I am well pleased : Hear ye Him." Surely, to hint a doubt as to whether, on any matter of sacred history, the Saviour possessed "full and accurate information" then,—to dare, at such a period of His life, to put His transcendent intelligence on a level with that of "the most pious and learned adults of His nation," is not more audacious than it is weak; not more irrational than it is blasphemous and profane. For where can the application of the principle stop? If the intelligence of Christ were not equal to the detection of false history, how know we that it was equal to the discernment of false doctrine? If He could err about the mission of Moses, when coming to bring us the law, what confidence can we have in His own mission, when giving us a dispensation of grace and truth?

From this part of our subject, one conclusion follows at all events. The books of Moses and those of the New Testament must stand or fall together. A man cannot consistently hold to the one, if he have made up his mind to despise the other. To deny Moses, is manifestly to deny Christ: and with the same pen-knife, as, in the spirit of Jehoiakim, a man cuts up the roll of the Pentateuch for the burning hearth, does he cut up the Gospel of our Lord Jesus Christ, to become fuel for the same flame. No; the union of the documents is indissoluble. And of the man who, when offered the books of the Gospel, and the books of Moses, desires that the one may be taken and the other left, we can only say that he has faith in neither. The converse of sacred words might with all reverence be applied to him, " Ye *would* have believed Moses if ye *had* believed Me."

IV. As a concluding corroboration of the view taken in the present chapter, we urge that such as the Jews have always believed the Mosaic writings to be, and such as the words of our Divine Lord plainly imply they are, such also have they been allowed to be in EVERY AGE OF THE CHRISTIAN CHURCH.

No doubt exists as to the belief of the Jews in the highest form of inspiration. The persuasion of it underlies all those minute precautions we have adverted to, in retaining every large or small letter exactly as it is, and in the superstitious dread of a change of one of them from its place above, to a place below the line. Later Jews, such as Aben Ezra and Maimonides in the twelfth century, began to introduce views upon the subject of a more lax kind; but they were condemned as heretical. The more learned and pious of the nation held then, as they hold now, that the sacred writings were absolutely and infallibly true, in all their parts; and that, in the case of Moses especially, without reliance on extraneous aids of any kind, and beyond the use of his own personal knowledge of the facts, every word came down from him to their fathers, as though written fresh from the mouth of God.

These views we find very strongly participated in by the early Christian Fathers. Irenæus declared that the Scriptures were " perfect as dictated by the word of God and His Spirit." Clement of Rome said, "The Scriptures are the true words of the Spirit." The Alexandrian Father of that name declares that "the whole Scriptures are the law of God, and that they are all Divine;" while Origen goes even further, saying "that every word is Divine, and that there is not a syllable which has not the wisdom of God in it." As the science of biblical criticism advanced, and was supposed to bring to light slight variations in the narratives, some modifications upon the subject appear in the language of St. Chrysostom and St. Jerome, but never without the clearest recognition of a Divine influence, supervising every part of the record.[1]

Nor less conclusive is the language, on the same subject, employed by the great writers of our own Church, from the time of the Reformation downwards. Cranmer calls the Scripture "the sure rock of God's word written:" Bullinger terms it "the very true word of God . . . . absolutely perfect:" Jewell, "the very sure and infallible rule . . . . the heavenly voices whereby God hath opened unto us His will;" Hooker, "heavenly truth uttered by Divine inspiration;" and Stillingfleet, "the infallible records of the word of God."[2]

Such, then, has been the belief in the Divine authority of the Pentateuch, from the day of its first

[1] See Professor Browne's Essay, *Aids to Faith*, p. 299, Lect. on *Inspiration*, p. 82.

[2] See other examples in an *Address on Inspiration*, by Rev. E. Garbett. London, 1862.

publication until now. Of its canonical authority we, as Christians, are not required to offer proof. We take the books of Moses, as we do the other Old Testament Scriptures, in full, and without hesitation, at the hands of God's ancient people;—take them as part and parcel of their religion. "To them were committed the oracles of God." And therefore, on the evidence which was satisfactory to them, and on the internal evidence of the books themselves, we accept the entire record, as a Divinely-penned exposition of the purposes and will of God; made to the Jews first, and, through them, to be proclaimed to the world at large. Theories of inspiration, especially in relation to the Old Testament, we have no occasion to invent, and are not concerned to offer. We know that holy men of old were moved by the Holy Ghost, but we do not profess to know how they were moved. For proof in controversy, for settlement of doctrine, for support in temptation, for guidance of life, we are content to rest as the pious of the ancient nation rest on the one foundation, 'It is written.' And, in thus resting, we put no difference between their sacred writings and our own. To us, as much as to them, every great announcement in the Pentateuch comes as with a voice from the cloud; as with the authority of a message direct from the eternal throne; as with the distinctness of words, proceeding out of the burning centre of the Tabernacle glory, and speaking audibly, "Thus saith the Lord God."

SECTION VI.

THE INSPIRED AUTOGRAPH AND THE RECEIVED VERSIONS.

" There may be mistakes of transcribers, there may be other real or seeming mistakes, not easy to be particularly accounted for ; but there are certainly no more things of this kind in the Scripture, than what were to have been expected, in books of such antiquity; and nothing in any wise sufficient to discredit the general narrative."— BISHOP BUTLER.

" 'Tis some relief, that points, not clearly known,
Without much hazard, may be let alone."— DRYDEN.

" GOD who at sundry times and in divers manners spake, in times past, unto the fathers by the prophets, hath in these last days spoken unto us by His Son." Such is the language in which a believing Jew, writing for the instruction of believing Jews, refers to that collection of ancient writings, which he knew to be dear alike to him and to themselves. In relation to the subject of our last section, the striking feature of this passage is that it assumes the Old Testament to be the *actual Word of God*. It is not a history, containing the Word; not a treatise, explanatory of the Word; but it is God Himself, speaking ; very truth of very truth ; a collection of utterances, proceeding direct from the excellent glory, and reproduced, in all their Divine purity, on a written page, as if "graven with an iron pen, and with lead on the rock for ever."

Moreover, in regard of their Divine authenticity, it is further assumed by the Apostle, that there is no difference in these writings. The communications may have been made "at sundry times;"—before the flood to Enoch; after the exodus to Moses; during the captivity to Daniel; after the return therefrom to Ezra and Nehemiah,—but in all cases, it was God speaking. "In divers manners," also may the revelation have been made,—by rapt ecstasies, by midnight dreams, by dark parables, by immediate impulses from the Divine Spirit, yet still it was God speaking. When the writings were first given to the world, and as they were first given, there was no place in them for misinterpretation or error. What agencies were employed to guard them from deterioration, in their passage from heaven to earth,—by what mysterious process Divine thoughts were made capable of being transmitted through a human mind, on to a human page, we are not informed. The Scriptures are the only source from which we could learn anything upon the subject, and they tell us nothing but the fact:— "Thy Word is truth;" "Holy men of old spake as they were moved by the Holy Ghost;" "All Scripture is given by inspiration of God."

Still, in relation to the forms of modern controversy, this question of inspiration is the pivot upon which many of the infidel objections turn. It may be that Christians have theorized too much upon the subject, and that adversaries have assumed too much; but, in one way or other, it has been the fruitful source of anti-Christian cavil, and will be so, until we are agreed, in some sort, as to what Inspiration is; and, in regard to the Scriptures, by what forms of proved inaccuracy the claim to such an influence could be invalidated.

I. The question has, first, to be fairly met, WHAT IS INSPIRATION?

To this inquiry, we have Professor Lee, of Dublin, returning the answer, "Inspiration is the actuating energy of the Holy Spirit, in whatever degree or manner it may have been exercised, guided by which, the human agents, chosen by God, have officially proclaimed His will, by word of mouth, or have committed to writing the several portions of the Bible." Another writer, Dr. Gaussen, defines it to be, "The mysterious power which the Divine Spirit put forth on the authors of the Scriptures, both in the Old and New Testament, in order to their composing these, as they have been received by the Church of God at their hands."

Of course, these are only opinions. Authoritative definition we have none. The subject has been left, perhaps wisely left, by learned Jews, by the early Christian writers, by the great Fathers of the Reformation, as one which, in their judgment, was not suited for the sharply defined precision of an all-binding dogma,—although they would one and all have laid down their lives rather than give up the doctrine that the Bible is the Word of God.

This absence of an authoritative ruling, however, has had its inconveniences. Writers and preachers have put forth hypotheses of their own,—not safe always, and not wise,—some claiming too much for inspiration, and some giving up too much; some contending for a rigorous severity of textual exactness which laid the Scriptures open to the most obvious exceptions, and others, allowing such an indeterminate license to the human element, in the writings, as to make it difficult to say, with certainty, how much of them is Divine; some supposing the influence on the minds of the sacred writers to have been absolutely mechanical, so that they became, as it were, mere instruments for photographing, with an enforced and blind fidelity, whatever might be traced out by the Spirit of God on the lens of their own mind; others supposing that the influence was informing, and generally directive only;· so that, the substance of the Divine communication being given to the writers, without any control over the choice of words, each was left to transmit the message to mankind in his own way.

Our safe pathway, in such inquiries, may reasonably be considered to lie between two extremes; between the false theories of the infidel, who denies all Divine communications to man, and the crude and hasty speculations of those, who presume to fix the measure, and determine the degrees of that heavenly illumination, which Scripture indeed everywhere supposes, but never minutely defines. Of course, the influence supposed must be of such a nature as to secure the ends of an authenticated Divine Revelation. But this by no means precludes the possibility that the influence itself might be different in degree, in different cases,—some subjects requiring more, and some less of Divine communication. Thus prophecy would seem to require the suggestion of distinct original ideas, of a new and often of a transcendental kind, according to the nature of the subject,—as in the visions of Isaiah, and Ezekiel, and Daniel; whilst, for narrative purposes, the influence might go no further than to secure an exact memory, accurate powers of observation, and, where the facts came through the medium of testimony, an ability to weigh evidence, together with a determined and controlling bias as to selection. Thus a special influence of the Holy Spirit was exerted over the minds of the Apostles to "bring all things to their remembrance," and to reveal to them, as Bishop Horsley observes, "whatever was requisite for them as disciples to know, and as Apostles to teach."

And so with regard to other portions of the sacred writings. We can well conceive, that, in relation to such momentous revelations as the creation of the world, the circumstances of the Fall, the first promise of a Saviour, and all the events connected with God's covenant selection of a peculiar people, a far higher degree of absolute Divine illumination must have been necessary than could be required for a biographer to transcribe the genealogies of the patriarchs, or to connect the domestic history of Ruth with the establishment of the royal house of David. In the one case, it was necessary that the mind and memory be freed from defect or error; in the other, that more than mortal wisdom should be communicated from above. It is a good rule to suppose so much of the supernatural as was needful for the ends proposed, and no more. What those ends are, to their full extent, we cannot know, and it is useless to speculate about the kind of influence requisite for them, until we do.

While, however, we may be anxious to keep clear of all technical or scientific theories of inspiration,— theories, that is, of the *modus* of the inspiring influence, of the method of the Divine illapse upon the human faculties, of the nature of those psychological operations, whereby God's thoughts are made to pass through man's thoughts, and yet suffer nothing in the process of transmission,—we are not, therefore, less earnest in contending for inspiration as *a fact*. A belief in such an influence,—suggestive, directive, corrective, and, wherever necessary to a right apprehension of the truth, extending to the very words employed, —is vital to our confidence in Revelation. Call it by what name you will, or suppose it to co-operate with the human medium in what manner you will, we cannot recede from the broad ground, that a special Divine superintendence was exerted over the minds of the sacred penmen, to enable them to make known to the world truths which could be discovered in no other way. How far the writer was, in some cases, at liberty to choose his own expressions; how far he might make use of his own knowledge, or other available sources of information; how far he was left to incorporate into the structure of his composition, the native colouring and characteristics of his own mind,—on such points we are not called upon to pronounce authoritatively. Enough, that we say that the writer is preserved, while the Spirit of God is upon him, from using any language, which would convey a mistaken sense of the Divine mind, whether in regard to facts, or precepts, or doctrine. Inspiration is this, or it is nothing. If we allow that the fabric of Scripture, as it was revealed, is such- an inextricable tissue of human thoughts and Divine thoughts, that Moses may err as Herodotus; that the provisions and enactments of the sacred code of Sinai, may be as liable to mistake as the institutions of Solon or Lycurgus, then heavenly doctrine is not; revelation is not; certain truth is not. Every man becomes a Bible to himself. The Holy Spirit is deposed from his sovereignty over the human conscience, and the "verifying faculty" is seated on the vacated throne.

II. Thus much may serve for a general answer to the inquiry, What do we mean by Inspiration? As will be seen, with certain necessary limitations, it commits us to the conclusion, held up to such scornful reprobation in a recent work, and expressed in the words, "The Bible is none other than the word of God,— not some part of it more, some part of it less, but all alike the utterance of Him who sitteth upon the throne,—absolute, faultless, unerring, supreme."[1] It remains that we consider what some of these limitations are; in other words, that we state, more definitely, what are the particular writings for which this inspiring influence is claimed, and then consider whether anything which is, or which is supposed to be, found in the copies, can reasonably set these claims aside.

i. And first, obvious as the limitation is, it is necessary to say that, in its rigid, absolute, and stringently literal sense, the inspiration contended for is claimed for the *inspired autographs* only, as distinguished from any *copies*, which might be made of the writings subsequently, or from *translations* of them made into any other tongue.

The reasonableness and fitness of this distinction will be apparent to any mind having the slightest acquaintance with the rules of argument; and yet it is one which Christians have been very apt to overlook, and which, therefore, objectors have found it conve-

---

[1] Bp. Colenso on the *Pentateuch*, quoting from Burgon on *Inspiration and Interpretation*, p. 6.

nient to ignore. It is easier to take the whole Bible as it stands. In this way the translator's ignorance, the transcriber's mistakes, the annotator's explanations, have all been passed off as integral portions of a Divine work,— the unreasonable demand being made upon us, that, according as these extraneous elements are able to abide a searching criticism, must the whole work stand or fall. Now, we are not going to apologize either for our translations or our copies. Happily they do not require it. But, in regard of infallibility, we must separate, by a measureless distance, the dictations of the infinite Spirit, and the renderings or copyings of a human hand. "The prophet that hath a dream, let him tell a dream; and he that hath my word, let him speak my word faithfully. What is the chaff to the wheat? saith the Lord."

But allowing the claim to inspiration, as a fact, to be unaltered by the necessity of relying on translated or copied versions, are not the practical securities for infallibility lost to us, by our receiving the Scriptures through such a medium? To this the best answer is furnished by the history of the more celebrated versions themselves, as glanced at in a former chapter. As against material error in the copies, particularly in the case of the Pentateuch, no better guarantee could be afforded us than the bitter feuds existing between the Jews and the Samaritans; whilst, for the Divine perfectness of the first and great translation of the Hebrew Scriptures, which is still extant in the world, namely, the Septuagint, we can desire no better warrant than the use of it by our blessed Lord Himself.

Hence, while still limiting to the original document the distinguishing theopneustic influence, whatever that influence be, we yet say that, even in our own English Bible, are to be read what, to all practical purposes, may be regarded as the exact revelations of the Divine Spirit. The purity of the sacred text to so great a degree, after the lapse of so many ages, is itself a phenomenon, of which the annals of written literature exhibit no like example; whilst, as to translations, the checks and counter-checks of rival creeds, the lynx-eyed jealousies of competing exegetical schools, the constant rendering of the Scriptures into some new language, have all conspired to secure, for the Divine thought, its most accurate human presentment; insomuch that, as the Scriptures of our own national version are read in our churches, we feel, that "not in the words which man's wisdom teacheth, but which the Holy Ghost teacheth," we do hear them "speak in our own tongue the wonderful works of God."

ii. In relation to these copies, however, we advert to another inquiry. How far is the claim to inspired truthfulness, in the Scriptures, impaired, or our confidence therein rightly shaken, by the many *various readings* found in our existing copies?

The existence of such variations in numerous transcripts of an ancient manuscript, we must feel to be inevitable. Nothing but the intervention of a constantly repeated miracle could have made transcribers true to every letter of the original words; or have secured for posterity an absolutely pure and unvitiated text. The same thing occurs in the great productions of classical antiquity. Scholars, to this day, are collating authorities to find out the true text of a Greek or Roman author; and we are not to wonder, if, while exercising a marvellous superintendence over the sacred record, in everything that was vital to a knowledge of the truth, yet that, in relation to casual and unimportant words, God should not exempt the Scriptures from those errors in transcription, which we are accustomed to meet with in the writings of uninspired men. We believe that the records of our faith were given from God to man; but it is quite in consonance with the course and law of Providence, to allow much for human agency, in their transmission to after times.

Nor were the ordinary mechanical lapses of a transcriber the only source of danger to the perfect purity of the holy text. Little as the Jews were likely, from their intense veneration for their sacred writings, to be guilty of any intentional falsification,—indeed, except by the Samaritans, no such charge has ever been brought against them,—yet they are believed to be open to the blame of a well-meant but unwise officiousness, in the insertion of explanatory words, or the filling up of supposed ellipses, as a guide for the public reader. These critical supplements were at first inserted in the margin; but, by degrees, and in the hands of later and uncareful copyists, they became incorporated into the body of the writing,—thus furnishing employment, at all events, for the industrious searcher after discrepancies, though utterly immaterial to the substantial accuracy of the text.

But what is the general character of these various readings? In number they would seem to be formidable enough. Including points of spelling and punctuation, and such like, we have them computed by thousands. Nor has there been any sparing of learned labour in the matter. In relation to this department of biblical science, we read of the four folios of Houbigant; the thirty years' labours of Michaelis; the four years' study of Dr. Kennicott, with his laborious collation of five hundred and eighty-one Hebrew manuscripts; and of the six hundred and thirty copies subjected by Professor Rossi to the same test. And with what result? The value of the answer depends so entirely upon the critical authority of the person giving it, that it may be better to quote direct testimonies. "As to the different readings of the Hebrew manuscripts collated by Kennicott," says the learned rationalist Eichhorn, "they hardly offer sufficient interest to compensate for the trouble they cost."[1] Professor M. Stuart, after reckoning up the numbers of various readings,— so many as to the consonants, and so many more as to the vowel-points,—

---

[1] *Einleitung*, 2; *Th.* 5, 700. See Gaussen, *Theopneustia*, p. 169. Ed. 1830.

adds, "But at the same time it is equally true that all these taken together do not change or materially affect any important doctrine, precept, or even history."[1] "Choose out of the whole MSS. as awkwardly as you will," says the acutest of English critics, Bentley; "choose the worst by design out of the whole lump of readings, and not one article of faith or moral precept is either perverted or lost in them. Put them into the hands of either a knave or a fool, and even with the most sinistrous and absurd choice, he shall not extinguish the light of any one chapter or so disguise Christianity, but that every feature of it will remain the same."[2]

Of course, those who are at all familiar with the processes of critical and philological science, will understand on what insignificant issues this mighty array of textual discrepancies would chiefly turn. Points of grammatical construction; the spelling of proper names; the insertion or omission of an article; the putting of one conjunction for another; the position of an adjective before its substantive or after it,—

[1] Professor Stuart, *Critical History and Defence of the Canon.* Andover, U. S., p. 169.

[2] Art. in *Quarterly Review*, Jan. 1863. The testimonies may be strengthened by the well-authenticated anecdote of Dr. Kennicott and George the Third. The monarch had participated in the fears of many pious people, on learning that the Doctor had discovered so many variations in the sacred copies, and inquired of the divine, "What was the upshot of it all?" To which the great Biblical scholar replied, that, by these discoveries, not a doctrine was touched, not a precept was altered, not a fact was left in less certainty than it existed before.

would all yield their contingent of spoil to the critical labourer, although, when gathered in, he should find only a harvest of nothingness for his reward. On questions of numbers, chiefly, could the differences be regarded of any moment; and these are found only in relation to the subordinate details of some narrative statement. To errors of this kind the copies were peculiarly open. The use for some time, of a letter to represent a numeral, the general uncertainty as to what the principles of Hebrew notation were, and even the fact that the omission or insertion of a cipher, in form representing our period (.), would, according to some methods of notation, make a difference to the extent of a decimal place,[1] must always make us afraid to speak with absolute confidence of the Hebrew arithmetic. Not that the fault is peculiar to Jewish scriptures. Writings, of much later date, are notoriously deficient in numerical accuracy. Thus we read that an army of five millions of men accompanied the expedition of Xerxes; and that, in the Diocletian persecution, twenty thousand persons were shut up in a temple at Nicomædia, and burnt to death; statements which, however palpably exaggerated, in respect of numbers, are never supposed to leave the general moral credit of the document containing them other than it was before.

[1] Dr. Kennicott accounts for the discrepancy between 2 Sam. viii. 4-8, 1 Chron. xviii. 4, in this way.—*Dissertation on the State of the Hebrew Text*, p. 533.

The very limited extent also to which our confidence in the purity of our present text could possibly be disturbed by these various readings, would become more apparent, if we were to shew, as a comparison of the most recently published "Recensions" with those of former years, would enable us to shew, that the further these Biblical critics carry their inquiries, the more closely does the result accord with what is found in our received copies.[1] But the matter can hardly be worth pursuing. The results, obtained by the collation of various readings, while, by their mere numerical strength, they can do nothing *against* the truth, may, we submit, do much *for* the truth by their collective insignificance. At a conclusion "so lame and impotent," the friends of revelation may well take courage. In relation to the books of Moses, and the other Old Testament writings, when we remember that more copies have been made of them than of any books in the world; remember how they were exposed to all the dangers and disasters of the captivity; remember how the people who had the care of them have been the objects of persecution, from the age of the Philistines to the time, when Rome, in her insulting pride, was wont to say to them, "Give up your sacred books, or die;" and remember, finally, those centuries of darkness the writings have had to pass

---

[1] Tischendorf's *Revision of the New Testament*, published in 1859, restores to the received text of St. Matthew's Gospel 187 readings which he had disallowed in his edition of ten years before.

through, when all that was precious in European literature was either corrupted, or destroyed, or lost,— and yet find that, against the integrity of our received text, not a single suspected reading can be quoted which touches the faith or hope of the Christian,— are we not entitled to say of the argument from these various readings, that it is one more for the believer than the sceptic? that they are not an objection, but a testimony?

iii. In relation to the Mosaic books, we note again, that our practical confidence in their inspired truthfulness is not affected by the admission that they may contain *some minor interpolations,* the work of a later hand than that which penned the original documents.

It has long been customary with sceptics to cite certain passages or expressions, in the books of Moses, which could not have been written by himself, or even by any author of his reputed times. The instances commonly selected are so well worn and familiar, as scarcely to need recital. Thus there is the circumstance of Moses writing the account of his own death; the giving of the name "Dan" in the book of Genesis to the city of "Laish," whereas the name of the place was not changed until after the Jews had entered Palestine; the claiming by Moses of qualities, such as no man would claim for himself, as in the passage, "Now the man Moses was very meek above all the men which were on the face of the earth." And, once more, the passage in Genesis, where it is said, "These are the kings that reigned over the land of Edom before there reigned any king over Israel,"[1]—language which clearly implies that the writer must have lived after the monarchy in Israel had been established.

These, and other similar instances, are quoted as obvious proofs that the books could not be the work of Moses, and must be the forgery of a later age. But, we ask, does not the very obviousness of the anachronisms prove that the hand of the forger is not in them? For many of the subtle and exact accordances of the Mosaic narrative,—with history, with geography, with all that is peculiar and distinctive in Egyptian or Hebrew life,—the only solution possible, on the hypothesis of fabrication, is that the forger must have been a profoundly astute and far-seeing man. How is it that a verdict is to be taken against him now of being a blunderingly ignorant, or superlatively stupid man? not only blind to the great facts of his nation's history, but absolutely reciting the posthumous details of his own?

But now about the anachronisms or inconsistencies themselves? Are they the interpolations of a later hand, or are they not? By the general *consensus* of the Jewish and Christian Church, it is allowed that some such marginal additions there are. A list of passages, entitled to be so considered, including no inconsiderable number of those paraded in a recent work, with the air of a fresh discovery, will be found

[1] Gen. xxxvi. 31.

in the work of Dean Prideaux, published 150 years ago. And, in a series of chapters, of which every page is fringed with citations from accredited Jewish authorities, the writer supplies us with a satisfactory history of those very interpolated passages and corrections, which are made to present such insuperable difficulties in the estimation of modern sceptics. The substance of the explanation amounts to this:—On the return from the Captivity, Ezra received a Divine commission to re-institute and organize all things pertaining to the national worship; and therein, of course, to edit and superintend the preparation of a perfect copy of the Scriptures, as they had been written up to that time. And there were five things, which, under inspired direction, he set himself to do: first, to collect all the books together, and settle their canonical authority; secondly, to correct all the errors which had crept into the copies through the negligence or mistakes of transcribers; thirdly, to add, to interpolate, to supplement according as, at any parts of the writings, he should find anything requiring to be made more intelligible; fourthly, to change the names of places which had become obsolete, in order to replace them by names with which the people were then familiar; and, lastly, to write out the whole in the new Chaldee character.[1]

Powers, so large and varied, entrusted to a Jewish

[1] Prideaux's *Connection of the Old and New Testaments*, Part I. Book V. s. 1-5, fol. 1617.

scribe, would of course be fatal to all confidence in the infallibility of the record, if it were not, as the writer above referred to is careful to remind us, that, in carrying out his work, Ezra "was assisted by the same Spirit as that by which the books were first wrote." With this security, the reproduced copy of the Law, by Ezra, becomes as infallible, to us, as the original autograph laid up by order of Moses in the Ark. The interpolations, however anachronous, or out of order, tell for nothing. The returned captives needed plain teaching. Of what moment would it be to Ezra, whether the document should meet, at all points, the demands of a pedantic criticism, so only that it was presented in a form which the people themselves could understand?

Of a kindred nature to the objections now under consideration, is the argument derived from the double use, in the Pentateuch, of the two sacred names, attributed to the Divine Being, of Jehovah and Elohim;—the ground of exception taken, being that the name of Jehovah is found in several parts of the book of Genesis; whereas, in the book of Exodus, it is made to appear that the name was only first revealed to Moses, when just entering upon his Divine mission. "And God spake unto Moses, and said unto him, I am the Lord; And I appeared unto Abraham, unto Isaac, and unto Jacob, by the name of God Almighty, but by my name Jehovah was I not known to them."[1]

[1] Exod. vi. 2, 3.

Speculations upon this subject, coupled with attempts to prove that the Mosaic record is made up of fragments of different dates,—some being of the Elohistic, and some of the Jehovistic period,—have been rife in Germany for the last hundred years. The only thing, however, these speculations have been remarkable for, is the utter unpracticalness of the result, and the hopelessly irreconcileable differences among rationalists themselves.[1] With regard to the attempted proof of a later date for the Pentateuch, founded on the above passage in Exodus, nothing can be more inconclusive. We have no reason to suppose that the entire five books were written all at once. And, the sacred name of Jehovah having been once revealed, no reason can be shewn why, at the final revise, Moses should not put in the newly communicated name in any passages

[1] See a list of these contradictory theories in Dr. M'Caul's Essay V., *Aids to Faith*, p. 191. Bp. Colenso, in Part II., seems far to outstrip his German brethren. By means of an elaborate analysis of the book of Psalms, in regard to its Jehovistic and Elohistic elements, he tries to show that the name Jehovah was not introduced until about the middle of David's lifetime. At this point, however, his learned and unquestionably able apologist in *The Reader*, while claiming for Dr. Colenso the merit of " having accomplished more in this department of criticism than all the other Bishops together," is obliged to part company with his author. " Instances of the use in composition of the name of Jehovah, though few, are decisive in favour of its ante-Davidic existence." " We can really attach no weight to the arguments used against the early date and historical character of this unquestionably genuine song (of Deborah), or of those inimitably primitive chapters at the close of the book of Judges."—*Reader*, Feb. 14, 1863, Review of Colenso's Part II.

where the substitution would heighten the grandeur or impressiveness of his subject.[1]

IV. We advert to one other supposed objection to the absolutely perfect inspiration of the Mosaic books, namely, the possibility that, in certain portions of them, the author may have made use of UNINSPIRED *sources of information.*

There are three ways in which we may conceive Moses to have obtained the materials for his record;—namely, by immediate revelation from God; by oral traditions, handed down from the earliest ages; or by written documents, preserved as the common property of the Hebrew race. Now some portions of the record, we are sure, must have come to him in the form of revelation,—could have come in no other way; such as the history of the creation, and the events of the primeval weeks. For events after this, however, down to the time of Moses himself, there is nothing to forbid the possibility of oral traditions being used, and that without much danger of corruption. From Adam to Noah, a period of 1650 years, but one intermediate link was necessary; whilst, by comparing the ages of Shem, and Abraham, and Joseph, we can shew easily that six persons, between Adam and Moses, would have been sufficient to convey to

---

[1] See the subject discussed at greater length in an able article in *The Guardian,* Feb. 11, Review of Bp. Colenso's Part II.

Moses traditions from the very origin of the human race.

Still less are we prepared to deny the possibility that Moses may have availed himself of the documentary resources of his countrymen; that he should have consulted the traditional records, preserved among the family of Abraham; should have owed something to national annals for his account of places and genealogies in the antediluvian age; or should have made use of some carefully kept family record in registering the names of those who went down with Jacob into Egypt. References are made, both by himself and other of the sacred writers, to uninspired sources of information,— as, for example, to " the Book of the Wars of the Lord," " the Book of Jasher," and " the Book of Nathan the prophet;" and though it be only to corroborate their own assertions, it shews that the writings themselves were held in respect.

At all events, since, on this point, many of the friends of revelation and its adversaries are at one,— on the evidence for a variety of documents, Vitringa, and Calmet, and Rawlinson, being in agreement with Eichhorn, and Ewald, and De Wette,—it may be well to meet the question, fairly, how far the importation, into the sacred record, of such an extraneous element should destroy our confidence in the inspired truthfulness of the document itself.

And we give two reasons why it should not. In the first place, whatever use Moses might make of these extraneous aids, he would do it *under the direction of the Holy Ghost.*

It must be remembered, that the only principles of inspiration by which we allow ourselves to be bound, have respect, not to the psychological nature of the agency employed, but solely to the practical infallibility of the result. The influence on the mind of Moses, when writing the record of the Creation, might have been very different from that under which he was led (if he were so led) to make selections from certain national annals of things, needful for the instruction of mankind. But the influences were equally Divine, in both cases, and the matters written down equally true. Moses was, in no case, a mere transcriber of records,—we may be sure of that. To the inspiration requisite for the selection of his document, would be added the wisdom to enlarge, and to correct, and to purge of all faulty elements; and thus such a perfect superintendence over the whole document, from beginning to end, would be maintained by the Holy Spirit, that, practically, it might be said of it, in its composite form,—genealogies, statistics, numerical reckonings and all,—as was said of the covenant given to Moses on the Mount,—" And the tables were the work of God, and the writing was the writing of God, graven upon the tables."

The other reason for disallowing any weight to the objection we are considering, is that the entire Pentateuch, as it has come to us from the Jews, is one body.

What it is in one part, it is in all. Moses made no distinction between the different portions, when he ordered the whole collection of writings to be laid up in the Ark. The Jewish Church have never made any distinction, while bearing their unfaltering testimony to the Divine authority of the books, from the days of Moses until now. Our Blessed Lord never hinted at any distinction,—quoting as He did from the earliest portions of the books as unhesitatingly as from the latest,—and speaking of them as alike authoritative, and alike Divine. In regard, therefore, of their inspired veracity, we cannot separate any portion of the record from the rest. To disintegrate is to destroy. All that Moses delivered to the Church in the wilderness, he delivered as having come from God; and to take from it, is as presumptuous as to add thereto.

And thus, we think, we have shewn the compatibility of a true and proper inspiration, in the Mosaic writings, with any traces of imperfection which the most adverse criticism could charge upon our present copies. Imperfection in these, to a certain extent, is a necessity. An Almighty power might secure that Divine thoughts should pass rightly into a human mind; might secure that, from this mind, they should be passed correctly into the types and forms of human speech;—but there the preternatural influence must cease. For the purity of the canon, we must depend mainly on Jewish faithfulness. For faithful translations, we must rely on a correct philological scholarship. For accuracy in the copies, we must trust to the state of our critical and Biblical science. And yet so wonderful has been the providence which has superintended these agencies, that we search the Scriptures with all confidence, because in them we "think we have eternal life." We feel that He who gave the word has guarded the text. Translations may be faulty, various readings may abound, interpolations, assumed or proved, may leave all our critical explanations at fault,—yet all these, we feel, leave unassailable and unshaken, the Divine fabric of inspiration,—do not cast a shadow of defect or variableness on the majestic work of God.

SECTION VII.

AUXILIARY EVIDENCES.

I.—MIRACLE.

" When God Himself doth of Himself raise up any, whose labour He useth without requiring that men should authorise them, ... He doth ratify their calling by manifests, signs, and tokens Himself from Heaven."—HOOKER.

"RABBI, we know that thou art a teacher come from God; for no man can do these miracles that thou doest except God be with him." So spake Nicodemus, anxious to express, in a sentence, the reasons which had prevailed with him to look upon the mission of Jesus of Nazareth as Divine. In so speaking, he gave utterance to one of the first convictions of the rational intelligence,—to an inference, which the mind draws, with all the rapidity of intuition, and all the confidence of a demonstrative and attested fact. Among nations, in the lowest state of civilization, faith in the unity and orderly sequences of nature is the normal condition of human thought; and,

K

therefore, the power that can produce a disturbance or interruption of these sequences, it is felt, must be nature's superior, and nature's God. The next step in the argument is reached instantaneously. Omnipotence cannot be divided against itself. If it delegate its functions, it must be for some work of its own. *For* the truth only, and not *against* it, must its resources be employed, and the mission of him that wields them must be Divine.

This argument has peculiar force, in relation to the preternatural facts of the Pentateuch. In proof of the credibility of the books, these facts, as we have seen, have considerable weight, apart from their preternatural character. On the face of it, the record purports to be a contemporaneous narrative. And if the facts related had never taken place, — if the channels of the Red Sea had never been laid bare to the bottom; if the people had never been miraculously fed with bread; if water had never been made to flow out of the hard rock; if a migrating nation had never been conducted by the guidance of the fire and the cloud,—myriads of living witnesses were present to withstand the mendacious chronicler to the face.

But the introduction of a preternatural element into these transactions gathers round them an evidence for the books of a still higher kind,—proves them to be not historically true only, but absolutely, infallibly, Divinely true.

All revelation supposes the direct interference of Deity in the concerns of man; is, in fact, itself such an interference,—being neither more nor less than the communication of facts or doctrines to mankind, to which the mind could not, or would not, have attained by the exercise of its natural powers. And as revelation supposes miracles, so does it appeal to them, as the proper and absolute proof of its Divine origination and authority. No higher testimony, in support of His claims was urged by Christ Himself. "The works that I do in my Father's name, they bear witness of me." "If ye believe not me, believe my works." "If I had not come among them and done the works that none other man did, they had not had sin."

As might be expected, therefore, miracles have been the incessant object of infidel attack. And this in various forms. Thus, by some, elaborate attempts have been made to bring the preternatural effects recorded in sacred history within the range of known physical laws,—laws assumed to be known to those who were to profit by the result, but which, in their operation, would appear as a miracle to the lookers on. In this way, we have naturalists, accounting for the fall of the manna by exudations from the leaves of the tamarisk; and astronomers, referring the miracle of Beth-horon to an eclipse; and geographers, arguing that Moses knew of a time and place where the Red Sea was fordable, which, the Egyptians not knowing, and essaying to do the like, were drowned;—all so many speculations, not for minimizing the amount of Divine interference, which is lawful, but for proving that there was no miraculous interposition at all.

With regard to the Mosaic miracles, however, this ground is now less frequently taken up than formerly. The facts are too palpably out of course, to admit of being surrendered at the bidding of such preposterous and strained conjectures. The bolder position has been advanced that a miracle is *impossible;* that the Omnipotent is fettered by His own laws; that conditions, developing themselves according to an order of eternal sequence, have been impressed upon the physical universe, and that, even by Him who first gave them being, they are now beyond recall.

By whomsoever advanced, we hesitate not to say that this view involves rampant Atheism:—by which we mean that it is one which none but an Atheist, or a disbeliever in a personal God, can consistently maintain. And that for this reason. Every Deist, of whatever school, believes in the fact of creation. And creation, begin when it may, and be brought about how it may, innovates upon the constituted order of things; is a deviation from the law of observed sequences; is something contrary to all antecedent experience;—in a word, is a miracle. The geological Deist, for instance, who should ask millions of centuries as needful for the formation of his rocks, would be obliged to concede the possibility of a miracle, because there must have been a departure from the order of visible operations when the first crust began to be. The Atheist, however, is not troubled with this difficulty. His creed, or no-creed, may be attended with embarrassing consequences of other kinds. But grant him his first postulate, that this visible universe is an eternal fact,—without beginning of life or end of days,—all its laws being self-existent, self-evolved, self-sustained, and the alleged impossibility of the miracle must be allowed. Hence, between the philosopher that says with his lips, There is no miracle, and "the fool that saith in his heart, There is no God," we can see no difference.

We are, therefore, really weary to have to reply for the thousandth time to the stock-objection, that a miracle is impossible, and that the advanced state of science demonstrates its impossibility. The advanced state of science knows no more either for or against miracle, than the infantile state of science did, because it is equally out of the domain of either. Short of that which involves a contradiction, who shall say what is or what is not possible with God? The very attempt to draw the boundary line, over which the Omnipotent cannot, or should not, pass, presupposes the possession, on the part of the finite, of the attributes of the Infinite,—supposes not only a knowledge, by us, of the extent of the Divine resources, but also of those innumerable plans and purposes, for the furtherance of which those resources are to be employed. "Lo! these are parts of His ways: but how little a portion is heard of Him? the thunder of His power who can understand?"

But the positions taken up against miracles, of late, have been of a more moderate kind; such, for instance, as that they are improbable, difficult to believe—tend to disturb that confidence in the uniformity of Divine action, which is at the basis of all our science, as well as of our veneration for God himself, as for a Being incapable of violating His own laws. Here considerable confusion of thought, as well as much that is vicious in argument, will be found to have arisen from the mode of stating the objection; and especially from a want of carefulness in defining what a miracle is. We are obliged often to doubt the logical honesty of many sceptical men. For example: a century ago our metaphysical terminology was less exact than it is now; and, therefore, when Hume says, "A miracle is the violation of the laws of nature," we put it down to his bad philosophy. We cannot make the same allowance for the late Professor Powell. And hence, when, in a recent publication, we find him identifying the miracles of Revelation with "imagined interruptions of natural order," or "supposed suspensions of the laws of matter,"[1] we cannot acquit him of giving a view of the nature of miraculous agency, which he knew every intelligent theologian would repudiate. A miracle, in its received theological acceptation, is nothing more than an effect produced by Divine power, in some

[1] *Essays and Reviews*, p. 110.

way that is out of the ordinary course of sensible operations. In such a definition, we say nothing about the laws of nature being interrupted, but only that the manner of its visible operations is changed,—which change, however, we presume to be effected by some other law that we know nothing about. The miracle is no more contrary to nature than the ordinary phenomenon is. It is something in addition to nature; the introduction of a higher element of power which we do *not* see, into a lower element which we *do* see.

On this view, it will be seen how utterly impertinent and beside the question are all attempts to explain the *modus* of a miracle, or to free it from the consequences which, it is alleged, would follow if the great system of dependent causation, observable in the universe, were abruptly broken in upon, or changed. Yet, to this issue is modern scepticism trying to have the question narrowed. "The essential question of miracles," says Professor Powell, "stands quite apart from any consideration of testimony. . . . . It is not the mere fact, but the cause or explanation of it, which is the point at issue."[1] Now we contend that it *is* the fact of the miracle, and that only with which we have to do. We do not attempt explanations, because it is of the very essence of a miracle that explanations of it cannot be given. By hypothesis, we are dealing with the preter-

[1] *Essays and Reviews*, p. 141.

natural. A miracle, therefore, which natural causes could account for, would be no miracle at all.

Neither is it necessary to our belief in a scripture miracle, that we should be able to clear it of certain supposed harmful consequences to our physical system, which a sudden and forceful interference with the operation of natural causes might be expected to occasion. In a recent publication, the miracle of Joshua is cited as one which, as understood by the writer, must have been followed by a "total collapse of our material system," causing the instantaneous destruction of every living creature upon the earth. Now, without attaching much importance to any explanations of the phenomenon in question, it is but right to add, that except upon an assumption, which this author has no right to make, there is nothing, on any physical showing, to necessitate the catastrophe spoken of at all. The assumption we refer to is, that there was "an actual suspension of the motion of the heavenly bodies," and this he declares "the Bible speaks of to a common understanding."[1] But is this so? Joshua spoke only as other men would speak, only as we ourselves might speak, if, from any cause, the return of night should be intermitted, and the light continue through an entire diurnal revolution of the earth. But such an effect, it is allowed, might be produced, and yet the heavenly bodies continue in their appointed courses. Light, as

[1] Bp. Colenso on the *Pentateuch*, p. x., Preface.

modern science has abundantly proved, does not depend upon particles emitted from the sun at all, but upon a subtle fluid, a delicate luminiferous ether, which, at the Divine will, might have been made available for all the practical necessities of the Jewish leader, the heavenly bodies meanwhile pursuing their unbroken career as before.[1]

This explanation is not intended to supersede the reality of the miracle itself,—in which we fully believe, and without which this prolongation of the light for a whole day would have been impossible,— but merely to shew that such an event would not necessarily involve " the total collapse of the material system." Nor is there anything in the language of the sacred historian to necessitate such a view. As an able writer in the *Quarterly* has well observed, "The results of physical science, not being the purpose of the Revelation, its written record must, to be intelligible, speak the ordinary language of the time ; and all, therefore, which can be looked for when Revelation touches the domain of science, is that it should not propose to instruct us concerning science, and then instruct us falsely."[2] Tried by this rule, the language of the sacred narrative, in relation to this miracle, is just what we should expect it to be, and what, to be understood, it must be. Joshua, believing with his age, in the reality of the

---

[1] See this point ably illustrated in Professor Young's *Science Elucidative of Scripture*, c. v., 172.

[2] *Quarterly Review*, No. 217, Jan. 1861, p. 291.

sun's apparent motion, in the fulness of his faith in the God of Israel, called on the sun to stop in its course. This call is recorded by the inspired historian in his own language, and when the desired effect follows, he, in the same language, records the answer to the prayer. And the object of the Revelation does not require more than this. The design of the sacred writer was to excite the nation to gratitude for a notable instance of Divine interference on their behalf,—not to say by what means this interference was effected,—whether by arresting the heavenly bodies in their courses, or by one of a thousand ways besides.

Only, however, as showing the insatiable avidity of modern scepticism, in its search after flaws in the Bible, do we advert to these modes of removing an apparent difficulty. The miracle of Joshua might have been left to stand with all its bristling array of threatened consequences,—" the wreck of matter and the crash of worlds,"—and, in view of the power of God, to stem the desolating mischief, we should still have taken our stand upon that word,—" Is anything too hard for the Lord ?" Is God infinite to execute a miracle, and not infinite to avert any harmful consequences? Does He obey the laws of the material universe, or do they obey Him? Again do we see at work the spell of a withering Pantheism. All nature is left to be a God to herself, and the Great Mind of the universe is made to abdicate His throne.

With all confidence, therefore, we fall back on the

ancient argument for miracle. And, in relation to these writings of Moses, we hold such evidence to be all-powerful. It endorses the integrity of the author. It authenticates the divinity of his mission. It attests the infallible veracity of his statements. Miracle puts the seal of God on the whole work. By means of it we feel the Divine presence to be with Moses everywhere—in his words when he speaks; in his plans, when he acts; in his thoughts, when he writes. Whether applied to our Lord or to his servant Moses, that saying of Nicodemus is true:—" We know that thou art a teacher come from God, for no man can do these miracles that thou doest except God be with him."

II.—PROPHECY.

" For they (the Divine prophecies) resemble the nature of their Author, to whom one day is as a thousand years, and a thousand years as one day: and though the fulness and height of their accomplishment be many times assigned to some certain age, or certain point of time, yet they have, nevertheless, many stairs and scales of accomplishment, throughout divers ages of the world."—BACON.

THE argument from MIRACLE is strongest for contemporaries. For those who come after, the evidence of

FULFILLED PROPHECY has more of convincing force. A palpable instance of Divine interposition—nature seeming to go out of her way to put the seal on a human undertaking—commends that work to an eye-witness incontestibly. It is the highest form of moral demonstration. To all but an eye-witness, however, the miracle can but take the form of testimony,—in the present case, testimony of the highest kind, to be sure,—but still, as evidence, never to be reproduced with the vividness which attends ocular attestation, and even becoming weaker the further it has to descend down the stream of time. Not so with the evidence arising from the accomplishment of prophecy. This is germinant. It gathers strength with age. The force of it lies in the fact, that the things foretold must have been beyond the ken of human prescience to foresee, or the most skilful forecasting of human agencies to bring about. Every century that passes, therefore, puts the prophecy further and further out of the domain of human causation, and gives to successive fulfilments of it the force of a reproduced miracle. In regard to some of the Mosaic prophecies, we, of these last days, are on a level with those who ate of the manna, or drank water from the rock. The evidence comes not to us through testimony at all. It is the finger of God made manifest. "We have seen it with our eyes."

The prophecies of the Pentateuch are the more worthy of notice from the high and peculiar intimacy with Deity, which, even in comparison with the rest of the goodly fellowship, Moses appears to have enjoyed. The expression "there arose not a prophet since in Israel like unto Moses," was not without its special significance. It doubtless referred to the fact that a kind and measure of illumination had been granted to him peculiarly his own. "God spake to him face to face, as a man speaketh to his friend." Not so to others. Miriam and Aaron received divine communications;—in virtue of them, claimed to be heard as well as Moses. But the Lord reproved them, and vindicated His favoured servant's pre-eminence. "Hear, now, my words. If there be a prophet among you, I the Lord will make myself known unto him in a vision, and will speak unto him in a dream. My servant Moses is not so, who is faithful in all mine house. With him will I speak mouth to mouth, even apparently, and not in dark speeches; and the similitude of the Lord shall he behold."[1] Whether, by this last expression is meant, as some think, that on occasions of intercourse with His servant, the Lord assumed some visible form of ineffable splendour, causing that, when Moses descended from the Mount, his face shone with the undeparted radiance, we may not undertake to decide. Enough that, on any shewing, it vindicates the claims of Moses to an intimacy of surpassing and unequalled closeness with the mind and will of the Most High God.

With this fact in our minds, we turn with interest

[1] Num. xii. 6–8.

to some of the earlier prophecies in the Mosaic books. And we take, as an example, that sentence pronounced by Noah on his youngest son. It is no outburst of parental anger, but an efflux of the prophetical spirit, delivering itself in calm, solemn, and portentous words: —"Cursed be Canaan : a servant of servants shall he be to his brethren."[1] Four thousand years have passed away since these words were uttered, and during the greater portion of that time has the prophecy been in course of fulfilment,—is being fulfilled before our eyes to this day. Every nation has trodden with iron heel on the children of Ham. The malediction of heaven has pursued them through all the successions of human history. The Israelites, the Persians, the Grecians, the Romans, have each had the rule over them in turn, all because that word had gone forth with regard to Ham—"a servant of servants shall he be to his brethren." Are later evidences of fulfilment demanded? Let the descendants of Shem and Japheth blush while they read the words—Africa is the slave-market for the world.

We turn to another of these early prophecies,—that relating to the Arab tribes. The following is the language which the angel of the Lord, speaking of their ancestor Ishmael, addresses to Hagar:—"Thou shalt bear a son, and shalt call his name Ishmael, because the Lord hath heard thy afflictions. And he will be a wild man: his hand will be against every

[1] Gen. ix. 25.

man, and every man's hand will be against him : and he shall dwell in the presence of all his brethren."[1] Another prophecy, addressed to Abraham, runs thus:— "As for Ishmael, I have heard thee: Behold, I have blessed him, and will make him fruitful, and will multiply him exceedingly : twelve princes shall he beget, and I will make him a great nation."[2]

Now look first at some of the earlier fulfilments of these predictions. Thus there was to be a rapid increase among his descendants. How plainly is this borne out by a comparison with the descendants of Isaac. One hundred and sixty-nine years after, the sons of Jacob amounted only to twelve, while the children of Ishmael had already become so considerable as to form a trading nation. "Behold," it is said when the brothers were plotting the destruction of Joseph, "a company of Ishmaelites came from Gilead with their camels bearing spicery, and balm, and myrrh, going to carry it down into Egypt." Then, it was declared of Ishmael that he should beget "twelve princes." And in accordance with this, we find afterwards, that when Moses is enumerating the descendants of Ishmael, he says, "These are the sons of Ishmael, and these are their names, by their towns and by their castles; twelve princes according to their nations."

Yet more striking, in relation to our present subject, are the continuous and later fulfilments of these prophecies. The character of the Ishmaelite is given,

[1] Gen. xvi. 11, 12.   [2] Gen. xvii. 20.

and from that time to this, in all its leading features, it has never changed. " He will be a wild man," it was said,—literally, a "wild-ass man."[1] The qualities of the wild ass we find described in a magnificent passage in the book of Job: " Whose house I have made the wilderness, and the barren land his dwellings. He scorneth the multitude of the city, neither regardeth he the crying of the driver. The range of the mountains is his pasture, and he searcheth after every green thing."[2] How true for all time this description is—true for the outcast son of Hagar himself, as well as true for his wandering posterity of the desert to this day—it seems almost needless to point out. Such as Ishmael was, such the Arab tribes are now,—fiercely independent, tied to no settled home, scorning the arts or comforts of civilized life, living in sullen clanship apart from their kind, and, except in their dealings one with another, without honour and without law.

Equally conclusive is the testimony of all history to the fulfilment of that part of the ancient prophecy which foretells the wild and untameable independence of the Ishmaelitish race, the posture of permanent antagonism they should maintain against all the ruling powers of the earth. " His hand shall be against every man, and every man's hand against him." Now, in reference to the fulfilment of this prediction, we may ask confidently, Is there another community, or kindred,

[1] See Dr. Benisch's *Jewish School and Family Bible*, in loc.
[2] Job xxxix. 6-8.

or people, or tribe, among all the inhabitants of the world, that can boast, as these Arabs can boast, a three thousand years' history of successful resistance to the army of the invader, the ambition of the tyrant, to every attempt of fraud or force to bring them under the power of a foreign yoke? Their history, in this respect, is surely without parallel. It is not that no attempts have ever been made to bring them into subjection. These attempts were made again and again, by the Assyrians, the Medes, the Persians; by Sesostris when in the zenith of his glory; by Alexander, when all the world was bowing to him; by Pompey, in the time of the republic; and by Trajan and Severus under the empire: but always in vain, or, if not in vain, with only the most partial and temporary success. Even Gibbon himself admits this. In one of those melancholy passages, which must disfigure to all time one of the noblest products of human thought, after speaking of "the perpetual independence of the Arabs," he hints that "the attempt to transform this singular event into a prophecy and a miracle in favour of the posterity of Ishmael," is, on account of some exceptions which he cites, " as indiscreet as it is superfluous." But in the very next sentence we have an admission, as satisfactory and complete as any advocate for the truth of the Mosaic prophecies could desire. "Yet these exceptions," the historian goes on, " are temporary or local; the body of the nation has escaped the yoke of the most powerful monarchies; the arms of Sesostris and Cyrus, of Pompey and Trajan, could never achieve the conquest of Arabia: the present sovereign of the Turks may exercise a shadow of jurisdiction, but his pride is reduced to solicit the friendship of a people whom it is dangerous to provoke and fruitless to attack." [1]

Other testimonies of like import might be cited from historians of the highest credit. They all prove incontestably that those words of the angel to Hagar were the revealings of the Omniscient mind,—of Him with whom prophecy is as history, and the future the same as the past. "Oh! that Ishmael might live before Thee!" was the prayer of the aged patriarch. In another sense, Ishmael does live. Thirty-seven centuries have made no difference in the general features of his character. Untamed in spirit, seeking no home beyond his own barren sands, with the brand of an ancient sentence upon him, unobliterated and unchanged, the outcast son of Hagar still stands before us, a witness for Moses, a witness for prophecy, a witness for the inspired truth of God. "And he will be a wild man: his hand will be against every man, and every man's hand will be against him: and he shall dwell in the presence of his brethren." [2]

But let us proceed to a notice of prophecies bearing more directly on the history of the Jewish Church and

---

[1] *Decline and Fall*, vol. ix. pp. 229, 230. Ed. 1797.

[2] For other illustrations of fulfilment of the earlier Mosaic prophecies, see Bishop Newton's *Dissertations*, vol. i.

nation. The Messianic prophecies, found in the books of Moses, need not be insisted on. Bold, figurative, darkly enigmatic as they are, they must, in their fulfilment, and when the veil was taken away, have burst upon the mind of the Jewish converts, as the sun shining in his strength. As the government of their nation passed into the hands of the usurping Idumean, what a divinity of foresight would they see in those words of their great ancestor, "The sceptre shall not depart from Judah, nor a lawgiver from between his feet, till Shiloh come:" and how clearly would they understand that enforced visions of the Almighty were resting upon the perfidious Balaam, in that, through the long vista of intervening centuries, he should have glimpses of "the bright and Morning Star."

More striking still are those prophecies of the Mosaic books which foretell the future fortunes of the Jews themselves. We have a summary of them in the 28th chapter of the book of Deuteronomy. They anticipate the defection and ingratitude of the people, and set forth what shall follow—defeat, disgrace, dispersion, poverty, sickness, want—all that could make the country a desolation, or the homes and hearts of the people sad. But this is not all we find contained in these prophecies. Minute and graphic touches are introduced, beyond all human power of prescience. The salient national characteristics are pointed out of peoples that were yet to be;—foreshadowing the armies of Nebuchadnezzar coming down like a wolf on the fold, and the Roman legions hasting as the swift eagle to its prey. Sieges are foretold, in which parents should be driven to eat the flesh of their own children for food,—an extremity of suffering which Moses had been a bold guesser to anticipate, but which his descendants were more than once destined to experience. Still more wonderful is the prediction that the very soil of Palestine should change; that, rich and exuberant as it then was, seed should not be sown in it, nor grass grow upon it; that the glory of all lands should become as the plain of Sodom, a withered, verdureless, parched-up thing, smitten by the fire of the wrath of God.

One or two of these prophecies may be noted more particularly, as instances of what are called germinant or continuous fulfilment, in relation to the present condition of the Hebrew race.

Thus, there is the prediction twice given that "Israel shall dwell alone."[1] For some generations after its utterance, it may be said, such a prophecy, with regard to the Jews, might have been made with safety. Their laws enjoined separation from other peoples. The peculiarity of their institutions made any great admixture with surrounding nations all but impossible. Whilst as to their religion, conscious as they were that they alone had the knowledge of the true God, we cannot wonder that, with pity or with proud disdain, they should look down upon all the world besides. Thus far, therefore, it might appear

[1] Deut. xxxiii. 28. Num. xxiii. 9.

that Moses incurred little hazard. He had merely foretold a continuance of national isolation, which it was the very tendency of the constitution he had given to the people to perpetuate and encourage. But, apart from the uncertainty whether this constitution itself would always be observed by the people, the hazard, attending this prediction of continued separateness, was increased, by its being made to stand side by side with other prophecies, which, if fulfilled, threatened to destroy this unity;—prophecies of dismemberment, and captivity, and scattering to the ends of the earth. That both predictions could be, and were fulfilled, the history of the subsequent disruptions and captivities proved abundantly. But would any conceivable degree of political sagacity, allow a man to predict beforehand, that his people should become mixed with other peoples, and yet all the lines of national demarcation remain as defined and palpable as before?

In like manner, it may be asked, would any leader, however far-seeing and observant of national tendencies, have ventured to promise to his people, that, after their deportation to an enemy's country, they should return and settle down again in their own land? This Moses does, in language most unhesitating and decisive. Conditionally on their repentance, he says to them, "If any of thine be driven out unto the outmost parts of heaven, from thence will the Lord thy God gather thee, and from thence will he fetch thee: And the Lord thy God will bring thee into the land which thy fathers possessed, and thou shalt possess it; and he will do thee good, and multiply thee above thy fathers."[1] All observation and all history would go to prove, that such a return of an entire community to a land, from which they had been forcibly expelled years before, was a thing least to be expected. Every year would increase the difficulty. The springing up of new ties and interests, in the land of their enforced adoption; the difficulty of collecting together the remains of a broken and scattered nation; the hopelessness of recovering those territorial rights and possessions, which, during their captivity, had been seized upon by other hands,—would all create difficulties, only to be overcome by the raising up of some powerful deliverer;—one whose unpurchased aid it would be the wildest of chances to calculate upon, and yet whose assistance, on any other terms, an impoverished and enslaved people would never be likely to command. Such a deliverer, as we know, was raised up in the person of Cyrus,—the Lord guiding him, though he knew it not, in order that He might turn again the captivity of His people, and, in honour of the word of His faithful prophet, might bring them again to their own land.

Other captivities and other dispersions have followed since then, and, in due time, we may believe with all confidence, will follow another and more

[1] Deut. xxx. 4, 5.

complete restoration of the Jews to the land of their fathers. It was an emphatic mark of the Mosaic prophecies, that the plagues entailed upon their disobedience should be "of long continuance."[1] And we must wait. In the meantime, in the past and present condition of the Jewish people, we have a constant and continuing witness to the truth of the predictions we have been considering. Dispersed among all parts, yet naturalized in none; living under every variety and form of civil polity, yet retaining everywhere the marks of an unchanged national distinctness; dislodged and driven from every place where they have attempted to settle down,—the sport of a military fanaticism at the time of the crusades, the victims of a lawless rapacity, and legalized extortion, for several centuries afterwards,—yet, amidst all these unparalleled persecutions and sufferings, ever loyal to the law as their statute book, to Moses as their prophet, to Jerusalem as their home,—what can we see, in all this, but a fulfilment of that prophecy in Deuteronomy, "And the Lord shall scatter thee among all people, from the one end of the earth even unto the other .... among these nations shalt thou find no ease, neither shall the sole of thy foot have rest?"[2]

In the prophecies of Moses, therefore, in relation to his people, taken in connection with their present condition in the world, we discern a strong proof that

[1] Deut. xxviii. 59.   [2] Deut. xxviii. 64, 65.

the writings which he has given us are both historically and divinely true. The present condition of the Jews, without extinction as a race of themselves, and yet without amalgamation with other races, is an unique fact. They are a people to be accounted for. Take from us the book which does account for them,— which leads us back to the tent of their great ancestor; which shews us how, under the fostering shadow of an Almighty presence, the family, the community the great nation came to have a place in all the histories of the earth,— and we feel that a leaf is torn from the records of the human race, beyond the power of a sceptical philosophy to replace. Accept the history, and with it the testimony of its daily unfolding prophecies, and all is plain. We ask not Moses for further witnesses. His best witness for the truth of his books is the Jew himself: the Jew, as we see him now. This witness speaks to us as no abstract reasonings can speak. We cannot look upon one of God's ancient people, without seeing one, whose history, whose institutions, whose very countenance must carry us back to the cradle of civilization, and to the infancy of the world. His features, cast in a mould of unaltering primeval type; his destinies, a connecting link with the facts of universal history; his laws, the same as they were delivered, three thousand years ago, from the burning fires of Horeb,—the very " seal not railed from the bond," make the Jew stand alone in the world. It is his to have seen the birth and death of nations. Race after race of his oppressors have disappeared, without leaving any trace of their national existence. Deeply buried in the earth, are the cities where his forefathers sojourned in captivity; and only the broken column of the desert remains to tell the story of their magnificent decay. But the Jew is as a column unbroken,— standing indeed among the vestiges of forgotten nations, and seeming to be as one of them,— but still not forsaken, and not destroyed. He is a relic of that grand past, when the angel-Redeemer spake face to face with the fathers,— a pledge of that glorious future, when this same Redeemer shall speak face to face with us, and "shall stand at the latter day upon the earth."

III.—CONNECTION OF THE DISPENSATIONS.

"The law with all its ordinances, is like a grain of seed, which contains in itself the whole law of formation of the plant."—
OLSHAUSEN.

We advert to a third form of auxiliary testimony to the Divine original of the books of Moses, arising from the preparatory character of the dispensations he was commissioned to reveal, and their *connection with the dispensation of grace and truth.*

The whole period of time, from the creation until now, is occupied by three principal dispensations, which we usually denominate as the Patriarchal, the Levitical, and the Christian. Of these, the characteristic feature is that they are all marked by unity of design; constitute, of themselves, a gradually developing and harmonious scheme; and are occupied, especially, with the coming of a Divine person into the world, in whose work and mission, all that was distinctive and external in preceding systems, was to have its accomplishment and consummation. Hence, of all these economies, with whatever difference of revealed form, the central object is Christ. He is conspicuously introduced under the patriarchal dispensation; is more fully shadowed forth under the Law; covers the whole field of vision in the disclosures of the Gospel.

As an argument for the Divine authorship of the Mosaic institutes, however, the point, in these successive developments of a revealed scheme, we would specially select for illustration is the ADAPTATIVE or CORRELATIVE character of the Levitical and Christian dispensations; the one being the complement of the other; the natural germination of the other; that, without which the other would seem to be a superfluous and unmeaning thing. The force of the argument from adaptation, in the department of natural theology, when we wish to establish Divine authorship or contrivance, we all feel instantly. Take a familiar example. I deduce the fact of intelligent design, from the structure of the human eye. I deduce the same conclusion, from observing the uniformity which obtains in the phenomena and properties of light. And I should claim to have adduced two independent proofs of contrivance, even though the eye were not suited to the light, nor the properties of light adjusted to the delicate mechanism of the eye. But suppose it were next proved, that this eye was constructed upon strictly optical principles: that it opened or closed, dilated its pupil or contracted it, in perfect accordance with all known optical conditions,—how demonstrable would be the argument, not for intelligent design only, in respect to the eye and the light, but for their having proceeded from a common original,—their being the joint product of the same contriving mind?

The illustration may be applied to the two great dispensations of revealed religion. The one is made for the other. Each supposes the existence of the other. Each one has uses, functions, allusive references and appointments, which, if, either in fact or in anticipation, the other were not, would be as void and meaningless as the eye would be in a world where there was no light, or the ear in an atmosphere which had never vibrated with the sounds of melody.

Hence, in the way of a reciprocated corroboration of each other's Divine original, it may be difficult to say whether the New Testament is the more indebted to the Old, or the Old Testament to the New; whether the Jew should have been more convinced by what he might learn from the Christian, than the Christian is convinced by what he is too thankful to learn from the Jew. To us, however, from whose eyes the vail has been taken away, it is enough to know that the two dispensations, like the two dreams of Pharaoh, are one—their design the same, their authority co-equal. Judaism was the ground-plan, of which Christianity is the completed edifice. The Law was the outline, of which the Gospel is the filled-up picture. Progression, growth, development, in bringing the work about, there must be. It is the standing law of the Divine administration. "The brook became a river," says the son of Sirach, "and the river became a sea." But still, while sacrifices, feasts, institutions, types, were throwing forward into the future their broken but emblematic shadows, all the devout of the ancient nation knew—aye, while rejecting Jesus of Nazareth, do know now—that "the body is of Christ."

And this, as we all know, is the great argument of St. Paul, both in his Epistle to the Hebrews and elsewhere. Unlike many who turn to another faith, and who are usually prone to heap contumely and scorn on the religion they have left, the apostle, on becoming a Christian, feels that the holy ground of the ancient sanctuary has become holier still. Every part of it stands out with a new and sacred significance.

As mute "patterns of things in the heavens," he had reverenced these ancient appointments always. There was eloquence in their dumbness, and a hidden brightness in all their clouds. But, under the action of Gospel light, the whole scene had changed. Dumb things spake. Painted figures started into life upon the canvass. It was as if a touch of some magic wand had put sense and motion into their phantom-forms, till the whole scheme was laid out in sacred drama: —Christ, the radiating centre of the scene, and His sacrifice the key to all that had been unsolved before. And now He beholds Christ everywhere. He beholds Him in history—in the fire, and in the cloud, and in the sea. He beholds Him in ritual—in the hyssop, and the sprinkled blood, and the scarlet wool. He beholds Him in type—in the uplifted serpent, and the falling manna, and the smitten rock. All is enigma without Christ; all, in the light of Christ, is manifest as a blazing star.

Much weight, we venture to submit, is due to this form of argument, in favour of the position that the Levitical and Christian dispensations must have had a common original. It is as if we had found, in one age of the world, the scattered members of a body, having its minute articulations and joints, and then, 1500 years afterwards, had found the very body to which, by the most rigid anatomical tests, those members must have belonged; as if, in one age, there had come into our hands a wax impression, sharp in its lines, and deep in its cuttings, and, ages afterwards, there had been dug up the most minutely-corresponding seal. Still more forcibly would this idea of a common authorship be forced upon us in the case of any literary or intellectual production. Of the poet Virgil we read in our school histories, that, on finding the merit of an anonymous literary compliment he had paid to Augustus, meanly laid claim to by another, he wrote four half-finished lines on the palace-gates, which the pretender was challenged to complete. Of course he was not able. The mind which had begun was the only mind which could finish; and the ending of the lines established the true authorship of the beginning.[1]

We say the same of the five books of Moses. They are five unfinished commencements of a grand scheme of grace and truth. But no pretender can take up the work. He that conceived the thought must work out the thought. And therefore, if, in the person, and offices, and work of Christ, we see the expansion and complete development of the Mosaic

[1] Few readers, it may be supposed, will have forgotten the incident here referred to. The mean appropriator of the poet's honours was Bathyllus. On discovering the fact, Virgil wrote on the gates, "Hos ego versiculos feci, tulit alter honores," and then added, four times over, as commencements of other verses, " Sic vos non vobis," which, on Bathyllus failing to complete, were completed by the real Author, thus: —

Sic vos, non vobis, nidificatis aves;
Sic vos, non vobis, vellera fertis oves;
Sic vos, non vobis, mellificatis apes;
Sic vos, non vobis, fertis aratra boves.

idea—the former half of the line, as given in the Law, answering to the latter half of the line, as contained in the Gospel—how shall we withhold our assent from the conclusion, These separated lines are the product of the same Almighty intellect; the hand that penned them is Divine?

SECTION VIII.

MODERN OBJECTIONS.—FORCE OF THE ARGUMENT
FROM ADMITTED DIFFICULTIES.

"Philosophers, who darken and put out
Eternal truth by everlasting doubt;
* * * * *
Discoverers of they know not what, confin'd
Within no bounds,—the blind that lead the blind."—COWPER.

"The mistakes of scientific men have never injured Christianity, while every new truth discovered by them has either added to its evidence, or prepared the mind for its reception."— COLERIDGE.

SLENDER as are the claims of modern Rationalism to have advanced anything very new in their objections against the Scriptures, the concession is to be made that an appearance of novelty is given to recent attacks, in that, as compared with those which had gone before, the objections are made to take a more critical and scientific form. Exceptions to the leading facts of the primeval history—the scheme of a six days' creation, the declared universality of the Deluge, the descent of all mankind from one human pair—had furnished materials for the Deists of an older school; for that class of sceptics, more *honest*, at all events, who, when making onslaught on the Old Testament, without paltering, or bated breath, told us plainly that they meant to falsify and subvert the New. The policy of modern scepticism is to drive out old beliefs as the children of Israel did the Canaanites, "by little and little." Dealing substantially with the same objections as the Deists of the seventeenth century, it proposes to look at the difficulties as they appear from a modern stand-point; from the advanced ground of modern science, modern scholarship, modern criteria of the possible, or the credible, or the true. Whether with any greater success than aforetime remains to be seen.

i. Foremost among the more recent attacks on the Pentateuchal history is a special repudiation of the *book of Genesis*, as being a composition wholly destitute of any historic pretensions, and one which could never have been written by Moses at all.

The exception is made to rest chiefly on the contents of the first *eleven* chapters of the book; on the ground, first, that these chapters abound with miracles, which are antecedently assumed to be impossible; secondly, that they deal with facts which, as lying out of the domain of any human knowledge, must have come to the writer through the uncertain channel of tradition; and, lastly, that they bear undisputed marks of a varied authorship, and even of having been compiled from documents which could not have been written in one and the same age.

On some of these grounds of objection we have touched already. The alleged impossibility of miracles

M

we have shown to be a mere assumption; and a very atheistical assumption, too. Whilst, as to the possibility that, for any unimportant details, Moses may have availed himself either of oral traditions, or of written documents, extant at the period, it is manifest that if the hypothesis of a Divine influence be granted, that influence would be just as available for making Moses an infallible compiler of the materials of others as an infallible inditer of his own. Thus, for all the purposes of a divinely verified revelation what difference can it make in the moral evidence of the case if the account, suppose, of the Creation and the Deluge were originally given to Adam and to Noah, and thence transmitted through faithful hands from Enoch to Shem, from Shem to Abraham, and from Abraham to Joseph and to Moses?

Besides this, however, the whole argument, from a supposed difference in the style and tone of a literary work, is one which, when opposed by any reasonable amount of contrary evidence, the ablest scholars have pronounced to be untrustworthy. Professor Moses Stuart quotes the theories of two of the most learned Rationalists, Ewald and Lengkerke, in regard to the number of distinct authors which they allege must have been at work on the Pentateuch. No language of modest hesitation is used on the matter. Each is quite sure that he can appreciate all those niceties and peculiarities of diction which enable him to pronounce authoritatively that *this* portion is the work of one hand, and *that* the work of another. And yet, in spite of this same confident boasting on the part of these two representatives of Teutonic criticism, one makes out that the Pentateuch is the work of *six* authors, the other that it is the work of *three*.[1]

But what are the positive evidences of authenticity to be urged in answer to these allegations? Well, first it is to be observed that the book of Genesis as we have it now, with its first eleven chapters, is found in every copy of the Old Testament, in every copy of the Pentateuch, and in every version of both. The Targums of Jonathan and Onkelos make no distinction of authorship between the first and second chapters of Genesis, or between the fourth and fifth; the whole is evidently regarded by them as the work of one author. Indeed, in all ages of the Jewish history, from the time of Joshua downwards, whenever the books of Moses are quoted or alluded to, the entire Pentateuch is assumed to be the divinely inspired composition of Moses. The

[1] *Critical History and Defence of the Old Testament Canon*, sect. 3, p. 48. The Professor also quotes a notable illustration of critical fallibility as having occurred not very long ago. A learned German, Dr. Reinhold, disgusted with the arrogant pretensions of Strauss, Ewald, and others, that they could discriminate infallibly between the ancient and modern, in a written style, composed and passed off as " a tale of olden time," the story of *The Amber Witch*. The critics were satisfied. In particular, the Tübingen Reviewers, the compeers and friends of the Rationalists, pronounced their infallible sentence, grounded on their skill in discriminating the age of a writing, in favour of the book as a genuine ancient chronicle. The vexation of the critics on hearing of the hoax was unmeasured; nor would they believe it, until the author produced the testimony of his neighbours that he was the veritable writer of the work.

name given to it was not meant to imply that there were five different books. It meant simply the *five-fold volume*.

Next, we urge in support of the genuineness of this part of the Mosaic record, that the book of Genesis is the *foundation* of all the rest; is necessary to an intelligent understanding of the history that is to follow; connects the call of Abraham with the beginnings of the human race, and supplies us with the reasons for the religious and political segregation of the Jews from all the families of mankind. Whether to the Jews, or to ourselves, the four later books without the first would have been an inexplicable enigma. Take Genesis from the Pentateuch, and you are left with only a mutilated literary fragment, a book wanting its introductory chapter, a story without a beginning.

Whilst, once more, we urge in behalf of retaining Genesis in all its integrity, that the book is constantly referred to both in the succeeding books of Moses and in the other Scriptures. Proofs of references to the later chapters would fill several pages. We limit ourselves to examples from those *earlier* chapters on which modern suspicion has specially fastened. Thus, in inculcating the observance of the Sabbath on the Jewish nation, we have Moses referring to the Sabbath of Paradise;[1] in enforcing the duty of abstaining from the eating of blood, we have almost in the same words the

---

[1] Compare Exod. xx. 11, xxxi. 16, 17, with Gen. ii. 2, 3.

precept which had been before given to Noah.¹ Both Hosea and Job are found referring to the circumstance of Adam's transgression;² whilst Isaiah not only alludes to the facts of the Deluge, but to the gracious promise which succeeded, that the waters should no more go over the earth.³

In the New Testament, also, the references to these earlier chapters are frequent, distinct, and unequivocal. Our Lord, in express terms, makes mention of the institution of marriage in Paradise;⁴ and assumes as facts, with the history of which all who listened to Him would be familiar, the entrance of Noah into the ark, and the destruction of the cities of the plain.⁵ For references to Genesis in the apostolic writings, it may suffice to direct attention to the brief but striking summary of its contents, from the very beginning, as given in chap. xi. of the Epistle to the Hebrews.

For the authority of the book of Genesis, then, as for that of the other books of the Pentateuch, we again fall back upon the united, constant, undeviating testimony of the Jewish Church. A certain collection of writings purports, on the face of them, to have been prepared by Moses for the instruction of his nation under Divine direction. Without disintegration and without difference, this entire body of writings is also

¹ Compare Lev. xvii. 14 with Gen. ix. 4.
² Hos. vi. 7 (margin); Job. xxxi. 33.
³ Isa. liv. 9.
⁴ Comp. Matt. xix. 4, 5, with Gen. ii. 24.
⁵ Matt. xxiv. 38, 39, and x. 15.

by Divine direction delivered to the Church in the wilderness,—to be believed in as a truthful record, to be watched over as a sacred trust, to be venerated as the oracles of God. If the book of Genesis constituted a part of this body of writings, then, unless the ancient nation were the most credulous dupes in the world, and their leader one of the greatest impostors, Genesis must be an inspired book, and Moses was its author.

ii. The next form of modern sceptical objection we may advert to, in relation to the Pentateuchal record, is based upon its alleged disagreement with the facts and discoveries of PHYSICAL SCIENCE, more especially of GEOLOGY.

The history of the conflicts between religion and science is very instructive. According to a very common view, the two things have always been afraid of each other, always jealous of each other, always fancying it impossible that they should sit side by side together on the throne of eternal truth. The strife is foolish, because what Kepler beautifully calls "the finger of God and the tongue of God"—His works and His word—can never be contrary the one to the other. Whatever the discrepancy be, it must be of our own making. We have either generalized too hastily upon the facts of science, or have interpreted too superficially the statements of Scripture. Such has been the history of all past disagreements; and if we will but in patience wait for it,—wait till our knowledge of science is more perfect, and perhaps, as Bishop Butler suggests, our knowledge of the Bible too,—such we nothing doubt will be the solution of any discrepancies which may yet remain. By rapidly converging lines will Scripture and science be brought into more entire coincidence with each other; whilst every fresh light thrown upon the true teaching of either, will tend to confirm our belief that the Scriptures are a revelation from God.

The remark will not unfitly apply to some of the earlier geological objections to the Mosaic record, in regard to the work of creation, and especially to the commonly assumed date of our world's beginning. The interpretation was undoubtedly a hasty one which assumed this date to be coeval with the creation of man. The first verse in our Bibles tells us only that this world had a beginning, but does not profess to inform us when that beginning was. The existence of a previous condition of our globe before man appeared upon it was no new hypothesis, invented to quadrate with the discoveries of geological science, but was suspected and anticipated even by the early Christian fathers.[1] And now all intelligent commentators are agreed that, between the first and second verses of the book of Genesis, a margin is left for any conceivable number of geologic cycles, enough on that score, at all events, to free the Mosaic narrative from blame.

But on other grounds, besides that of the age of our terrestrial system, have geologists excepted to the

[1] See *Edinburgh Review*, xc. Oct. 1849, p. 352.

Mosaic cosmogony; and the formation of the earth in six days, and the sudden emergence of the land from the waters, and the covering of earth's surface with a matured vegetation, are all declared to be at variance with the most accredited theories of modern science. Now we are far from wishing to undervalue the results of scientific investigation of any kind. With respect to geology we have always regarded it as one of the noblest fields ever opened for human thought; and to the cause of truth and social progress we feel it is bringing in fresh aid continually. But when successive theories in relation to it are urged as being at variance with Scripture, is it not competent to us to ask, Have all these geological systems been in accordance with one another? Has not system risen against system, and theory displaced theory, till the disciple of a science, itself but of yesterday, finds himself already walking among the fossil remains of extinct philosophies,—obliged to relegate the speculations of the early founders of the science to the same shelf with arguments for the Ptolemaic system of the universe?

Allowing therefore, as we may and do, for the value of scientific investigations, we ask, Is it reasonable to require that revelation, which must from its nature be a fixed and everlasting thing, should contain the unfolded germs of physical speculation, which must be a shifting thing; and in the case of geology, as we have seen, a very rapidly shifting thing too? Assume that we have got hold of the right theory at last, that "the testimony of the rocks" will never give forth more truthful utterances than those made for them by Hugh Miller; and assume further, that in putting "days" for *eons*, and other methods of interpretation, the book of Genesis could be shown to be in exact accordance with the modern state of geological science,—yet since the modern rod swallows up all other rods, and since two things which disagree with each other cannot agree with a third, we should be found to have a revelation which was right for Hugh Miller, but wrong for all the geologists which had gone before; in other words, Moses would be made to have written an account which for thirty-three centuries would have appeared to mankind as false, but in the thirty-fourth century would begin to be hailed as true! This is no fanciful hypothesis. The thing might have taken place in relation to the science of astronomy. Suppose that, in accordance with the demand for the most rigid scientific accuracy in Scripture, Moses or Joshua had expressed themselves in the language of the Copernican theory. Then, since that theory was to all appearance at variance with the evidence of man's senses, we should have had statements, by Moses or Joshua, believed to be demonstrably absurd up to the time of Copernicus, but acknowledged to be scientifically exact for ever afterwards.

Hence, in relation to the objection now under consideration, we think it enough to urge that information is to be sought for in Scripture only on matters bearing on its own proper subject.[1] It cannot be too often repeated that whilst there is an accordance, and except on the hypothesis of an inspiring influence on the mind of the sacred writers, a wonderful and inexplicable accordance, between Scripture and science, yet that he who looks into Scripture for a scientific summary of all the physical phenomena connected with the formation of the universe will assuredly look in vain. With elaborately constructed theories for bringing Scripture into harmony with the discoveries of modern science we have no sympathy. Peace-making schemes have been put forth with more or less success by different divines, — by Buckland, by Pratt, by Sedgwick, by Hitchcock, by Pye Smith,— but since Moses cannot be made to agree with all of them, and since we know not how soon we may be called upon to force his record into adjustment with some newer hypothesis, it seems better that we do not hastily commit the sacred narrative either to conflict or to agreement with any specific theory at all; but contend only for that general harmony with observation and fact, which would make the document intelligible to all readers, and in its leading

---

[1] De Quincey well observes, " GOD by a Hebrew prophet is sublimely described as the *Revealer*. . . . But of what is He the Revealer? Not surely of those things which He has enabled man to reveal for himself, but of those things which, were it not for special light from heaven, must eternally remain sealed up in inaccessible darkness. On this principle we should all laugh at a revealed cookery. But essentially the same ridicule, not more and not less, applies to a revealed astronomy or a revealed geology."—*Miscellanies*, p. 208, 1st edit.

and essential features, true for all times. And this we confidently aver it is.

iii. The lesson sought to be engrafted on the last kind of objection, namely, the duty of suspending all rash judgments upon Scripture, till the facts alleged to be at issue with its statements have been indisputably ascertained, will apply to some other forms of scientific objection, taken from the department of *language*, and *history*, and *antiquities*.

Experience has shown that the source of most of these objections is to be found in inaccurate or insufficient knowledge. One after another of them have we seen cleared up, only that they should lay a fresh offering at the footstool of the truth of God. A few instances may be cited. In the last century some learned writers on the formation of language pretended to have discovered proofs that it was not possible for all the dialects of the world to have had one common origin. Whereupon Sir William Jones and others addressed themselves to the task, and demonstrated affinities between all the languages of the earth, which only the supposition of one primary root could possibly explain. Again, when the celebrated tables of Indian history were first produced, and Christians were becoming alarmed at the finding of historic records, having every appearance of being anterior to the Mosaic era, it was permitted to Laplace, no special friend to Christianity, to show that some of the facts on which these tables were based were astronomically impossible. In like manner when objections to the sacred record were urged by Volney, founded on some exhumed monumental remains at Denderah, and Esneh, and Thebes, it was discovered by Champollion that, not only had there been a false reading of the characters, but in one instance that a temple, for which an antiquity of many thousands of years had been claimed, was really erected in the reign of the Emperor Tiberius![1]

Nor less conclusive have been the testimonies in disproof of some later objections. Modern rationalism, in its quest of a field where the local information of Moses might be expected to be at fault, not unnaturally fixed upon Egypt. Our limited sources of information about everything belonging to that country, in Mosaic times, promised to make charges of inconsistency against an author easy, and recklessness of counter-assertion safe. By Von Bohlen and Tuck both these expedients were had recourse to very freely. Bricks were not used for building at that early period of the world, it was declared. It was contrary to all the known habitudes of the nation that Pharaoh's daughter should think of bathing in the Nile. The sacredness attached by the Egyptians to animal life would never have allowed them to slay and prepare flesh for the table of Joseph; whilst, as to the ripe grapes of Pharaoh's butler, it was advanced confidently, that not until many centuries

---

[1] For fuller information on these and like illustrations, see Hamilton's *Pentateuch and its Assailants*, p. xix. Introduction, and Dr. Wiseman's *Lectures*, pp. 69–73.

afterwards was the vine cultivated in Egypt at all. To the utter confusion of these objectors, however, nearly all these statements have been falsified by sculptured remains and painted sepulchres. The Egypt of Pharaoh's time has been unearthed. The stones of the Desert have found a tongue; and by the mouths of Hengstenberg and others, as their interpreters, have borne witness that all which Moses has told us of their ancient country is faithful and true.

Such corroborations surely ought to give us strong confidence, whenever a new assault is made on our cherished beliefs. Time and human progress we see are great interpreters. The objections to our sacred writings which remain, whether new or old, are not more formidable than those which have fallen before the sword of God's truth already, and in due time will perish in the same way. As it was done to Jericho and her king, so shall it be done to Ai and her king. All human wisdom is grass, and "all the goodliness thereof is as the flower of the field." "The grass withereth, the flower fadeth, but the word of our God shall stand for ever."

FORCE OF THE ARGUMENT FROM ADMITTED DIFFICULTIES.

" Difficulty is a severe instructor, set over us by the supreme ordinance of a powerful Guardian and Legislator, who knows us better than we know ourselves, as He loves us better, too. *Pater ipse colendi haud facilem esse viam voluit.* He that wrestles with us strengthens our nerves and sharpens our skill. Our antagonist is our helper. This amicable conflict with difficulty obliges us to an intimate acquaintance with our object, and compels us to consider it in all its relations. It will not suffer us to be superficial."—BURKE.

"Whatsoever things were written aforetime were written for our learning," we read in one place; and in another, "All scripture is given by inspiration of God, and is profitable for doctrine, for reproof, for correction, for instruction in righteousness." A question not unnaturally arises hereupon, Does it comport with this declared purpose of giving us information that a revelation should contain things hard to be understood? in other words, are the difficulties of Scripture fatal to its claims as a religion sent from God?

Now to this it might be sufficient to answer generally, that from the nature of the subjects dealt with, considered in all their complex relations towards the finite and the infinite, towards God and towards man, difficulties of the kind referred to were to be expected in a revelation. Quoting from Origen, Bishop Butler says, "He who believes the Scriptures to have proceeded from Him who is the Author of Nature, may well expect to find the same sort of difficulties as are found in the constitution of nature. And in a like way of reflection, he adds, He who denies the Scripture to have been from God on account of these difficulties, may for the same reason deny the world to have been made by Him."

In the case of that portion of revelation, however, we are now endeavouring to vindicate, other and special considerations are to be offered as calculated to lead to certain forms of difficulty in our mental apprehensions.

i. Thus, one source of difficulty is to be found in *the brief and elliptical character* of the Mosaic writings.

The record itself is of the most abridged and condensed form. Five chapters contain the world's history for 1500 years. The succeeding five tide us over 500 years more. Only a very few chapters are given to the actual details of the forty years' wanderings, and two or three verses are often made to comprise the incidents of an engagement, which in the hands of a modern historian would have furnished material for the history of a great war. Yet more does this feature of the books strike us if we take into account the immense variety of subject they are made to embrace; history, morals, polity, doctrine, ritual, prophecy,—each according to its admitted importance, having demands upon the writer's narrow space. Could the writer amplify and enlarge upon all these topics? And if there were some upon which he must be more full and copious,—because complete information upon them respected the plan of human redemption for all time,—must not such amplification on particular subjects necessitate the language of conciseness, approaching even to obscurity, in the treatment of all the rest? Can we wonder that little facts should be allowed to drop out of the recital, when the author's highest aim is evidently to develope the principles of a great theocratic system? Or that the history should be abridged somewhat of its illustrative details, in order to make room for those minutiæ, in the economy of the daily sacrifice, which were designed to keep the eye of faith and hope fixed continually on the coming of the world's Redeemer?

We notice this point the more particularly, because it is in this inevitably laconic terseness of Moses, in matters not essential to his revelation, that we have had set forth, of late, the head and front of his offending. He stands arraigned at the bar of modern criticism, not for what he has said, but for what he has stopped short of saying. Instances will be given more fully in another part of this work, but an example or two may be quoted here. Thus it is *not said* that Jacob took down with him into Egypt any part of the large households common in the East, and therefore all calculations of the number of the population at the time of the Exodus must proceed upon the literal basis of seventy souls,— neither less nor more. It is *not said* that the Israelites obtained any weapons of war from the Egyptians, or that they picked them up on the shores of the Red Sea after their overthrow (though Josephus asserts that they did), and therefore the history is responsible for the inconsistency of supposing that a great victory was obtained over Amalek by a people unequipped with arms. It is *not said* that the priests in the wilderness had any helpers in the various departments of the Tabernacle service, and therefore Moses is guilty of asserting the demonstrative impossibility that three priests did all the work themselves. No plea is urged, that if the ellipsis were thus supplied, it would not make the narrative perfectly clear. The proffered explanation, it is allowed, is not inadequate, and, of course, is not impossible. But it is not "so nominated in the bond," and such gaps in a history, according to these critics, are fatal to its credibility. In that the oracle does not speak, it lies!

ii. But the brevity of the narrative is not the only source from which obscurity or difficulty in our understanding of the Mosaic writings might be expected to arise. The fact that the record deals with the transactions of a *very remote antiquity*,—with races which have passed away, with countries whose localities we can no longer define, with habits and usages which we have no contemporaneous literature to illustrate, and with dialects which have so long died out from ordinary use among men, as to be difficult of reproducing, with precision, in the language of modern thought,—must increase the difficulties of interpretation still more.[1]

---

[1] The following passage is from the work of Professor Stanley:—
" The Jewish history has suffered from causes similar to those which

Especially, among elements tending to induce an inadequate apprehension of the writer's meaning, we cannot overlook the fact, that, in anything of primitive purity or perfectness, the original language of the Mosaic books has ceased to exist. A great source of textual elucidation is thus lost to us. We all know, from the labours of Dean Trench, what treasures of history, of topography, of science, of social life, are frequently locked up in single words. How interesting is it often to trace the genealogy of a metaphor! What force of meaning, when thoroughly entered into, is found to reside in some vernacular idiom! But, in the case of the Mosaic books, these secondary historic lights are nearly all gone, their beauty lost in a translated baldness, their force and fire subdued to the commonplace of a later age.

Very difficult is it for us to say how much our apprehensions of many matters relating to sacred antiquities, to points of civil polity, social usage, tribal arrangements, domestic economy, may have suffered from these unavoidable causes, introducing a degree

still, within our own memory, obscured the history of Greece and Rome. Till within the present century, the characters and institutions of these two great countries were so veiled from view in the conventional haze with which the enchantment of distance had invested them, that when the more graphic and critical historians of our time broke through this reserve, a kind of shock was felt through all the educated classes of the country. The same change was, in a still higher degree, needed with regard to the history of the Jews. Its sacred character has deepened the difficulty already occasioned by its extreme antiquity."—*Preface to Lectures on the Jewish Church.*

of obscurity into our entire conceptions of Asiatic life, which a nearer proximity to the times, or access to any contemporaneous history, might have tended to dispel. At all events, the facts may serve to show how large an allowance, on the principles of a fair literary criticism, should be made for writings coming to us under such circumstances; and therefore how gratefully any reasonable explanation of a seeming difficulty should be welcomed by us, before we either attribute ignorance to the author, or cast a suspicion of untruthfulness upon the books.

Yet herein do we see the perverseness of modern rationalism. It first taxes its critical ingenuity to the utmost to discover a difficulty, and then retorts upon us that we have recourse to conjecture for taking the difficulty away. But, on the supposition that the Mosaic narrative is not complete and full in all its historical details,—which no one supposes it to be,—what, we have a right to ask rationalists, are their own alleged difficulties but conjectures? For example. It is *not said* that the sons of Aaron had any sons of their own, and therefore Bishop Colenso *conjectures* that the number of officiating priests in the wilderness could not have exceeded three. On the other hand, it is *not said* that Eleazar and Ithamar had *not* any sons of their own, and we therefore conjecture that the number of officiating priests may have been many more than three. In the absence of positive data, why is not one conjecture as good as the other?

In spite, therefore, of the taunt of infidelity, we maintain that, as against these alleged difficulties, it is quite competent for us to make any supposition, not unreasonable or improbable in itself, which would make the narrative consistent. And this to an indefinite extent. We are not tied to one chosen solution. If one explanation does not meet all the conditions of the case, it does not follow but that some other may. Whilst, if some event or phenomenon in the narrative should to the last appear insoluble,—incapable of accomplishment by any human resources we could think of,—it is to be remembered that there is a higher ultimatum to be pressed into the service, before faith in the Mosaic record should be given up. For though we would not needlessly or lightly invoke the agency of miracle, yet, inasmuch as those wilderness journeys were entered upon under the shield of a Divine promise, and by the authority of a Divine command, who will say that, in case of the absolute failure of all natural appliances, some form of preternatural agency might not have been employed? In no instance, perhaps, has the limited reading of a recent objector shown itself more than in his assumption, in face of the strongest contrary proofs,[1] that the desert in which the Israelites wandered was nothing but a vast expanse of gravel, and stone, and sand,—a place where they and their cattle could not have subsisted for forty years, nor

---

[1] See remarks on Bp. Colenso's Eleventh Objection in the Appendix.

even for one. Yet suppose the case, that the physical characteristics of the desert had been universally such as this superficial writer supposes, is it conceivable that He who suffered not the raiment of the people to wax old for forty years, would let all the herbage wither, and dry up every springing well? " Is not the life more than meat, and the body than raiment? "

iii. Lastly, as against the supposition that the difficulties of Scripture could in any way militate against its Divine claims, we urge the fact that such difficulties may serve, and have served, the highest interests of the Revelation itself.

Grant the possibility that a Revelation might have been given to mankind, in which nothing obscure or perplexing should appear. Grant that the Divine Author of the Scriptures might have left such overpowering demonstrations of His own handiwork on every page, and verse, and line of the Bible, as should have laid the whole intelligent race under the compulsions of an irresistible assent,—is it quite certain that both we and the faith too might not have been great losers thereby? Thus has it been no gain to us, to the intellectual claims of revelation upon the reason and faith of men, that in consequence of difficulties in the Scriptures,—whether in the department of history, philology, morals, or doctrine,—it has become needful to employ, in the study of them, the highest endowments of humanity, the profoundest scholarship, the most varied knowledge, the greatest critical acumen, all that science could contribute, and all that learned industry could collect?

Or, again, has it been no advantage to us, to the establishment of our hearts in the faith, that by reason of the alleged presence in the Scripture of hard things, and incomprehensible things, and startling things, its defenders have been set on the discovery and exploring of entirely new fields of evidence,—laying open, in the subtle and hidden agreements of the record, a mine of internal wealth, and, in fact, so causing all the resources of a skilful advocacy to be laid under tribute, that bread has come forth of the eater, and out of his own mouth has been condemned the caviller against the truth of God?

Whilst if, to these incidental benefits, we add the powerful accession which has been brought to the strength of our Christian evidence, when, as we are constantly finding, some of these obscurities become cleared up;—the vivifying flash of heaven-sent light which comes upon the mind, when, by the discoveries of a riper criticism, the alleged difficulties are proved to be no difficulties, and the long-controverted statement turns out to be true, after all;—we ask, is not the question at least an open one, whether, even if it had been possible, a revelation absolutely free from difficulties, would have been expedient for ourselves? Would not the absence from the sacred page of every obscure or perplexing statement have caused to be lost, to the believer, many supports to his faith, many incitements to his diligence, many motives to his prayers for Divine guidance and illumination, while yet, it is morally certain, that such freedom from difficulty would neither have restrained the objector from his cavils, nor cured the unbeliever of his pride?

SECTION IX.

RECAPITULATION.—CONCLUSION.

" It seems to be of the greatest importance, and not duly attended to by every one, that the proof of Revelation is not some direct and express things only, but a great variety of circumstantial things also: and that, though each of these direct and circumstantial things is indeed to be considered separately, yet they are afterwards to be joined together; for that the proper force of the evidence consists in the result of those several things, considered in these respects to each other, and united in one view."—BISHOP BUTLER.

A SUMMARY of that which is itself a summary may not promise much in the way of further elucidation, but it is added in order to indicate the general course our argument has taken, as well as to shew by what steps we have reached our ultimate conclusion, that the five books of Moses are not only part of a Divine Revelation, but are also the necessary and indispensable foundation upon which all subsequent revelation rests.

In our PRELIMINARY OBSERVATIONS, it will be remembered, we endeavoured to settle the antecedent question to what class of literary conposition the Mosaic record should be considered to belong. A *fasciculus* of tractates upon many subjects clearly ought not to be dealt with as a formal treatise upon one. If, in its general structure, a book be found true to its avowed design, the laws of the most rigid criticism can require no more. Livy or Julius Cæsar might compose a more scientific narrative than the author of the Pentateuch, and Justinian, with more of technical precision, might draw up a code of written law: but Moses had to prepare something more than a history, and something more than a statute-book,—namely, a text-book for all time of the dealings of God with our fallen race, and His plans for restoring them to more than their lost estate. Convict the book of unfitness for that end, and the argument is yielded. As a divinely authorized record the Pentateuch must fall. But who, and where is he, who is prepared to stake his unbelief on this issue?

In the SECOND SECTION, our aim was to establish the REMOTE ANTIQUITY of the Mosaic books;—to bring together the concurrent testimony of all history, all literature, all peoples, and all tongues, to bear witness that Moses, and the institutions of Moses, were well known in their times, and in the old times before them. Be it that these allusions to the Mosaic usages or records were made, by some only to be carped at, by others to be falsified, by some to be made the ground-work of a new religious system, and by others to be held up to scorn,—the fact attested was still the same. If any reliance is to be placed on the verdict of universal history, the inference cannot be gainsaid. The Pentateuch is an UNDOUBTEDLY ANCIENT BOOK.

In the THIRD SECTION, our object was to establish

the credibility of the Mosaic record, on evidence supplied by THE DOCUMENTS THEMSELVES;—in the minute and familiar acquaintance discovered by the author with all the scenes and transactions he describes; in the artless particularity with which he enters into the smallest details of Asiatic and Hebrew life; in the confidence with which he deals with pre-historic facts,—a confidence which the results of archæological discovery are daily continuing to affirm; and, more than all, in the proofs everywhere patent in the record, that it was penned by a fearless, upright, honest, and impartial man. No unprejudiced reader can fail to discern this evidence. The touches of an eye-witness are palpable in every page. The several dependencies of the narrative hang together with the easy consistency of truth and fact. Between separated portions of the record, we have subtle and delicate shades of agreement, which we feel must have been undesigned, so deeply embedded are they, and indirect, and out of sight. Throughout the work we see none of the devices of the literary impostor, nothing of his caution, nothing of his reticence, nothing of his studied avoidance of topics, which might be hazardous to an unsure and tripping step. All is natural, straightforward, transparently and unsuspectingly honest. If there be force in internal evidence at all, the Pentateuch is a thoroughly TRUSTWORTHY AND TRUTHFUL BOOK.

In the FOURTH SECTION, we endeavoured to give proof of the FAITHFUL KEEPING of the books. The lapse of ages and the revolutions of kingdoms lay, on most things, a corrupting or destroying hand. How know we that, in all their pristine and unmutilated integrity, the Mosaic documents have been kept safely? The endeavour to unravel this inquiry led to a twofold tracing of the external custody of the books,—*down* the stream of time, from the age of Moses to our own; *up* that same stream, till we come to the age of Moses again. The conclusion arrived at was, that a special Providence had watched over the writings. Checks and counter-checks, official rivalries and tribal feuds, made mutilations or substitutions impossible. To any who should urge the contrary, or allege that the entire record might be the invention of a later age, the challenge is thrown out to name the time when;—in other words, beginning with the day when the books were first laid up in the ark, and coming down to the time when they began to be translated into a hundred tongues, they are challenged to find in the chain of communication one missing link. If they are not able to do this, our second step is gained. The Pentateuch, in all its essential features, is a FAITHFULLY TRANSMITTED BOOK.

Undoubtedly ancient, transparently truthful, faithfully preserved,— such attributes, belonging to a written document, should alone shield it from the impertinences of a pedantic criticism, at all events: but in our FIFTH SECTION we put forward for the books much higher claims. They spake with authority. The spirit of INFALLIBLE TRUTH breathed through their utterances. They were voices from the Throne. So, at least, believed the assembled fathers of Israel, who first heard the words. So have testified all pious Jews ever since,—in defence of the divinity of their holy writings, loving not their lives unto the death. So taught the Omniscent One in the days of His incarnation, in order that nothing might be wanting, even as nothing has been wanting to secure the *consensus* of all churches and all times, to the fact, that unto the Jews were committed the oracles of God. And from the Jews, as God's librarians,—as the nation selected by Him, to guard a sacred deposit,—we, as Christians, are content to receive these oracles. Such as God taught them to regard the books, such we believe the books to be. Unfaithful have the chosen nation been in many things, but they have never been unfaithful in this, in preserving intact from human mutilations the Book of the Law of the Lord. Hence, if that which is infinite can come to us safely through a finite channel, the Pentateuch is a DIVINELY INSPIRED BOOK.

From this point, our argument took somewhat more of the defensive form. If we could have been content to have claimed for the Mosaic narrative the credit of being a generally veracious record,—a true book, the work of a true man,—room had been left for those many forms of inaccuracy and defect, which are inseparable from every human authorship. But, in our vindication of the writings of Moses, we had taken up ground, compelling us to say, "A greater than Moses is here;" one who could not, as Moses could, even to the estimation of a word, misrepresent the teachings of eternal truth. Hence the line of argument adopted in our SIXTH SECTION. The Divine infallibility which might be claimed for the Mosaic AUTOGRAPH, could not be communicated to all subsequent copies. All ages, after the first, must be content to have the treasure in earthen vessels, and, of consequence, to have therewith a portion of inherent human frailness. Yet, when all has been said that can be said, whether of translators' or transcribers' lesions, how inappreciably small does this inhering imperfection seem ! how little, with all that Christian scholarship has done *for* us, and sceptical criticism has done *against* us, is there to shake the confidence of the most unlettered man among us, that the Bible, in his hands, is the WORD OF GOD!

In the SEVENTH and EIGHTH SECTIONS, we brought together a few AUXILIARY TESTIMONIES, calculated to build up the general argument, the rather, as the evidence they are commonly supposed to furnish has been largely vilipended by modern critics as a mode of proof which is behind the age. Followers of Strauss, they hold with axiomatic certainty that " the climax of the wonderful is the climax of the unthinkable." Hence the right they claim to blot out certain chapters of our Christian evidence. Nature, in the calm order of her eternal sequences, it is alleged, revolts from "Miracle." The possibility of a man giving forth the utterances of prophecy, is foreign to all our laws of thought. Judaism is an effete thing of the past, and such fragment of a history as it pretends to give us, is laughed by our scientific analysis to scorn. Briefly, and but slightly, have we touched upon these objections; and that partly out of respect to the intelligence, or the remains of religious principle, which may be found in the objectors themselves. For if any weight at all is to be allowed to their allegations, it is not faith in the Pentateuch only that has to be given up, not faith in the Old Testament Scriptures only, but faith in the evidence of the senses, faith in the testimony of history, faith in the Divine origin of Christianity, faith in the very being of a God!

Indeed, the difficulties which beset the path of the philosophical unbeliever should, of themselves, suffice to make him pause. To say nothing of the fact that he has the testimony of ages against him; that the wisest and best men the world ever saw have taken the opposite side; that the Bible has created a literature of its own, a philosophy of its own, a morality of its own, the acceptance of which, by any people, has always initiated a new era in the nation's mental life,—he has, in his assaults on the Pentateuch, difficulties of a peculiar kind to surmount. The Jew of the *present*, as he exists before our eyes now, we have argued, is a phenomenon to be accounted for. Not less so is the Jew of the *past*. We throw out the challenge to the unbeliever boldly. Detach the Jew from his connection with the religious history of mankind, leave the pages blank which connect his annals with those of the most renowned empires of the earth; suppose the Pentateuch "unhistoric,"—its author a myth, its miracles a fraud, its ritual and institutes no more than old wives' fables,—and when, "deeper than did ever plummet sound," you have drowned the book, tell us what you are going to put in its room? How is this gap in the world's life to be filled up? Whence will you derive your new material for the missing chapters of a universal history? For surely it is not enough for our boasting advocate of the "higher criticism" to avow or assume his disbelief of the system he opposes; he is clearly bound to afford us an adequate explanation both of the facts of its history and of the extraordinary character of its results. In the department of physics, he is wont, in the case of any alleged result, to insist much upon the adequacy of the causation employed. We demand an adequate causation for certain moral results likewise. And if the books of Moses be not historic, and be not Divine, we ask him, who so regards them, to tell us how it has come to pass that falsehood has done the work of truth, and out of thick darkness has come a flood of light; how ignorance was enabled to frame a moral code, before which the wisdom of the wisest bows, and how the dim and broken shadows of the Jewish ritual should have prepared for that final dispensation of our perfected Christianity, for which the whole earth panted, as the hart for the water-brooks? Let him address himself to this task, and we mistake if he will not find that to build up is not quite so easy as to destroy, and to invent adequate explanations of what Revelation has done more trying to the mind than to believe in its Divine origin, and to admit its patent facts:—

"Faith is not reason's labour, but repose."

But we have done. Our leading object, it will be seen throughout, has been to present the evidence for the Mosaic record on its positive, historic, self-commending, and self-approving side. The problem may not be easy to solve, antecedently, by what kind or amount of objection, this solid wall of evidence could, by possibility, be shaken; but, certainly, by the force of any assaults, which it has had to sustain as yet, it is as little disturbed as the tall rock by the dashing of the ocean spray. Still, both in number and variety, though probably not in force, we must expect these assaults will increase. The controversy will not end with the silencing of a modern heretical prelate. His perverse zeal will provoke very many,—morbidly anxious for a part in his notoriety, and not caring, for the sake of it, to share in his unhonoured fall. Classical fable attributes the origin of the serpent-brood of Africa to the blood which dropped from the slain Medusa's wounds. From the same ill-fated country may spring up vipers of another kind, each slain heresy of her unfaithful prelate raising up a new foe to the truth of God. It is well, therefore, that we should be both forewarned and forearmed. We should not, when the alarm is sounded, have our weapons of controversy to seek; but, whether teachers or hearers, should be ready to give to every man both a justification of our creed and a reason for our hope.

Only in this, our bounden duty, of searching the Scriptures as well as the grounds on which the Scriprures rest, let us be ever mindful of the spirit in which we approach our task. When, in that book, whose Divine claims we have been considering, Jehovah is represented as revealing Himself from the top of Sinai, the people were commanded to sanctify themselves and to make ready, in order that, on the third day, they might behold the glory of the great I AM. Nor less requisite is it for us, if we would see God in His written Word, to remember, as we bend over the inspired page, that the place whereon we stand is holy ground. We should come to the study of the sacred oracles, meek in spirit, pure in heart, too conscious of ignorance to disown its statements, too thankful for the blessed hope it gives us, to complain that we cannot enter into all the deep things of God. Above all, must we pray for the assistance of the Holy Spirit, the Source of all light, the Author of all goodness, the Leader into all truth,—that so the eyes of our understanding being enlightened, and the statutes of the Lord having been our song in the house of our pilgrimage, we may hereafter have our part with those, who stand with their harps upon the crystal sea, and whose delight it is to recite continually "THE SONG OF MOSES, THE SERVANT OF GOD, AND THE SONG OF THE LAMB."

"In mentioning ecclesiastical history, Lord Bolingbroke gives his opinion very freely upon the subject of the Divine origin of the sacred books, which he supposes to have no such foundation. This new system of thinking, which he had always propagated in conversation, and which he now began to adopt in more laboured compositions, seemed no way supported, either by his acuteness or his learning. He began to reflect seriously on these subjects too late in life, and to suppose those objections very new and unanswerable, which had been already confuted by thousands. 'Lord Bolingbroke,' says Pope, 'is above trifling : when he writes of anything in this world, he is more than mortal. If ever he trifles it must be when he turns divine!'"—GOLDSMITH's *Life of Bolingbroke.*

"I see no reason to entertain a doubt of Moses being the writer of the first five books of the Old Testament. It was the belief of all Jews and all Christians, till of late years ; and all that is alleged against it is that certain passages were inserted of events subsequent to his own time, which may well have been added afterwards, for the benefit of after-times ; and being inserted as notes, in the margin, would in turn, be thought worthy of being incorporated in the text."—DR. PRIESTLEY.

APPENDIX:

OR, REMARKS ON SOME RECENT OBJECTIONS; PARTICULARLY THOSE CONTAINED IN A WORK ENTITLED "THE PENTATEUCH AND BOOK OF JOSHUA, CRITICALLY EXAMINED, BY THE RT. REV. JOHN WILLIAM COLENSO, BISHOP OF NATAL."

"A regardless contempt of infidel writings is usually the fittest answer; *spreta vilescerent*. But where the holy profession of Christians is likely to receive either the main or the indirect blow, and a word of defence may do anything to ward it off, there we ought not to spare to do it."—COLERIDGE.

As intimated in the Preface, it is no part of our design in this Appendix to go fully and minutely into all the points of difficulty, raised in a closely printed octavo volume, and collected industriously from all sources. To all needful purposes this has been done already, by writers eminently qualified for such a task by their peculiar line of study, such as Dr. McCaul, Dr. Benisch, Isaac Taylor, and several others, of whose labours we have availed ourselves in drawing up the present Appendix. We are not sorry to be able to cite the testimony of such writers. In inquiries of this kind, involving questions of Hebrew scholarship, Hebrew ritual, Hebrew life, everything turns upon the approved authority of the witness appealed to. And in this respect the substantially accordant testimony of the authors we have referred to, when opposed to the half-read surmises of a modern rationalist, will, it is believed, carry with it all suffrages.

To these writers, therefore, as well as to some others, noted at the foot of the page, would we refer those of our readers who may wish to see the objections of Bishop Colenso discussed with more particularity and fulness.[1] The purpose of the following remarks will be sufficiently answered if, without professing to furnish a complete answer to the objections specified, they serve to indicate lines of argument, in the proper following out of which a complete and satisfactory answer may be found.

FIRST OBJECTION.

THE BEATING OF THE SLAVE.

(*The Pentateuch Examined*, page 9.)

We select this instance for consideration, first, because, although occurring in the "Introductory Remarks" of the Bishop's book, and before entering upon the chapters which

[1] Especially do we commend for its complete answer to the Bishop, on all points involving mathematical or scientific questions, the able letter of the Rev. C. Pritchard. The pamphlet only came into the author's hands as these pages were passing through the press, but he is glad to be able to introduce a few references to it in the present Appendix. The other replies to which he is glad to call attention, are those of Mr. Drew, Mr. Hoare, Mr. Knight, and those contained in the work of Mr. Birks on the Exodus. Several of the newspapers also have devoted each a series of articles to the Colenso controversy, all distinguished by considerable ability; particularly those of the *Guardian*, the *Record*, and the *Weekly Review*. The articles in the two former of these journals have been published in a separate form; the able and scholarly character of the papers in the *Weekly Review*, it is hoped, will procure for them a like permanent distinction.

present us with his more scientifically formulated objections, it is his palmary case, and was evidently among his earlier stumbling-blocks;—one of the first " strains upon the cord" before it snapped. It seems also to have been a practical impediment to his mission work ; an accelerating inducement with him to change that mission for another, and a less enviable one,—namely, that of becoming the Apostle and Coryphæus of modern rationalism.

The objection is thus presented. After speaking of "the feelings which must be started in most pious minds when such words as these are read, professedly coming from the Holy and Blessed One, the Father and 'Faithful Creator' of all mankind," two texts bearing on slavery are quoted, the following being especially singled out for comment :—

"If a man smite his servant, or his maid, with a rod, and he die under his hand, he shall be surely punished. Notwithstanding, if he continue a day or two, he shall not be punished : for he is his money." (Exod. xxi. 20, 21.)

" I shall never forget," the author adds, " the revulsion of feeling with which a very intelligent Christian native, with whose help I was translating these words into the Zulu tongue, first heard them, as words said to be uttered by the same great and gracious Being, whom I was teaching him to trust in and adore. His whole soul revolted against the notion that the Great and Blessed God, the Merciful Father of all mankind, would speak of a servant or maid as mere ' money,' and allow a horrible crime to go unpunished, because the victim of the brutal usage had survived a few hours."

Let us see what considerations should have mitigated this revulsion of feeling in an educated Protestant Bishop.

i. In the first place, slavery, as an institution, was a *normal appendage of Asiatic life.* Moses did not create the system, as the Zulu from the Bishop's ignorant horror might have supposed, but found it on his hands. In the case of the Israelites, the institution was so bound up with their relations with neighbouring nations that its abrogation by Moses would have been impossible, even if he could have made the people believe it to be expedient. For without it, it is evident that a captive taken in war would have been atrociously murdered in cold blood. As between Israelite and Israelite, Moses might disallow any such proprietary right of one man over the person and services of another, and he did. But, in the case of prisoners of war taken from the Gentiles, or in that of distressed strangers voluntarily giving themselves up to a condition of personal servitude for what *they* considered an equivalent, at all events,—namely, the means of subsistence,—Moses could not oppose himself to the invariable usages of the age. But it is most untruthful to charge upon him that he did anything to strengthen the evil. As a property of man in man, Moses neither enacted slavery, nor sanctioned slavery, nor encouraged slavery; he only acquiesced in it as a necessary evil, which was beyond any power of his to annihilate. In so doing he did but follow the example of all prudent legislators. "I make laws," says Solon, "not according to my own standard of what is perfect, but according to the measure of what I know Athenians will bear." Moses, we believe, hated slavery as much as he hated divorce. Yet he gave bills of divorcement. And why? Infinite Wisdom has supplied the answer: "Moses, because of the hardness of your hearts, suffered you to put away your wives: but, from the beginning, it was not so,"[1]

[1] Matt. xix. 8.

which means, as Michaelis suggests, that "the executive was weak:" for, notwithstanding their acknowledgment of the Divine legation of Moses, the Israelites frequently rebelled against his authority.

ii. But, in the second place, the whole tenour of Mosaic legislation on this subject, as compared with all legislation then or since, is *on the side of mercifulness and humane consideration.*

As Moses could not extinguish the evil, he did all that man could do to mitigate its severity, till the world should be ripe for its overthrow, which could only be after the lapse of ages. Yet see what he did. Man-stealing, the familiar crime of our own age, was punished as a capital offence. Every slave was protected, both as to life and limb. An act of mutilation by a master was followed by the forfeiture of all further right in the servant, and if of malicious intent he took life away, his own life went for the servant's life. In the case of a *Hebrew* servant particularly, both during the time of his voluntary servitude and at the close of it, the utmost consideration was shown. He could claim the rest of his Sabbath, insist on participation in religious ordinances, could not be kept a day beyond seven years, and, on his emancipation, must be supplied liberally with the means for his future sustenance. Will the slave legislation of that or of any other age, on the score of humanity or kindness, bear any comparison with this? Will that of Athens, only allowing a slave's evidence to be taken at all under stress of torture? Will that of Rome, allowing an irresponsible right in the patrician master to chastise his slave even unto death? Will that of —— but the blush of a scarcely yet departed national shame forbids us to challenge further comparisons, and makes us content with saying that, before Bishop Colenso proceeded to arraign the harshness of Mosaic slave-law, it is a pity he did not make inquiry of times nearer to modern times, and of countries nearer home.

iii. Once more, in mitigation of this ebullition of Episcopal and Zulu horror, we urge that the Bishop has failed to enter *into the true meaning* of the condemned passage itself.

The former verse sets forth the conditions under which the master's life shall become forfeit for that of his servant, namely, that he have killed him of malicious purpose. "And if a man smite his servant, or his maid, with a rod, and he die under his hand, he shall be surely punished with death." But actual proof of malicious purpose may be wanting : and then it was ruled, that any circumstances favouring doubt upon the subject,—as against the extreme penalty of the law, at all events,—should weigh in the master's favour. "Notwithstanding, if he continue a day or two, he shall not be punished, for he is his money." Now would a modern law court disallow such mitigating considerations ? The issue to be tried is, Did the master intend to kill his servant ? And it is answered, No. For, first, the instrument used for beating was "*the* rod" (not *a* rod, as in our English version), being the cane which was allowed by the custom of the times to be used by a master in the correction of his slaves. Secondly, if there had been any premeditation on the part of the master to take away the life of his servant, he would have "died under his hand." Thirdly, it is noted that the servant "lived for a day or two" afterwards, which, at least, leaves room for the possibility that he might have died from some other cause besides the beating. And, lastly, it was against all probability that the master should have intended the death of his servant, because it was his interest to keep him alive, " for he is his money." On these grounds, it is allowed by Moses that the death of the master, which would have followed if the servant had died on the spot, should, on the possibility that the taking away of life was not intended, be commuted to a punishment of milder form, and that he should be amerced for the offence.

And why, while on the subject of Mosaic slave legislation, did not the Bishop lead his convert four verses onward, and bid him read as follows :—" And if a man smite the eye of his servant, or the eye of his maid, that it perish, he shall let him go free for his eye's sake ; and if he smite out his man-servant's tooth, or his maid-servant's tooth, he shall let him go free for his tooth's sake."[1] We wonder whether there is any slave-holding power on earth that would have made or yielded to a regulation so stringent upon the proprietor and so humane towards the slave ?

We may add that the going *unpunished altogether* is an unauthorized assumption of the Bishop's own. The words in the twentieth verse, " shall be avenged," mean, as all commentators admit, " avenged by death :" and it is only from *that* extreme penalty that reprieve is pronounced under the circumstances mentioned. Similar cases must have occurred in Israelitish courts of justice, and the prevailing practice, it is believed, was based upon this passage. Happily, some of the ancient rabbis, who lived near enough to the period when the Jewish state existed, distinctly inform us that the slayer of a slave under the

[1] Exod. xxi. 26, 27.

circumstances described in verse twenty, *was put to death by the sword.*[1] (Sanhedrin, 52–6.)

SECOND OBJECTION.

THE FAMILY OF JUDAH.

(*The Pentateuch Examined*, c. ii. p. 17.)

In this objection, the chief point of glaring inconsistency which the Bishop labours to establish is, that the narrative, making Judah to have been twenty years old when he was married, and forty-two when he went down into Egypt, yet represents him to have become *a grandfather* in relation to Pharez in the course of twenty-two years.

[1] Dr. Benisch, p. 29; also the second article of the *Weekly Review*, Jan. 10. The writer, Mr. Paton, thus concludes his remarks upon the *so-called* Hebrew slavery:—" Such, then, being an exact description of Hebrew servitude, it cannot fail to be matter of surprise that the terms *bondage, bondmen,* have been allowed to enter our translation, to denote this service; and that the notion still prevails of slavery as being a recognized institution amongst the Hebrews. Michaelis has confirmed this notion by applying the general title of slavery to the system of Hebrew service. It is with great pleasure, however, that we refer to the great work of Saalschutz, *Das Mosaische Recht*, Berlin, 1846, who has wiped away the unjust reproach from the code of the Jewish law-giver, which vindicated and guarded personal liberty against every possible encroachment by numerous and most stringent enactments. In exposing the injustice of Michaelis' imputation, Saalschutz asks, 'With what justice could the appellation of *Leibeigenshaft*, servile thraldom, or slavery, be applied to such a system of servitude? Servants that were free by law in the seventh year, and universally in the year of jubilee, could not be called slaves; they were in no sense such. With what propriety or justice can any or all these classes of servants be called bondsmen or slaves?'—SAALSCHUTZ, vol. ii., note in sec. 12, pp. 714, given by Dr. Cheever.—See also article in Kitto's *Cyclopædia*, p. 774."

The objection is thus set forth. After a series of calculated events, by means of which the writer thinks he proves that, at the time of Jacob's going down into Egypt, Judah was forty-two years old, he goes on—

"But, if we turn to Gen. xxxviii., we shall find that, in the course of these forty-two years of Judah's life, the following events are recorded to have happened :—i. Judah grows up, marries a wife—'at that time,' v. 1—that is, after Joseph's being sold into Egypt, when he was 'seventeen years old,' Gen. xxxvii. 2, and when Judah, consequently, was, at least, twenty years old, and has, separately, three sons by her. ii. The eldest of these three sons grows up, is married, and dies. The second grows to maturity (suppose in another year), marries his brother's widow, and dies. The third grows to maturity (suppose in another year still), but declines to take his brother's widow to wife. She then deceives Judah himself, conceives by him, and in due time bears him twins, Pharez and Zarah. iii. One of these twins also grows to maturity, and has two sons, Hezron and Hamul, born to him before Jacob goes down into Egypt. The above being certainly incredible, we are obliged to conclude that one of the two accounts must be untrue."

Either the accounts, or the Bishop's *mode of stating them*, is untrue, no doubt. But in this latter, two or three assumptions are made which, while doubt remains upon them, must affect the resulting conclusions greatly.

i. First, the assumption that Judah was twenty years old at the time of his marriage, resting, as it does, upon the expression "at that time" (Gen. xxxviii. 1), is one which cannot be maintained. The old rabbinical explanation of the phrase in question, and one endorsed by modern scholars, makes it to mean a certain indefinite period, and fairly rendered "*about* that time." The word is so used in Deut. x. 1, where the context requires a latitude of eight-and-thirty years to be left, and therefore no complaint could be urged if in this case we ask for a margin of six or seven. Yet let this margin be conceded, and the difficulty all but disappears. For Judah might then have married at the age of fourteen, a circumstance in the East by no means uncommon, and allowing the same thing to have taken place in the case of Shelah and Pharez, there is nothing absolutely impossible, at all events, in Hezron and Hamul being born when Judah was as yet but forty-two.

ii. But again, only by means of unsupported assumptions can it be shown that, at the time spoken of, Judah's age was *only forty-two*. The calculation rests upon certain parallelisms in the histories of Judah and Joseph, leading, in our objector's opinion, to the conclusion that Judah must be just three years older than Joseph. Dr. M'Caul, however (Exam. p. 14, 15), by a much more elaborate chronological tracing, has shown that Judah was the elder by *seven* years at least, and perhaps by *eight or nine;* a conclusion which, if accepted, would make the fact of his having grandchildren, under the peculiar circumstances mentioned, by no means an improbable occurrence.

Similar views are taken by the Jewish rabbis, who had seen the difficulty, such as it is, a long time ago;[1] the admission, however, being allowed by all commentators, whether Jewish or Christian, that, for an exact critical chronology, the data supplied by the history are not sufficient. Doubt rests upon the very first link in the chain; how long was Jacob in Padan-aram? It is common to assume he remained there *twenty* years. Without any view

[1] See Dr. Benisch, Art. 4, *Jewish Chronicle*.

to this difficulty, Dr. Kennicott has put it down at *forty*. But if we suppose him to have remained nearer thirty years, all difficulty vanishes, and there is nothing to contradict such a supposition, seeing that Jacob was 130 years old when he died.

Mr. Pritchard gets rid of the Bishop's objection by an entirely different process. His arguments are too long for citation ; but he shews that Hezron and Hamul may, from the narrative itself, be fairly supposed to have been *born in Egypt*, and consequently, when Jacob was *more* than forty-two years old. Manasseh and Ephraim, he argues, were clearly among the seventy persons spoken of as having *come into Egypt*, although, as we all know, they were *born* there ; why may not the same thing be said of Hezron and Hamul?

THIRD OBJECTION.

THE SIZE OF THE COURT OF THE TABERNACLE.

(*Pentateuch Examined*, c. iv. p. 31.)

" And Jehovah spake unto Moses, saying, . . . Gather thou the congregation together unto the door of the Tabernacle of the congregation. And Moses did as Jehovah commanded him. And the assembly was gathered unto the door of the tabernacle of the congregation." (Lev. viii. 14.)

In reference to this summons, the Bishop objects that, taking the term *all* the congregation to mean " the whole body of the people," "at all events, the adult males in the prime of life among them,"—we have to suppose that 603,550 warriors were required, at the command of

Jehovah, to assemble at the door of the Tabernacle of the congregation; that, further, this expression must imply that they were to come within the court, and, therefore, that if they obeyed this consequence would follow—

"Allowing two feet in width for each full-grown man, nine men could just have stood in front of it. Supposing, then, that 'all the congregation' of adult males in the prime of life had given good heed to the Divine summons, and had hastened to take their stand side by side as closely as possible, in front, not merely of the door, but of the whole end of the Tabernacle in which the door was, they would have reached, allowing eighteen inches between each rank of nine men, for a distance of more than 100,000 feet, in fact,—nearly twenty miles!"

To this twenty-mile objection it is to be replied, that it contains three assumptions,—contradicted, one by sound criticism, another by all reasonable probability, and the third by common sense.

i. It is contrary to all principles of *sound criticism* to assume that the terms "assembly" and "congregation" must, of necessity, mean the entire body of 600,000 men. The words may be so interpreted in some cases, and even made to take in the women and children too. But whatever this objector may say to the contrary, the same words are sometimes used in a limited sense. For example, in Exod. xii. 3, the command is given to Moses and Aaron, "Speak ye unto all the congregation of Israel, saying," &c.; and yet when Moses proceeds to carry out the command, we find (v. 21) that " he calls for all the elders of Israel," these elders *representing* the congregation, and to whom, in giving the instructions, Moses felt the Divine command was fulfilled as faithfully as if recited to the whole body. For other instances of the word here translated "congregation," but yet having the force of a representative body only, see Dr. Benisch, s. 4, p. 12.

ii. Again, it is contrary to all *reasonable probability* that the whole assembly, of however many it may have been composed, should be confined to the space *within the court*. The Bishop has evidently not understood the true structure of the Tabernacle, which was not shut in by closed doors, as he supposes, but was open at the end; and, as the object was chiefly to witness an imposing religious ceremony, there might be a large number of spectators without, over and above the numbers which assembled within the court. And the verbal construction of the passage, it is alleged, favours this view : " And the assembly was gathered *towards the opening* of the Tabernacle of the congregation." (See Dr. M'Caul, p. 19.)

iii. The third assumption, we have said, is directly opposed to *common sense*. We feel it to be beneath criticism. It is that the word "all" being used in the summons to the congregation to attend the consecration of Aaron, it must be assumed that, if not every individual of the number, yet the main body of the 603,000 actually came. Why, is there a language on the earth in which the word has such an absolutely literal and determinate meaning? Or a people upon the earth with whom "all" is not an understood convention for a very large number? Suppose some chronicler, writing an account of our pageant the other day, should say, " All London turned out to give the welcome to the Princess Alexandra," would our arithmetical critic hold him guilty of " unhistoricalness " if it should be proved that out of three million Londoners some two millions, on the day in question, stayed at home?

FOURTH OBJECTION.

Moses and Joshua addressing all Israel.

(*The Pentateuch Examined*, c. v. p. 35.)

The objection begins thus :—

" These be the words which Moses spake unto all Israel. (Deut. i. 1.) And Moses called all Israel, and said unto them. (Deut. v. 1.) And afterward he read all the words of the law, the blessings and the cursings, according to all that which is written in the book of the law. There was not a word of all that Moses commanded which Joshua read not before all the congregation of Israel, with the women and the little ones, and the strangers that were conversant among them. (Josh. viii. 34, 35.)"

On this a statement follows, making the population of Israel, on the Bishop's computation, to be equal to that of London, or nearly three millions, upon which he asks—

" How, then, is it conceivable that a man should do what Joshua is here said to have done, unless, indeed, the reading every ' word of all that Moses commanded,' with ' the blessings and according to all that is written in the book of the law,' was a mere dumb show, without the least idea of those most solemn words being heard by those to whom they were addressed. For surely, no human voice, unless strengthened by a miracle of which the scripture tells us nothing, could have reached the ears of a crowded mass of people, as large as the whole population of London." [1]

---

[1] Upon which Mr. Pritchard shrewdly observes, "And if this stentorian voice could have reached them all, I would ask, what

The objection might have been grouped with the one last considered, as another example of petty arithmetical pedantry ; and capable of being disposed of in the same way. But the objection has some negligences and ignorances of its own. For example :—

i. Let it be granted, even if of those who did attend on the occasion,—call them all Israel, or half Israel, or only a tithe,—some could not hear every word that was spoken, it by no means follows that the entire recital would be a "dumb show." One purpose of the great meeting spoken of is well expressed in the preface to our Commination service, where we read, " It is thought good that, at this time, in the presence of you all, should be read the general sentences of God's cursing against impenitent sinners, gathered out of the seven and twentieth chapter of Deuteronomy and other places of Scripture, and that ye should answer to every sentence, Amen." Now many may have been present, in our cathedrals, at the reading of this service, who, without exactly catching the words of each separate sentence, would join in the general response of the congregation, at the bidding, " And all the people shall say, Amen." And so on the present occasion. It was the Ash-Wednesday of the Jewish nation,—a day, when they were to ratify and seal, by their own public acknowledgment, their acceptance of the Divine Law, as well as declare their determination to flee from such vices for which " they affirmed with their own mouths the curse of God to be due." Knowing, therefore, as all did, the general substance of the readings, the act might be an intelligent act, even to those who could not hear.

ii. But the peculiar facilities for hearing, furnished by

would have become of the ears of those who were unfortunately near to the speaker ?"

P

the special locality selected, seem to have been entirely overlooked by this objector. Half of the tribes stood on Gerizim, the other half on Ebal; in the narrow space between, stood Joshua and the Levites. Now, on the testimony of several modern travellers (see Dr. McCaul, pp. 30, 31,) it is affirmed, that there is a remarkable echo, and that, to such a distance, and with such clearness, may sound be conveyed, that it is quite a common thing for the villagers to call to each other from the opposite hills of Ebal and Gerizim, and that the voice is heard quite distinctly. Of course, in citing this testimony, we are not trying to provide for Bishop Colenso's auditory of two or three millions, but merely to shew, that quite as large a number, as it would consist with all historic truthfulness to speak of "as all Israel," might be gathered on the slopes of these two opposing hills, and hear from a voice in the valley between them, even though unstrengthened by miracle, " the words of the Law of the Lord."

iii. But even if these explanations were insufficient, we have still, as Mr. Pritchard remarks, the express words of Scripture itself, explaining the manner and the amount of the help which Moses received in his addresses and exhortations *to all Israel.* The elders, the priests, and the Levites, assisted him, Deut. xxvii. 1 and 9: "And Moses, *with the elders* of Israel, commanded this people to keep the ordinances." "And Moses and the priests and the Levites spake unto all Israel." Thus, instead of a prodigious multitude to be reached by " one human voice," it quite consists with the narrative to suppose that " all Israel " was broken up into manageable groups,—each one addressed, in the same words, by a Levite or a priest.

FIFTH OBJECTION.

THE EXTENT OF THE CAMP COMPARED WITH THE PRIEST'S DUTIES.

(*Pentateuch Examined*, chap. vi. p. 58.)

This objection is introduced by the text:—

"And the skin of the bullock, and all his flesh, with his head, and with his legs, and his inwards, and his dung, even the whole bullock shall he (the priest) carry forth without the camp, unto a clean place, where the ashes are poured out, and burn him on the wood with fire: where the ashes are poured out, there shall he be burnt." (Lev. iv. 11, 12.)

Proceeding then upon his computation of two millions, as the amount of the population, and then upon a view of the camp, as a moveable mass covering an area of twelve miles square, the objector goes on to point out, how impossible it would be for three priests to perform all the ritual offices for so great a multitude,—pointing his difficulty with the following piece of profane and unwarrantable ridicule:—

"In fact, we have to imagine the priest, having himself to carry, on his back on foot, from St. Paul's to the outskirts of the Metropolis, the skin, and flesh, and head, and legs, and inwards, and dung, even the whole bullock."

Passing over the attempt, in this passage, to heighten the grotesqueness of the description by a direct falsification of Scripture,—not a word being found there of the purveyor, whoever he may have been, carrying the bullock *on his back*, or even of his going on feet at all,—we need only call attention to the fact, that the whole point of the objection turns upon the question, whether the priest per formed the various offices connected with the removal of the offal *himself*, or only superintended the performance of it *by others*? And again is the Bishop found placing himself in opposition to the Hebrew grammar, to the analogy of Scripture, to the common usage and intelligence of mankind.

i. The *grammatical construction* of the Hebrew is, on the admission of all scholars, against the interpretation that by the words "he shall carry forth," is meant he shall do it in his own person.[1] The Hebrew language allows of a modification in the use of a verb, called hiphil, of which the effect is to give the original verb a *causative* form;—*e. g.* "to fall," under this modification would become "cause to fall;" "stand," changes into "cause to stand." This modification is adopted in the passage before us; so that the expression for "he shall carry forth," would be critically and exactly rendered "he shall cause to be carried forth." It may be by wagons, it may be by other persons, but no scholar would interpret the language as implying that the priest must necessarily do the work himself.

ii. The *analogy of Scripture* also is against such a forced interpretation. The same word is found in cases where the idea of subordinate agency is necessitated by the circumstances of the case; as, for example, in Lev. xiv. 44, 45, where, on Dr. Colenso's shewing, we should have to suppose that the priest, with his own hands and on his shoulders, carried the stones, and timber, and all the *débris* of the house of leprosy, out of the city into an unclean place! (See also Exod. iii. 10.) But indeed it is no matter of inference that the priests were largely assisted in all Tabernacle duties. It is affirmed in the record again and

[1] See Letter of Rev. J. B. McCaul, reprinted from the *Record*.

again. Thus, in Numb. viii. 24, we read : " This is it that belongeth unto the Levites ; from twenty and five years old and upward they shall go in to wait upon the service of the tabernacle of the congregation." (See also Num. iii. 6, and iv. 16, and viii. 19.)

iii. Once more, the *common usage* and intelligence of mankind are against the Bishop's interpretation. All languages and all nations have some expression for the word " carry ;" which, though used as if denoting a personal act, is always understood to imply instrumental agency. A victorious general is said to " carry" his prisoners to the capital. A merchant " carries " his commodities to a distant market. A colonist " carries " his household to a foreign settlement. What, if in order to prove persons unhistoric who should express themselves in such language, we should have the ludicrous suppositions made, as critically deducible from the language employed, that Stonewall Jackson carried his prisoners into Richmond one by one upon his back? or that every Manchester importer had to bear on his back the burden of his own bales of cotton ? Or that, unless we suppose Bishop Colenso to have taken all his living belongings on his shoulders, it must be historically false that he carried his family to Natal ? We owe some apology for illustrations, which even the bad taste and offensive provocation exhibited in the picture of a priest carrying a bullock on his back from St. Paul's to Highgate is hardly sufficient to excuse.

This chapter contains another objection, which for its utter coarseness we should have abstained from noticing, were it not that the objector says of it that " it is itself a very convincing proof of the unhistorical character of the whole narrative." We refer to the alleged impossibility of maintaining purity in the camp according to the directions given in Deut. xxiii. 12–14. The short answer to the objection is, that the directions spoken of did not apply to the camp life of the wilderness at all. They will be found among several other directions which bear internal evidence of having a *prospective* reference, and of being intended to come in force after the settlement of the people in Canaan.

SIXTH OBJECTION.

THE NUMBER OF THE PEOPLE COMPARED WITH THE POLL-TAX.

(*The Pentateuch Examined*, chap. vii. p. 41.)

The exception is found in the following passage:—

"And Jehovah spake unto Moses, saying, When thou takest the sum of the children of Israel after their number, then shall they give every man a ransom for his soul unto Jehovah when thou numberest them, that there be no plague among them when thou numberest them. This they shall give, every one that passeth among them that are numbered, half a shekel after the shekel of the sanctuary; an half shekel shall be the offering of Jehovah." (Exod. xxx. 11–13.)

On this passage are founded the two following objections:—first, that the term "shekel of the sanctuary" is used before there was any sanctuary in existence; the second, that in two takings of the census of the people, with an interval between them of six months, the improbable result is given, that there had been no change in the number of the population, 603,550 being the numbers on both occasions.

i. To the former objection two replies are offered. In the first place, the term "shekel of the sanctuary" is not the necessary rendering of the original. It is rendered in Benisch's Bible, "shekel of holiness," or, "holy shekel;"—the expression setting forth that all religious dues were to be paid in coin of full weight, as distinguished from the alloyed and depreciated currency which was so much in use at the time. Abraham was careful, in paying his money to Ephron, to pay him in shekels that were current money with the merchants. Dr. McCaul, however, sees a confirmation of the writer's truthfulness in the use of the word, for, as if conscious that up to this time the sacred shekel was unknown, Moses introduces the parenthetical explanation, "A shekel is twenty gerahs."

ii. The other objection put forth in this chapter, namely, the unlikely coincidence of the numbers taken at one census with those yielded at a census taken six months afterwards, must take rank among the Bishop's assumptions; his facts not proved. A poll-tax was collected with a view to meet the expenses of erecting the Tabernacle, and for this some form of numbering must have taken place. Six months afterwards, when the Tabernacle was reared, an official census was taken, and the result registered and declared. But to say that there were two official numberings, at an interval of six months, and yielding the same result, is, to say the least of it, more than can be proved from what appears in the narrative itself.

SEVENTH OBJECTION.

THE ISRAELITES DWELLING IN TENTS.

(*The Pentateuch Examined*, chap. viii. p. 45.)

On this incident two objections are founded; one critical, and the other arithmetical. It will appear on examination, that the criticism of the Bishop is unsound; and the arithmetic, if sound, no more relevant to the point in hand than would be one of his own imaginary problems.

i. The critical objection is adduced to establish a contradiction between the passage, Exod. xvi. 16, "Take ye every man for them which are in his *tents;*" and Lev. xxiii. 43, where it is assigned as a reason for their dwelling in booths for seven days, " that your generations may know that I made the children of Israel to dwell in *booths*, when I brought them out of the land of Egypt." But there is no contradiction whatever. Our best Hebraists have shown that the Hebrew word comes from a verb which means " to cover" or " afford shelter to," and might mean a " booth" for cattle, or a " tent" for a warrior, or a " lair" for a wild beast; in short, a moveable habitation of any kind. The contradiction, therefore, exists in our English version only.

ii. Then comes the arithmetical objection; and for this, assumptions are extemporized rapidly. (1.) First, the coverings they had were *tents*, and nothing else. (2.) Then these tents were of a *heavy construction*, made of skins, with a strong apparatus of cords and poles. (3.) Then *all* the people must have had them; and, as decency would not allow more than ten persons to occupy one tent, everything is ready for our arithmetic. The people would require 200,000 tents, and upon the calculation of one ox carrying 120 lbs., the service of oxen for transport would be 200,000.

To which it is answered, (1.) First, it is not true that the coverings must have been "tents" in the Bishop's sense. Some of the wealthier people would have such accommodations, no doubt; but the poorer among them would avail themselves of booths or sleep under cover of the wagons (Num. vii. 3), or betake themselves to any shelter they could find. (2.) Neither is it true that those who had tents, invariably used the cumbrous structures which this objection describes. A garment, stretched over a few poles, is often made to afford sufficient nightly shelter in the East now; can we doubt that many such extemporized contrivances would suggest themselves to a people in haste, and under stress of difficulty? (3.) Whilst, lastly, as showing all the above figures to be a mass of irrelevant and wasted arithmetic, it is reasonably conjectured that the great body of the emigrants would not, at first, require any tents or coverings at all. Hardy sons of toil as they were, and taking their departure at the most genial season of the year, it would be nothing to them to spend their nights in the open air for the first part of their journey, and then, as the heat of summer advanced, by degrees, they might procure for themselves the means of shelter. Will the Bishop still abide by the necessity for his imaginary 200,000 oxen, to carry his imaginary 200,000 tents, of imaginary weight and size?

EIGHTH OBJECTION.

THE ISRAELITES ARMED.

(*The Pentateuch Examined*, chap. ix. p. 48.)

After quoting the passage, " The children of Israel went up harnessed out of the land of Egypt" (Exod. xiii. 18), and contending from some other passages in which the word occurs that harnessed *appears* to mean " armed," or, " in battle array," the Bishop proceeds,

" It is, however, inconceivable that these down-trodden, oppressed people should have been allowed by Pharaoh to possess arms, so as to turn out at a moment's notice 600,000 armed men."

He next turns to the solution suggested by our marginal word, in which, for harnessed, we have " by five in a rank ;" but this, he alleges, only makes matters worse, as, after allowing reasonable marching room, we should have to suppose a column of 68 miles long.

Here, it will be observed, that the whole pith of the objection is contained in the proper rendering of a single word,—a word of very early use,—of entirely doubtful etymology,—occurring in only four other places, and quite obsolete in the later Bible times. Its true meaning, therefore, has long been one of the hard knots among Hebraists ; —one interpretation or another being put upon it, according to the view taken of its derivation. How, then, does the Bishop proceed in this case ? Why, he singles out one of these various renderings,—one, of which the best he can say is, that such "appears" to be the true meaning,—and upon this he builds up certain conclusions, which he considers proves the Mosaic history to be untruthful. Ignorant of other meanings having been given to the word he is not, because he even mentions some of them. Why were not some of these discussed, as well as " armed," or " five in a rank?" The answer is plain. The two renderings he selected encumbered the passage with an apparent difficulty ; several of the others, even that of Gesenius, for instance, which he quotes, would have left no difficulty at all. "Prepared," "equipped," "in orderly array," are among the accepted renderings of the word ; and the substitution of any one of these, in the passage under consideration, would have spared the Bishop and his readers all speculations about the mighty host, "nearly nine times as great as the army of Wellington at Waterloo." That some of the people were armed in the literal sense, there can be no doubt; and, however perversely rejected by this critic, rational explanations can be given of the means by which such arms might be obtained. But the 600,000 warriors is no asserted Pentateuchal fact, and therefore, not a matter which we are required to go into,—to the weariness of the reader's patience, and of our own.

NINTH OBJECTION.

The Institution of the Passover.

(The Pentateuch Examined, chap. x. p. 54.)

After quoting the directions for keeping the Passover, as given in Exod. xii. 21–28, the Bishop proceeds,—

" That is to say, in one single day, the whole immense population of Israel, as large as that of London, was instructed to keep the Passover, and actually did keep it. I have said, 'in one single day;' for the first notice of any such feast to be kept is given in this very chapter, where we find it written, ver. 12, 'I will pass through the land of Egypt this night, and will smite all the first-born in the land of Egypt, both man and beast.' "

And again, " How could the order to keep the Passover have been conveyed, with its minutest particulars, to each individual household in this vast community in one day,—rather, in twelve hours, since Moses received the command on the very same day on which they were to kill the Passover at even, Exod. xii. 6?"

Both these objections, it will be observed, turn upon a question of time; upon the possibility not only of conveying to so vast a multitude these minute instructions for a religious observance, but of having them carried out "in one single day," or, according to the Bishop's second objection, "in twelve hours."

To this the challenge is thrown out to the Bishop to prove that "twelve hours," or even a single day, was all the time allowed either for communicating the instructions, or for carrying them out? The Bible says no such thing. In Exod. xii. 3, we read, "Speak ye unto all the congregation of Israel, saying, In the tenth day of this month they shall take to them every man a lamb, according to the house of their fathers, a lamb for an house." Here it is plain that the command was given some time *before* the tenth of the month,—might have been even on the first or second,—but certainly was not on the fourteenth, as the Bishop alleges. But take the mean of *five* or *six* days, where could be the difficulty of conveying the information to a large community, organized and divided into tribes as the Jews were, and all in hourly communication with their respective chiefs? Besides, it is clear, from Exod. xi. 1-8, that Moses knew that the death of the first-born was to be the last plague, and that immediately after it, he and his people must be ready for departure.

This direction to take the lamb on the tenth day of the month had not escaped the notice of the objector; but, perversely enough, instead of so plain an assertion leading him to suspect the correctness of his own conclusion, that the first intimation was given on the fourteenth day, he superciliously dismisses it as one of those "perplexing and contradictory" statements of which the examples in the Pentateuch are "many."

But what makes him so confident that, not until the fourteenth day,—the day on which the Passover was to be killed, at even,—and therefore "within twelve hours," was the slightest intimation given to the people of what they were required to do? Why, because it is said in the 12th verse, " I will pass through the land of Egypt *this night;*" and again, in the 14th verse, *This day* shall be unto you for a memorial,—expressions, which it is contended must mean the time present, and can mean nothing else. But we have the authority of the best Jewish and Christian Hebraists for saying that it often *does* mean something else : and quotations are cited, again and again, where the same Hebrew word is used, not in relation to the time then present to the speaker or writer, but to a time already past (see Gen. vii. 11; Josh. v. 11, and, as a converse case, Lev. xvi. 30).

So melts into air, "thin air," the first part of this difficulty, in relation to the Passover. The *twelve hours'* notice, so utterly insufficient for purposes of inter-communication, for anything which appears in the narrative, may have been a notice of twelve days.

But this keeping of the Passover presents another difficulty. According to the directions that there should be a "lamb for a house," and that they were "all to be male lambs of the first year;" the Bishop finds, on inquiry among experienced sheep-masters, that the Israelites must have had a flock of two million of sheep — a fact nowhere said in the Pentateuch — and that for the pasturage of such a number 400,000 acres of pasture-land would be necessary. Again, however, is the Bishop's calculating ingenuity expended to no purpose. It is based entirely upon a misinterpreted reading of a passage in Josephus, to the effect that, on the *average*, the partakers of the Passover were " ten persons for each lamb ; " whereas ten was only the *minimum* of persons who might so partake, —that being the number to make a congregation ; but the law specified no *maximum* number. And since its requirements were satisfied if each person ate " a morsel of the size of an olive," the Bishop's basis of *ten* for a lamb might, with far more reason, have been put down at a *hundred*. So dwindles, to one tenth of their original magnitude, this formidable array of Passover figures.

TENTH OBJECTION.

THE MARCH OUT OF EGYPT.

(*The Pentateuch Examined*, chap. xi.)

This objection is introduced by the quotation : " And the children of Israel journeyed from Rameses to Succoth, about six hundred thousand on foot that were men, beside children. And a mixed multitude went up also with them ; and flocks and herds, even very much cattle." (Exod. xii. 37, 38.) Having referred to his former computation, that this moving body must be estimated at two millions, the Bishop proceeds,—

" Here, then, we have this vast body of people of all ages, summoned to start, according to the story, at a moment's notice, and actually started, not one being left behind, together with all their multitudinous flocks and herds, which must have been spread out over a district as large as a good-sized English county."

But this, he adds, is but a very small part of the difficulty. We are required to believe that this vast population, in one single day,—

" Came in from all parts of the land of Goshen to Rameses, bringing with them the sick and infirm, the young and the aged ; and, lastly, that having done all this, since they were roused at midnight, they were started again from Rameses that very same day, and marched on to Succoth, not leaving a single sick or infirm person, a single woman in childbirth, or even a 'single hoof' (Exod. x. 26) behind them."

i. For the leading fallacy involved in these extracts, it may suffice to refer to what has been advanced under the last objection. There is no warrant whatever in Scripture for saying that the departure out of Egypt was undertaken at a moment's notice; and therefore the whole picture of the "midnight summons," and the inevitable "confusion," as deduced from the helter-skelter of the Bishop's household at Natal, when the alarm of a Zulu irruption woke them from their slumbers, is a sheer impertinence. The Israelites knew of their departure weeks before; and had been preparing for it weeks before. The directions with regard to the Passover, given, as we have already shewn, *five* days before, at least,—and it may have been even *thirteen*,—implied the necessity of readiness for departure, together with an intimation that midnight would be the time when the order for commencing it would be given. For the command was, that they were to eat the Passover "with their loins girded, with their shoes on their feet, and their staff in their hand, and they were to eat it in haste, because, at midnight, the Lord would pass through the land, to smite the first-born and execute judgment against all the gods of Egypt." Such a command, previously given and confidently believed, would require a careful preparation by all the heads of families, and the leading men of the various tribes; and the Hebrews were not wanting to the occasion.

ii. The other part of this objection has reference to the ordering of the march itself; the aggravated difficulty, occasioned by first collecting the whole population from all parts to meet at Rameses,—and then, from Rameses, all starting together for Succoth. Whilst, in relation to the two millions of sheep and oxen, it is urged, "such grass as there was, if not eaten down by the first ranks, must have been trodden under foot and destroyed by those that followed them mile after mile."

Now with regard to this latter difficulty, it will be time enough to set about solving it when it has been shewn that there were two million cattle. At present, it rests upon a calculation of the Bishop's, deduced from the numbers required for Passover purposes,—a number which, as we have seen, he has put down at ten times greater than it probably was. As to the assembling at Rameses first, and then marching out from thence in one organized host to Succoth, it is sufficient to say of it, as of so many others of the Bishop's facts,—not proved. The history says generally, "The children of Israel journeyed from Rameses to Succoth,"—a statement which would be true, if interpreted to apply to the principal men and representatives of the nation, who, at that time, would of course be at Rameses, as being the head-quarters of the leaders of the Jews. The rest of the nation, settled down at spots between Rameses and Succoth, might either fall in with the rest of the moving body, as they came up, or have started in separate detachments from their respective places, on first receiving the order from Moses. At all events, nothing is said about any large portions having come first to Rameses, and then having to travel back over the same ground; and to allege that they did so, is a mere excuse for dragging in a little more of the Bishop's misemployed arithmetic, in proving that the marching host would present a column of twenty-two miles long.

ELEVENTH OBJECTION.

THE SHEEP AND CATTLE OF THE ISRAELITES IN THE DESERT.

(*Pentateuch Examined*, chap. xii. p. 65.)

On this objection the Bishop lays out his strength. His longest chapter is devoted to its consideration. He opens it thus,—

" The people, we are told, were supplied with manna. But there was no miraculous provision of food for the herds and flocks. They were left to gather sustenance as they could, in that inhospitable wilderness. We will now go on to consider the possibility of such a multitude of cattle finding any means of support, for forty years, under these circumstances."

And he does go on. Holding fast by his assumed number of two millions of sheep and oxen, he collects every testimony he can find, from the Pentateuch, from the prophets, from modern travel, in favour of his view, that the desert was a vast outspread of " bare and barren plains of sands," " destitute of anything that can perhaps be called soil," with great scarcity of water,—" in short, a waste howling wilderness." Some of his modern testimonies he finds very intractable for the purposes of his hypothesis, as exhibiting proof in the multitudinous wadys they speak of, that the country in former times must have been much more favourable to vegetation than it is now. But no wadys can provide for his formidable, but nowhere asserted, two millions; and so all modern testimonies, and ancient too, are thus complacently disposed of:—

" Bearing in mind that two millions of sheep and oxen, allowing a space of three feet by two feet as standing ground for each, would require, when packed together as closely as in a pen in a cattle-market, nearly 300 acres of land, it seems idle to expend more time in discussing the question, whether they could have been supported in the wilderness by the help of such insignificant wadies as these, which a drove of a hundred oxen would have trampled down into mud in an hour."

Let us proceed to consider what there is to justify this tone of contemptuous confidence.

i. In the first place, not one of the modern travellers, even of those from whom our objector quotes, when speaking of the look of wild desolation and sterility which now characterizes the desert, ever supposes his language would be applied to the whole 18,000 square miles constituting the Israelitish desert, and least of all to that portion in which the people passed thirty-eight out of their forty years. The Sinaitic peninsula, where the Israelites were for a year, is indeed allowed to present features of peculiar desolateness; but even Ewald admits that it must have been very different, in Mosaic times, from what it is now. Canon Stanley's account also, from which the Bishop so largely quotes, will be acknowledged, by every unprejudiced reader, to contain proofs in abundance, that both water and vegetation existed, to an extent quite adequate to the support of large populations, together with their cattle. His reference to the remaining vegetation of the innumerable wadys,— to the trunks of palm-trees, washed up on the shore of the Dead Sea; to the reckless waste of the Bedouin tribes, carrying on a traffic in charcoal derived from the acacia-trees; and to the fact, that places are pointed out, which, though now absolutely bare, have within historic periods been green and fertile,— are all strongly negative of the position, confidently taken up by our objector, that " the country through which the Israelites passed, has not undergone any material change from that time to this."

Moreover, even in its present state, we have proof from modern travellers, that there are portions, and extensive portions too, of this very Sinaitic peninsula, where there is excellent pasturage. Burckhardt, speaking of a ridge of mountains, says, " These chains form the northern boundaries of the Sinai mountains, and are the pasturing places of the Sinai Bedouins." In another place near to this, he says, "We entered the Wady Genne, a fine valley several miles in breadth, and covered with pasturage." Whilst Miss Martineau, speaking of this most barren part of the desert, says, " Here I came upon a clump of palms . . . in the midst of this clump was a well ; and along the deep water-course, for a considerable distance, tamarisks, acacias, and palms were scattered and clumped . . . . Soon after remounting we came upon a string of muddy pools, where our camels drank. Everywhere in the desert we were surprised by the number of water-courses, and the traces of torrents."[1]

ii. So much for modern testimony, in disproof of the Bishop's notion, that the desert was an unrelieved expanse of barrenness. Can he make out his case by anything found in the Bible itself ? He quotes two texts in support of his view. First, Deut. viii. 15, "Who led thee through that great and terrible wilderness, wherein were fiery serpents, and scorpions, and drought, where there was no water; who brought thee forth water out of the rock of flint." And next, Jer. ii. 6, " Neither said they, Where is the Lord that brought us up out of the land of Egypt, that led us through the wilderness ; through a land of

[1] See Bishop Colenso's *Examination Examined.* G. S. Drew.

deserts, and of pits; through a land of drought, and of the shadow of death; through a land that no man passed through, and where no man dwelt?"

Now these passages are proof that *portions* of the country through which the Israelites passed, were of this desolate character, but by no means prove that it was *all* so. So far, otherwise, both passages furnish evidence of their having only a limited application. For " the great and terrible wilderness " is expressly described as the portion lying between Horeb and Kadeshbarnea,—a district of about 100 miles, barren, waterless, infested with reptiles,—and, in passing through which, the Israelites no doubt endured great privations. The allusion is made to it here, therefore, by Moses, to remind the people of the Providence which had preserved them in that most terrible part of their journey.

So also with regard to the passage in Jeremiah. Whether, as Dr. Benisch, from one particular word introduced, supposes, the reference be to a portion of the desert extending from the Dead Sea to the Gulf of Akaba, or to the same region of which Moses spoke, certain it is that the allusion cannot be to the *whole desert*, because the words are expressly introduced, " a land that no man passeth through, and where no man dwelt,"—language, which, it is manifest, the prophet would not use in speaking of the whole desert through which Israel passed.

But, besides this, there are proofs in abundance on the face of the Mosaic narrative itself, that the desert, as a whole, was no desert in Bishop Colenso's sense of the term. The very etymology of the Hebrew word (Midbar) is " pasture-ground," suggesting to a Jewish mind " uncultivatedness," no doubt, but certainly not " barrenness." And it could not have been barren. It was the permanent residence of whole populations; some settled, and some migratory, but, whether one or the other, incapable of living in such a region as our objector takes the desert to have been. From Shur, the first station from the Red Sea towards Sinai, to Kadesh, the last station in their journey towards Canaan, the territory was in the hands of the Philistines,—probably a branch of the Phœnicians,— but certainly a people who had a king, an army, and all the other accessories of a settled community. And Amraphel, king of Shinar, finds nations settled to the south of the Dead Sea, and extends his conquests to places known as stations of the Israelites in the desert.

So also with regard to the existence of water,—a want, which if supplied, the Bishop admits would overcome the difficulty about vegetation,—proofs occur, that, though not abundant, and in some places not to be found at all, yet water there undoubtedly was. How else could the Israelites have been commanded to "wash their clothes" before the solemn meeting before the Lord on Sinai?" How came it that Moses was enabled to draw water for the flocks of Zipporah? Nay, how plainly does it appear that Mount Sinai itself had a *brook*, since in Deut. ix. 21, we read, " And I took your sin, the calf which ye had made, and burnt it with fire, and stamped it, and ground it very small, even until it was as small as dust : and I cast the dust thereof into the brook that descended out of the mount."

Indeed, it is abundantly evident that this writer has entirely failed to enter into *the nature of Israelitish life in the desert*,—failed even to obtain such a view of that life as might have been gathered from a careful perusal of the history itself. Intimations will be found in the books, constantly, shewing that the Israelites had friendly intercourse with the neighbouring populations; transactions of barter for water, food, spices, or whatever else they might require. Some instances of this kind are specified distinctly. Thus Moses, asking for permission to march through the country of Sihon, king of Heshbon, says, "Thou shalt sell me meat for money, that I may eat; and give me water for money, that I may drink: as the children of Esau who abide in Seir, and the Moabites who abide in Ar, did unto me" (Deut. ii. 28, 29); whilst in chap. xxiii. 3, 4, we have the sentence of Divine exclusion pronounced against the Ammonites and Moabites, "because they met you not with bread and with water, in the way when ye came forth out of Egypt,"—a passage, from which the only inference to be drawn is, that other nations had been accustomed to supply them with these necessaries, and that the case of the Moabites and Ammonites was a very *exceptional instance of inhospitality*. In like manner, the allusions to spices, certainly not the production of Egypt or the desert; to cinnamon, which must have been imported from India; to the clear olive oil, required for the service of the tabernacle,—all suppose forms of intercourse, either with the caravan traders, or some of the border-populations of the district. References to intimacies with some of these peoples,—those of Moab and Midian, for instance,—are given because of the painful consequences which followed; but, as a Jewish writer well asks, "If the Israelites had intercourse with two nations, why not with some more, not especially mentioned, because it was not marked by any particular feature that might have called for a special record?"[1]

We have dwelt the longer upon this objection, because the Bishop evidently regards this difficulty of providing

[1] Dr. Benisch, p. 48.

for the flocks in the desert, as his most demonstrative case. We believe it to be demonstrative of nothing but of the fulfilment of a divine purpose, first, in relation to the Jews, "to humble them, and to prove them, and to know what was in their heart;" and then in relation to others, that these wilderness wanderings, with all their trials, and difficulties, and deliverances, might be a type of the journey of life, for all time.

TWELFTH OBJECTION.

The Number of the Israelites, and the Extent of Canaan.

(Pentateuch Examined, chap. xiii. p. 32.)

This objection is of the following form. In Exod. xxiii. 27–30, God had declared that He would not drive out the ancient inhabitants of Canaan in one year, "lest the land become desolate, and the beasts of the field multiply against thee." Upon which the Bishop proceeds to shew that the land of Canaan, as divided in the time of Joshua, was about 11,000 square miles, and was occupied by more than two millions of people. He next takes three English counties,—Norfolk, Suffolk, and Essex,—as representing half the Palestine area, and having about half its population, and then proposes the question, "Are these counties (with some twenty large towns, which he enumerates) in any danger of lying desolate, with the beasts of the field multiplying against the human inhabitants?"

The points of failure, in the parallel here sought to be established, would be patent to a child. But take only the one which arises from the comparison being made between an *island* and a *continent*. In an island, after you have once exterminated the wild beasts, you are in no danger of their infesting the land again. In a continent, and that surrounded, as Canaan was, by extensive tracts of uninhabited country, you never know when you may be free from their irruptions. Especially would this liability increase if the population were sparse, and the original human inhabitants suddenly exterminated, which is the very case contemplated here. " But we are able to keep the wild beasts down in Natal ;" it is answered. Yes, but how much of the power to do this do you owe to the modern invention of fire-arms ?

But we cannot think it will be desired of us to bestow on this objection any further notice. The abounding of wild beasts, for a long time after the settlement in Canaan, is a plain Scripture fact. The imagery of the Psalms, Proverbs, and prophecies, is taken from them constantly. And the histories show how natural such images would seem. Think of David encountering a lion and a bear at once, as well as of the two she-bears devouring forty-two of the mocking children in the time of Elisha. Are we to reject a plain account of what actually *was*, for an unsupported hypothesis, taken from our modern experience, of what was likely to be ?

THIRTEENTH OBJECTION.

THE NUMBER OF THE FIRST-BORN AND ADULTS.

(*Pentateuch Examined*, chap. xiv. p. 84.)

Quoting from Num. iii. 43, where we find the number of first-born males to be stated at 22,273, the Bishop proceeds to divide the gross adult male population, estimated at 900,000, by this number, and, from the result, arrives at this conclusion; " so that, according to the story in the Pentateuch, every mother of Israel must have had on the average forty-two sons."

The fact does appear incredible: and if no other solutions were obtainable, we should, in this case, be obliged to take refuge in that liability to errors of transcription, to which the system of Hebrew notation laid the copies peculiarly open; in other words, we should admit that, in this instance, there must be some arithmetical mistake. But there are considerations which shew that the numbers may not be so very far wrong after all.

i. In the first place, the term first-born, in relation to the particular purpose for which this census was made, would be restricted, it is alleged, to the *first-born son of father and mother too*. Jacob had four families; David had six; Gideon had many. Yet each of these would have but *one first-born*, for the purposes of this particular numbering. Both polygamy and concubinage prevailed to a great extent, and must have reduced the disproportion complained of immensely.

ii. Other causes would bring up the divisor, in the present sum, to something far beyond these 22,273. For example, allowance must be made (1) for those who perished by order of Pharaoh; (2) for those who might have died from natural causes, between the Exodus and the time this census was taken; (3) for those whom the Levitical law declared disqualified for the tabernacle service—the cripple, the idiot, the blind.[1] We are wholly

---

[1] Mr. Pritchard makes a large deduction for the posterity of the retainers, who, as all being incorporated among the families of the Levites, would not be numbered among the first-born. Engrafting this upon some other close calculations, he comes to this conclusion, " I have estimated the entire population of pure descent at 638,976,

without data for saying, to what extent all these causes would throw the mere man of statistics out of his reckoning. Grant him his dividend of 900,000, how is he to arrive at his second term? He cannot arrive at it. His divisor is a conjecture, and therefore his quotient of forty-two sons to each mother of Israel, an absurdity, or a myth.

FOURTEENTH OBJECTION.

THE SOJOURNING OF THE ISRAELITES IN EGYPT.

(*Pentateuch Examined*, chap. xv. p. 91.)

The objection contained in this chapter, is raised, not for itself, so much as to prepare the way for something more formidable that is to follow. Quoting the words, therefore, " Now, the sojourning of the children of Israel, who dwelt in Egypt, was four hundred and thirty years," the Bishop proceeds to deduce, both from passages in the New Testament, and from interlineated clauses found in the Vulgate and other ancient versions, that the four hundred and thirty years must be reckoned from the call of Abraham, the whole period being bisected into two equal portions,—namely, two hundred and fifteen years,—from Abraham's call to the descent of Jacob into Egypt, and a like period from that descent to the Exodus. The interpretation has met with very general acceptance among commentators for a long time; and, therefore, regardless of any strength it may give to the Bishop's succeeding objections, the point is to be ceded, that the actual duration of the sojourning in Egypt did not exceed 215 years.

and this, divided by twenty-four, gives us about 26,000 as the equivalent number of first-born males,—a number not very discordant from that mentioned in the sacred record."

FIFTEENTH OBJECTION.

THE EXODUS IN THE FOURTH GENERATION.

(*Pentateuch Examined*, chap. xvi. p. 96.)

This objection, also, is designed to be subservient to the aggravation of the great difficulty of the seventeenth chapter, arising out of the number of the Israelites at the time of the Exodus; and the point of the objection is, that, whereas it is said in Gen. xv. 16, speaking of the seed of Abraham being strangers in a land which is not theirs, " in the fourth generation they shall come hither again," this fourth generation must be reckoned from the time of their leaving Canaan to go down into Egypt; and, consequently, we are presented with the astounding fact, that "in four generations seventy souls grew into two millions."

i. To this, it is replied, first, that the Hebrew word here used for " generation," sometimes stands for *seculum*, or one hundred years; and that the expression may not unreasonably be referred to the *fourth century* of those very four hundred years spoken of three verses before.

ii. But further, it is objected, that the attempt of the Bishop to prove that there were only four generations in the whole period of 215 years signally fails. There were five generations from Jacob to Moses and Aaron alone, the latter being then above eighty years of age; and, as the Orientals marry very young, it is probable that among the children, who went up at the Exodus, would be many of the *sixth*, or *seventh*, or even of the *ninth* generation. Some can be proved to be so. Bezaleel is shown, by his pedigree, to be of the *seventh*; the daughters of Zelophehad were of the *seventh*; whilst Joshua was certainly of the *ninth*, if not of the *eleventh*. So much for the astounding assertion of the Bishop, that the enormous increase in the population of the Israelites was accomplished " in four generations."

SIXTEENTH OBJECTION.

THE NUMBER OF THE ISRAELITES AT THE EXODUS.

(*Pentateuch Examined*, chap. xvii. p. 102.)

The reckless assertion, put forth in the last objection, as to four generations, bridging over the entire space of 215 years, was emphatically insisted upon by the Bishop, because it was a weapon, which, he thought, might do for him good yeoman's service. For, having made certain assumptions, as to the average number of sons, likely to be born to Kohath, as head of the first generation, then to Amram, and Aaron, and Eleazar, as heads successively of the second, third, and fourth, he is brought to the arithmetical conclusion, that, in order to the truth of Joshua's 600,000 fighting men, " we must suppose that each man had forty-six children (twenty-three of each sex), and each of these twenty-three sons had forty-six children, and so on."

Let us look at some of the assumptions here made,— assumptions which are not only not warranted, but are, in some particulars, positively and demonstrably false.

First, there is that which we may call the *basis-fiction* of the whole calculation—the *four* generations, instead of *seven* or *nine*. At each generation the Bishop calculates the population becomes trebled. By working out his own figures for five generations later, we get more than half the number of adult males required.

But this is on the further assumption of our objector,

that the males of the first generation were only fifty-one, because, reckoning from the number of children, born to the sons of Jacob, *at the time of their going down into Egypt*, he says we get an average of four-and-a-half sons to each. But what about the sons born to them after they went down into Egypt? The oldest of the sons of Jacob was, on his own showing, only about forty-six years old, and that none of them should add to their families, after their settlement in Egypt, is very improbable. Then no room is left for the children of Dinah or Sirah, in this calculation, who clearly have as much right to be included as any of the rest. Thus no rational difficulty stands in the way of the fifty-one males, which is taken as the starting-point of the calculation, being quite *double the number*, and thus yielding a result, in the ninth generation, quite equal to all that the Pentateuchal history requires.

Still, the increase in the population of the Israelites during their sojourning in Egypt, was, beyond all question, exceedingly great. But are there not adequate causes to account for it?

i. First, there was the *Divine promise* that it should be so. Surely no common rate of increase, among the posterity of Abraham, would satisfy such words as, " In blessing I will bless thee, and in multiplying I will multiply thy seed as the stars of the heaven, and as the sand which is upon the sea-shore." And no common rate of increase is implied in the words which describe their multiplication. Bishop Colenso begins this chapter by observing, " We nowhere read of any very large families among the children of Jacob, or their descendants, to the time of the Exodus." What, we ask, does he make of such a passage as this, " And the children of Israel were fruitful, and increased abundantly, and multiplied, and waxed exceeding mighty; and the land was filled with them?" the word for "increased abundantly" being strictly, "swarmed like fish."

ii. Then again, some of this large increase must be supposed to be *due to polygamy*. Its existence cannot be denied. And that which had been practised by Abraham and Jacob, we can hardly suppose, would be wholly abstained from by their descendants.

iii. But the consideration which most satisfactorily disposes of all objections against this increase in the number of the Israelites,—at least, so far as to make such increase compatible with historic probability,—is that the seventy souls from which the population at the Exodus is said to have sprung, includes only those from the loins of Jacob, taking no note of the *large retinue of servants*, which Jacob and his sons would carry with them into Egypt. Abraham, we are told, had more than 300 servants, born in his house and trained for war. Would Jacob and his grown-up sons be without such appendages? or would they, the great sheikhs of their time, think of settling down in a new country, with the purpose of doing all the menial work themselves? Now, these servants, being circumcised, would become incorporated with the families of their masters; would contract marriages with the Egyptians; and these circumstances, together with polygamy and other irregularities, would account for that "mixed multitude" which accompanied the Israelites at the Exodus; whilst the effect upon the aggregate of the population, would be such as to defy all our statistical reckonings to compute.

Nay, we may even do without these servants, and supposing the Israelitish mothers not to have been more prolific than Malthus has shown to be the case in some parts of Scotland,—where an average of six children to a marriage is not uncommon,—we should have in the *seventh* generation, as coming from Bishop Colenso's number of fifty-one males in the *first*, a population of upwards of two millions,—the number so demonstratively convincing that the Pentateuch is unhistoric.[1]

SEVENTEENTH OBJECTION.

THE DANITES AND LEVITES AT THE TIME OF THE EXODUS.

(*The Pentateuch Examined*, chap. xviii. p. 110.)

In this chapter, we have two forms of objection, both supposed to be freighted with demonstrable impossibilities. And so they are, if the Bishop's premises are granted unexamined, but not otherwise.

The first exception is to the number of the Danites, estimated in the narrative at 627,000. Now Dan had but one son in the first generation; and therefore, in order to his having this number in the fourth, " we must suppose that Dan's one son, and each of *his* sons and grandsons, must have had about eighty children of both sexes."

" In the fourth generation again :"— the same *proto-*

[1] Dr. M'Caul's *Examination*, p. 112. Mr. Pritchard, whose chapter on this subject is marked by singular acuteness, has well turned the tables on Bishop Colenso, by pointing out the absurdities which would follow on his own supposition. For instance. The Bishop says, that contemporary with the generation of Moses and Aaron there would be 1094 males. But whatever the number, the record states that the land was filled with them, a century before the Exodus; and even at the beginning of the Egyptian jealousies Pharaoh complained, " Behold, the children of Israel are more and mightier than we." Was the land filled with 1094 males ? or would such a number be a terror to the mighty hosts of Egypt?" (See Pritchard, chap. iii.)

pseudos, haunting our objector through several chapters. Suppose Dan's one son Hushim to have had a large, or even moderate family; and carry on the rate of increase to the *ninth* generation, how far short of the Pentateuch's sixty thousand will the result come then?

The objection with regard to Levi has respect chiefly to the relative fewness of his descendants.

"The two sons of Amram increased in the *fourth* (Eleazar's) generation to six, viz. the sons of Aaron four (of whom, however, two died, Num. iii. 2, 4), and of Moses two. Assuming that all the sixteen of the third generation increased in the same proportion, then all the male Levites of the generation of Eleazar, would have been forty-eight, or rather forty-four, if we omit the four sons of Aaron, who were reckoned as priests." (*Pentateuch Examined*, p. 108.)

But here assumptions are made, quite without warrant. First, the increase in the third generation may have been much greater than it was in the first and second, both of which, according to the numbers mentioned, were, as we see, much below the average. Secondly, the sons mentioned as having been born to Gershon, Kohath, and Merari, respectively, may not include the whole number. The names of the Levites are not always given, even in these early generations. Gershon is said to have sons; but, in the usual place, nothing is said of his having grandsons. But when we come to Num. iii. we find that he had them, and that they were heads of families. The assertion, therefore, that the number of Levites could not have exceeded forty-four altogether, is one absolutely devoid of Scripture foundation; even if, considering the duties to be performed by these officers, it were not one too palpably absurd for any forger to have put forth.

EIGHTEENTH OBJECTION.

THE NUMBER OF THE PRIESTS AND THEIR DUTIES.

(*The Pentateuch Examined*, chap. xx. p. 122.)

This chapter opens with a series of quotations from the book of Leviticus, setting forth the multifarious duties of the priests; in relation to burnt-offerings, meat-offerings, peace-offerings, sin-offerings; presiding over festivals, spreading over several days together; attending to lepers, and all matters of ceremonial pollutions; the whole being summed up with the mention of one class of duties alone—that of attending to the sacrifices of women after child-birth, which would have required, on the most moderate computation, fifty-two hours every day,—supposing the three priests, who, according to the objection could alone have taken part in such offices, to have been employed " from morning to night, without a moment's rest or intermission." On this ensues a recital of other difficulties, such as whence the requisite number of pigeons, could be obtained in such a place as the desert,— the chapter closing with some remarks, on the absurdity of the supposition that, for the use of three priests with their families, there should be set apart no less than thirteen cities.

Let us see what can be urged in abatement of the apparent inconsistency of these representations.

i. In the first place, no inconsiderable part of this elaborate ritual recited by the Bishop, belongs, not to the wilderness condition of the Israelites at all, but had a *prospective reference* to the time of their settlement in Canaan. With the exception of the Passover, we have no proof that any of the Jewish festivals were kept in the

R

desert at all: whilst the feast of ingathering, and that of the seventh month, quoted by this writer, as extending over seven days, imply, by their very name and purpose, that they had not yet come into operation.

ii. In the next place, it is not true that all this work devolved upon *three priests only*, namely, Aaron and Eleazar, and Ithamar. Eleazar had a son, we know, Phinehas; and, as mention is made of the posterity of Ithamar, in connection with the priesthood, he must have had sons too,—and sons too, from the advanced age of Aaron at this time, likely to be quite qualified for the duties of the priesthood. Priests also are spoken of before the consecration of Aaron (Exod. xix. 22), who, though probably not of the same priestly rank with him, may well be supposed to have been admitted to the subordinate ecclesiastical offices.

iii. Thirdly, on which the Bishop insists, the penalties against usurpation of the priestly function were never meant to extend to such subsidiary aids, as the priest, at his discretion, might think fit to obtain *from the Levites*. This is plain from such passages as that in Num. viii. 19: "I have given the Levites as a gift to Aaron and his sons, to do the service of the children of Israel in the tabernacle of the congregation, and to make an atonement for the children of Israel." Or that in 2 Chron. xxix. 34, where we read, "But the priests were too few, so that they could not flay all the burnt-offerings: wherefore their brethren the Levites did help them, till the work was ended, and until the other priests had sanctified themselves." Why, with such a body at their disposal, is the absurd fiction to be imagined of "three men working incessantly from morning to night?"

iv. The difficulty about *the pigeons* is one magnified,

if not created, by this objector's already-exposed ignorance of the physical geography of the desert. This desert, we have seen, was a place of human habitations, and thither birds of this description gather. Moreover, a modern traveller, already quoted—Miss Martineau—little thinking of the use which would be made of her authority, specially mentions the fact, in regard to the Sinaitic peninsula, " We saw a good many pigeons." But suppose the case that pigeons, in sufficient quantity for the Mosaic requirements, could not be obtained. What then? Why, as in the case of a man unable to present a pair of turtle-doves, something that he could obtain would be accepted instead. But in truth there can be no reason why this should not be included among enactments which, as we have said, had respect, not to the nomadic life of the desert, but to the settled condition of the Israelites in Palestine.

v. To the objection about the disproportion of the number of cities set apart for the priests, to the number officiating, it is to be observed (1), that these cities were a provision for a more established condition of the hierarchy; (2), that others, besides priests, lived in them; (3), that the residences, being a part of the sacerdotal remuneration, the priests were permitted to derive revenue from letting out to others any portions not required for themselves.

NINETEENTH OBJECTION.

THE PRIESTS AND THE CELEBRATION OF THE PASSOVER.

(*The Pentateuch Examined*, chap. xxi. p. 131).

This objection begins,—

Again, how did these three priests manage at the celebration of the Passover? We are told (2 Chron.

xxx. 16; xxxv. 11) that the people killed the Passover, but *the priests sprinkled the blood from their hands*, and the Levites flayed them. " Hence, when they kept the second Passover under Sinai (Num. ix. 5), when we must suppose that 150,000 lambs (70) were killed at one time, between the two evenings (Exod. xii. 6), for the two millions of people, each priest must have had to sprinkle the blood of fifty thousand lambs in about two hours, that is, at the rate of about 400 lambs every minute for two hours together."—*Pentateuch Examined*, p. 131.

Let us take, one by one, the several parts of this statement.

i. First, we have the assumption that *three* was the maximum number of priests, shewn to be without foundation before.

ii. Secondly, that there were 150,000 lambs killed. This number, it has been already intimated, may be divided by ten, no limit being fixed, by the Law, as to the number of persons who might partake of each lamb.

iii. Thirdly, it is alleged that the lambs were manifestly killed in the court of the Temple. Answer: Not necessarily, if the court would not contain them. A discretion was left in such cases to take in adjacent portions of ground. The case actually occurred at the consecration of the Temple of Solomon. An unusual number of sacrifices were brought, and we read, " The same day did the king hallow the middle of the court that was before the house of the Lord: for there he offered burnt-offerings and meat-offerings, and the fat of the peace-offerings: because the brazen altar that was before the Lord was too little to receive the burnt-offerings, and meat-offerings, and the fat of the peace-offerings."[1]

[1] 1 Kings, viii. 64.

Lastly, it is declared that the killing and sprinkling by the priests had all to be "done within two hours." To this, it is to be replied that the precise measure of time intended by the expression "at even," or "between the two evenings," is one of the most vexed questions of Jewish interpretation,—the several measures varying from one hour and a half, to five hours and a half, according to the period of the day when it is supposed to begin. Let one of the longer periods be taken, and, with such help as the Levites would give, and on the supposition of a reduction in the number of the lambs offered, there is no such very palpable evidence that the thing was impossible to be done.

TWENTIETH OBJECTION.

THE WAR ON MIDIAN.

(*The Pentateuch Examined*, chap. xxii. p. 139.)

The last objection in the Bishop's book, consists of a revival of the stale charge, brought against the Mosaic narrative in regard to the Midianitish destruction, in Paine's *Age of Reason*,—only supplemented by a little arithmetic.

I. The arithmetical objection is twofold. (1.) That a force of 12,000 Israelites should have slain all the males of the Midianites, taken captive all the females and children, seized all their cattle and flocks, burnt all their cities and castles, without the loss of a single man. (2.) That a succession of military marches, conquests, and other important events, is related as having taken place between the death of Aaron, and the day on which Moses addressed the people on the plains of Moab,—a period of six months only,—which it is utterly incredible could have been accomplished in so short a time.

(1.) To the first part of this objection, it is to be answered, that, while it is not a thing unknown, even to modern warfare, for great military successes to be achieved, without the loss of a single man (witness the case of Fort Sumter, two years ago, surrendering after almost a whole day's bombardment without the sacrifice of a life on either side), the whole affair of the Midianites was of Divine ordering; the design being not only to shew how the Lord fought for Israel, but also to make a judicial example of a people, who had become the pests of the human race. Is it wonderful, under such circumstances, that the enemy should be smitten with an overpowering terror and amazement, or that the Israelites, strong in the consciousness that they were only the divine executioners against Midian, should be able to pursue their advantage with such resistless force, that not one of their hosts should fall?

(2.) The second form of arithmetical objection exceeds, in the gratuitousness of its assumptions, anything to be found in the whole book. Thirteen events are selected from the history as having occurred between the death of Aaron and the address of Moses on the plains of Moab, a period of exactly six months. With the exception of the mourning for the death of Aaron, not one word occurs in the history of the time taken up by these several incidents, neither, is it said, whether in some instances the events might not overlap, and be simultaneous; and yet, in the very wantonness of bold and unauthorized conjecture, the Bishop supplies a time for every one of them. As thus; (i.) the mourning for Aaron,—"a month," which is granted. (ii.) The attack of King Arad, and the reprisal of the Israelites, "for which two transactions we may allow another month." (iii.) The journey from Mount Hor to the time of the plague of the fiery serpents, "for all which we must allow, at least, a fortnight." (iv.) The succeeding march with nine encampments, "for which we cannot well allow less than a month." (v.) The sending messengers to Sihon, and the taking of his cities, "for which we may allow another month." (vi.) The sending of spies to Jaazer, and taking its villages, "say in another fortnight." (vii.) The completion of the conquest of Og, king of Bashan, including the capture of all its cities and unwalled towns, "we must allow at the very least a month."

At this stage the Bishop halts, and calls out "time." Five whole "months" and "two fortnights" have had full work provided for them, and yet we have to bring within this same limit of six months six events more.. Of these, the war upon Midian is one which "surely must have required a month or six weeks."

"*Cadit quæstio;*" without information from the Bible, or from any source, we, the Bishop of Natal, can tell to a day how long it took, 3000 years ago, to send messengers, to employ spies, to chase an army from the field, to burn up cities, and to knock down walls, and we pronounce authoritatively that six months is too short a time for the work. *Therefore*, some of the events did not take place. *Therefore* the narrative is not historic. *Therefore* the Pentateuch is unworthy of all rational belief. Q. E. D.

II. The moral objection of the Bishop in this chapter, as already intimated, is simply a form of *Paine redivivus*, slightly modified, perhaps, in coarseness of expression, but hardly exceeded by the work of this arch-infidel himself in the utter revoltingness of its blasphemy. First, we say it is very difficult to acquit the Bishop of not intending to endorse that dreadful lie of Paine's, in regard to the younger Midianitish women "being consigned to debauchery by order of Moses." For why else, after quoting the expression "keep for themselves," does he speak of the age of these "women-children" as being "mostly, we must suppose, under the age of sixteeen or eighteen?" Why was he not content to abide by the generally accepted interpretation, that by "women-children" was meant *children* in the literal sense,—*infants*, incapacitated by age from all participation in the universal contamination, and for the same reason incapable of contaminating others? We shudder to interpret, in words, the meaning which the Bishop's allusion seems to point to, but, as far as we can understand his language, other meaning there is none.

"Methinks my Lord should be religious,
And know the office that belongs to such."[1]

Nor less offensive to all reverence and right feeling is the next sentence of the paragraph, in which Moses is compared to Nana Sahib, and the tragedy of Cawnpore is declared to sink into nothing by the side of that command of Moses, which ordered all the women and children to be "butchered in cold blood." On these words, by a Christian Bishop, we refrain from all comment. He could not have been ignorant of the circumstances under which the war with the Midianites was undertaken, or of the fact that moral ends were in the Divine contemplation, when ordering the destruction of all the adults among them, which nothing short of their destruction could possibly secure. The whole nation was wallowing in the very filth of sensuality and sin. Their women, especially, had been set on to employ all

[1] K. Hen. VI. part iii.

the arts of harlotry to draw the Israelites into sin,—not even into the sin of profligacy only, but into that, as part of a dark plot for inveigling them into systematic idolatry. Looking at the war-usages of the times, is the Bishop prepared with an expedient, short of extermination, by which the Divine hatred of sin could be vindicated, or Israel be delivered from a recurrence of the plague ? At all events, it is enough to vindicate the narrative from all such profane impertinences, as that exhibited in the comparison between Moses and the butcher of Cawnpore, to say that, for the supposition of personal revenge or brutality on the part of the Israelites, there is not the slightest foundation. They were but a sword in the Lord's hand. A judgment was to be visited on the enemies of God, and to Him must it be left to choose the most fitting instrument. It might be the sword, it might be the pestilence, it might be the earthquake. Enough that it would be seen and felt to be the Lord's doing, whether a military slaughter were ordered to be visited on the accursed pollutions of Midian, or the earth opened her mouth to avenge the gainsaying of Core. "So that a man shall say, Verily there is a reward for the righteous : verily he is a God that judgeth in the earth."

Rapidly and cursorily, have we gone through these twenty objections. Let us sum the worth of the series, and give the arithmetical result.

First, from these twenty objections we have to deduct all those which are due to the author's critical incompetency,— the force of the original Hebrew, as Jewish and Christian scholars alike testify, being entirely misunderstood. Secondly, we are to cast out those which rest on assumptions, for which there is no Scriptural warrant, but in so many instances the very reverse. Thirdly, we may well remove those objections, which a better acquaintance with the physical, or local, or moral circumstances of the history would have caused the Bishop never to have made. And lastly, we are entitled to eliminate those for which adequate explanations,—explanations uncontradicted by Scripture, by reason, or by common sense,—have been found already. When, from the gross sum, these deductions have been fairly made, we challenge our episcopal mathematician to disprove the correctness of the equation,

$20 -$ the number of vanished objections $= 0$.

But we may not speak more in this strain. Arrived at the last page of our book, we are constrained to give utterance to thoughts of a more tender and solemn character. The Colenso of the past is before our minds—the Colenso of our college days;—flushed with honours, intent on plans for good, loving the truth as it is in Jesus, and walking in the truth he loved. Not *then* had the presumptuous purpose been formed of dragging the revelations of the Most High to appear at the bar of human criticism; not *then* had the treasonable thought found place in his heart that the language of ignorance, or mistake, or accommodating falsehood, might fall from the lips of the Holy One of God; not *then* had come over his mind the shadows of that dark and disastrous Pyrrhonism, which would engulf, in its depths, the whole objective element of Christianity,—testimony, experience, moral evidence,— the historical, the inspired, the miraculous,—leaving us nothing in their stead, but the unauthorized speculations of the human intelligence,—it may be those of Moses, it may be those of the Sikh Gooroos. But will the Bishop forgive us for asking, Is he as happy *now*, as he was *then?* Is the mind haunted by no sense of privation, now that all which once ministered so abundantly to all the cravings of his religious nature is gone? Is the desolation he has created around him a victory? Is the reaction which has followed on his fancied success, rest?

Nor is this all. There is another solemn thought which oppresses us, and which will one day oppress Dr. Colenso too. We allude to the absolute irrevocableness of the mischief he has done. The annals of literature record nothing more painful than the efforts of repentant authors to recall a pernicious book, or counteract the evil it has wrought. They can do neither. The book will live in spite of them,—live the longer, the more it is known that the author wishes it had never been born. In this way all printed and published infidelity becomes immortal. The exposed sophistry and answered objection will be propagated from mouth to mouth, and from book to book to the end of time. From the youthful pretender to an intellectual scepticism are still heard the covert sarcasms of Gibbon : and the productions of Voltaire and Paine are as destructive now, as they were in the day when the first brood came forth of their empoisoned brain. Oh! would that the infidel could carry his work away with him, when he goes hence. But he cannot;

> " Sinking in the quicksands he defends,
> He dies disputing, and the contest ends—
> But not the mischiefs; they, still left behind,
> Like thistle-seeds, are sown by every wind."[1]

Has the Bishop of Natal realized this tremendous responsibility? or have his friends realized it for him? If they have, may we urge upon them the thought, that impossible as it may be, by anything they can do, to spare the Bishop his cup of bitter anguish,—impossible as it

[1] Cowper, *Progress of Error*.

must be altogether to arrest the spreading contamination of his book,—yet none can say what manifestations of an interposing Arm we may be permitted to see, if, with one heart and one mind, that prayer of the faithful go up daily before the throne,—" THAT IT MAY PLEASE THEE TO BRING INTO THE WAY OF TRUTH ALL SUCH AS HAVE ERRED AND ARE DECEIVED."

INDEX.

Adaptation of the Levitical and Christian dispensations, 156
Amber Witch, The, 163
Antiochus Epiphanes, destruction of sacred writings by, 68
Archaisms in the Pentateuch, 39
Archæological discoveries, corroborations obtained from, 173
,, ,, objections based on, 171
Ark, books laid up in the, 66

Benisch, Dr., referred to, 195
Berosus, testimony of, 20
Blunt, Professor, referred to, 54
Bolingbroke, Pope's account of, 194
Buckle, referred to, 5
Bunsen, Chevalier, referred to, 5
Butler, Bishop, on considering Revelation as a whole, 14
,, ,, Scripture difficulties, 174
,, ,, the mistakes of transcribers, 104

Camp, the, and the priests' duties, 211
Canaan, extent of, 231
Canaanitish races, extinct, referred to, 43
Chaldean mythology, referred to, 25
Chaldee character, the change of Hebrew into, 121
Chinese mythology, referred to, 25
Church, the, wounded by her friends, 2
Coincidences, undesigned, 54

Colenso, Bishop, earnest appeal to, 250
,,   ,,   his assumption in regard to our Lord's possession of limited knowledge, 99
,,   ,,   comparison of Moses to Nana Sahib, 249
,,   ,,   misconceptions about the Physical Geography of the Desert, 180
,,   ,,   want of acquaintance with Oriental life, x
,,   ,,   summary of his objections, 250
Commemorations, outward and visible, of leading events, 28
Continental criticism, tone of, 9
Criticism, historic, science of, 11

Darwin, referred to, 5
Deism of the 17th century, 8
Delitzch, referred to, xii
Deluge, universal traditions of, 26
Desert, Israelites dwelling in the, 229
Difficulties in Scripture, force of the argument from, 174
,,   ,,   shewn to arise from brevity of the narrative, 175
,,   ,,   ,,   ,,   our limited or inadequate information, 180
,,   ,,   ,,   ,,   the antiquity of the record, 177
,,   ,,   subservient to the interests of Revelation, 183
Dispensations, connection of, 154

Egypt, local peculiarities of, described, 41
Elohistic and Jehovistic titles, 123
Essays and Reviews, 3
Exodus, on the, 235
,,   success of the enterprise, 58
Ezra, his additions made under Divine authority, 121
,,   sacred writings collected and collated by, 67

Genealogies, the faithful keeping of, 45
Genesis, book of, foundation of the rest, 164
,,   ,,   sceptical objections against, 161
Geological objections, 167
Geology and Scripture, forced agreement between, 170
Gibbon, referred to, 145

Graves, Dean, referred to, 56
Grecian mythology, referred to, 25

Hebrew life, commonwealth, under an extraordinary providence, 61
,, ,, literal character, change in the, 67
,, ,, minute descriptions of, 51
,, style of the Pentateuch, 40
,, ,, ,, testimony of German rationalists concerning, 41
Hengstenberg, testimony of, 42
Houbigant, referred to, 115

Infidel publications, lasting mischief of, 251
Inspiration, claims to, not affected by errors of transcribers or translators, 112
,, danger of theorising upon, 107
,, definition of, 106
,, different kinds of, 108
,, needful for authenticating a revelation, 110
Institution of the Passover, 219
Intellectual activity of the age, 2
Interpolations, supposed, in the Pentateuch, 119
Israelites armed, 217
,, dwelling in tents, 215
,, sheep and cattle of, in the Desert, 225
,, sojourning of, in Egypt, 234

Jehovistic and Elohistic titles, 123
Jerusalem, supposed loss of Scriptures at the siege of, 69
JESUS CHRIST, His Divine testimony, how evaded, 99
Jews, prophecies relating to, 150
,, the present condition of, 153
,, their history a necessary part of the world's life, 190
,, veneration for the law, 81
Josephus, his books against Apion, 33
,, qualifications as a historian, 33
,, referred to, 32
Joshua, miracle of, considered, 136
Judah, family of, difficulty respecting, 202
Judas Maccabeus, his copy of the Scriptures, 69
Justin, testimony of, 23
Juvenal, testimony of, 23

Kennicott, Dr., referred to, 115
Kepler, referred to, 166

Leslie's four critical tests, 29
Levitical and Christian dispensations, their mutual adaptations, 156
Longinus quoted, 23

Manetho, testimony of, 20
March out of Egypt, the, 222
Masoretic text, settlement of, 71
McCaul, Dr., referred to, 195
Michaelis, referred to, 115
Midian, Paine and Colenso upon, 249
  ,,   the war on, 245
Miller, Hugh, referred to, 169
Minuteness of detail in the Pentateuch, 44
Miracle, appealed to by Christ himself, 131
  ,,   force of the argument from, 130
  ,,   special object of Infidel attack, 132
  ,,   the argument for their impossibility considered, 133
Mosaic Institutes, peculiarity of, 62
  ,,   Record, external testimonies to, 14
  ,,   ,,   history of its transmission, 65
  ,,   ,,   literary characteristics of, 39
  ,,   ,,   the special object of Infidel attack, 10
Moses, addressing all Israel, 208
  ,,   his competency as a writer, 47
  ,,   honesty and impartiality, 49
  ,,   utter unselfishness, 48
Mythologies, ancient, their coincidence with the Mosaic narrative, 24

Niebuhr, referred to, 12
Number of the Danites and Levites at the Exodus, 239
  ,,   ,,   first-born, 232
  ,,   ,,   Israelites at the Exodus, 236
  ,,   ,,   priests and their duties, 241

Olshausen, on the Law and the Gospel, 154

Passover, institution of the, 219
Pentateuch, corroboration of, from early documentary sources, 19

Pentateuch, Divine authority of, affirmed by all the writers of the
Christian Church, 101
,, ,, ,, by our Lord and the writers
of the New Testament,
95
,, ,, ,, by Philo and Josephus, 94
,, ,, ,, by the writers of the Apocrypha, 93
,, ,, always acknowledged by the Jews, 90
,, ,, claimed in the writings themselves,
88
,, external testimony to, 19
,, internal evidence to credibility of, 38
,, minuteness of detail in, 44
,, pure theology and morals of, 57
,, supposed interpolations in, 119
,, what kind of composition, 15
Philosophical infidelity, difficulties of, 190
Poll-tax and the numbering of the people, 214
Powell, Professor, referred to, 135
Priestley, Dr., quoted, 194
Priests, the, and the celebration of the Passover, 213
Pritchard, Rev. C., referred to, 196
Prophecies, Mosaic, the; —
,, ,, concerning the Jews themselves, 149
,, ,, Messianic, 147
,, ,, predictions concerning the Arabs, 143
,, ,, the curse on Canaan, 142
Prophecy, importance of the arguments from, 142
,, Lord Bacon on, 140

Quarterly Review, quoted, 116
,, ,, referred to, 137

Religion and Science, conflicts between, 166
Rossi, Professor, referred to, 115

Samaritan Pentateuch, the, 74
Sceptical attacks, more to be expected, 192
Scepticism, modern, one-sidedness of, 13
,, of popular literature, 3
,, progress of, 8
,, ,, in France and Germany, 8

S

Science, physical, its relation to Revelation, 166
Scriptures, diffused knowledge of, among all classes, 79
,, Jewish, official custody of, 78
Septuagint Translation, history of, 69
,, ,, quoted from by our LORD, 71
Slaves, treatment of, by Mosaic law, 197
Stephen, Sir J., referred to, 5
Stillingfleet, Bishop, referred to, 75
Strabo, testimony of, 23
Stuart, Professor M., referred to, 115

Tabernacle, Bishop Colenso on the size of, 205
Talmud, the—its minute directions to transcribers, 83
Targums, history of the, 80
,, Samaritan, 81
Taylor, Isaac, referred to, 51
Temple, sacred writings deposited in the, 66
Tents, the Israelites dwelling in, 215
Tischendorf's Recension, referred to, 118

Undesigned coincidences, 53
Uninspired sources of information, possibility of, 124

Various readings, Bentley's testimony concerning, 116
,, ,, Eichhorn's ,, ,, 115
,, ,, Stuart's, M., Prof. ,, 116
,, ,, their comparative unimportance, 113

Westminster Review, quoted, 1

Works by the same Author.

I.

Third Edition, in crown 8vo, price 7s. 6d., an entirely New and re-constructed Edition of

DAILY DEVOTION; or, Prayers framed on the successive Chapters of the New Testament, and arranged for Morning and Evening throughout the Year. Adapted for the Family or the Closet.

II.

Third Edition. in fcap. 8vo, price 5s.

CHRISTIAN CONSOLATION; or, Discourses on the Reliefs afforded by the Gospel under Different States and Trials of the Christian Life.

III.

In post 8vo, price 5s.

ROMANISM, as set forth in its own acknowledged Formularies.

IV.

In 8vo, price 3s.

SERMONS preached before the University of Cambridge.

V.

In fcap. 8vo, Second Edition, with Additions, price 4s.

THE CHRISTIAN SYSTEM vindicated against the more Popular Forms of Modern Infidelity. Being the Author's Three Hulsean and Norrisian Prize Essays.

VI.

In fcap. 8vo. price 5s.

DISCOURSES ON THE LORD'S PRAYER.

VII.

In fcap. 8vo, Second Edition, price 2s. 6d.

FAMILY DUTIES; or, Lectures on the Relations of Husbands and Wives, Parents and Children, Masters and Servants.

VIII.

In crown 8vo, price 7s. 6d.

THOUGHTS ON PREACHING, specially in relation to the Requirements of the Age.

IX.

Price 6d.

THE SPIRITUAL MIND; an Address delivered at a Conference of the Clergy of the Diocese of Oxford, held at Exeter College, July 28, 1862.

186, Fleet Street.
February, 1863.

MESSRS. BELL and DALDY'S
NEW AND STANDARD PUBLICATIONS.

New Books.

JERUSALEM Explored; being a Description of the Ancient and Modern City, with upwards of One Hundred Illustrations, consisting of Views, Ground-plans, and Sections. By Dr. Ermete Pierotti, Architect-Engineer to His Excellency Sooraya Pasha of Jerusalem, and Architect of the Holy Land. [*Preparing.*

Plan de Jerusalem Ancienne et Moderne. Par le Docteur Ermete Pierotti. On a large sheet, 41 in. by 29 in.; with numerous details. Price 10s. [*Ready.*

British Seaweeds. Drawn from Professor Harvey's "Phycologia Britannica," with Descriptions in popular language by Mrs. Alfred Gatty. 4to. 3*l.* 3*s.* [*Ready.*
This volume contains drawings of the British Seaweeds in 803 figures, with descriptions of each, including all the newly discovered species; an Introduction, an Amateur's Synopsis, Rules for preserving and laying out Seaweeds, and the Order of their arrangement in the Herbarium.

British Moths and Butterflies. Transferred in 195 plates from Curtis's "British Entomology;" with Descriptions by E. W. Janson, Esq., Secretary of the Entomological Society. 4to. [*Shortly.*

British Beetles. Transferred in 259 plates from Curtis's "British Entomology;" with Descriptions by E. W. Janson, Esq., Secretary of the Entomological Society. 4to. [*Shortly.*

Hymns of Love and Praise for the Church's Year. By the Rev.
J. S. B. Monsell, LL.D. Fcap. 8vo. 5s. [*Ready*.

The Story of Queen Isabel, and other Verses. Fcap. 8vo. 3s. 6d.
[*Ready*.

The Odes of Horace. Translated by J. Conington, M.A., Professor of Latin in the University of Oxford. Fcap. 8vo. [*In the press*.

Love and Mammon, and other Poems. By. F. S. Wyvill,
Author of " Pansies." Fcap. 8vo. [*In the press*.

The Book of Common Prayer. Ornamented with Head-pieces
and Initial Letters specially designed for this edition. Printed in red
and black at the Cambridge University Press. 24mo. Best morocco.
10s. 6d. Also in ornamental bindings, at various prices. [*Ready*.

Also a large paper Edition, crown 8vo. Best morocco, 18s. Also
in ornamental bindings, at various prices. [*Ready*.

Colenso's Examination of the Pentateuch Examined. By the
Rev. G. S. Drew, Author of " Scripture Lands," " Reasons of Faith."
Crown 8vo. 3s. 6d. [*Ready*.

Vindiciæ Mosaicæ : a Letter to Bishop Colenso in reply to his
Arithmetical and other Arguments against the Veracity of the Pentateuch. By the Rev. C. Pritchard, M.A., F.R.S., Secretary of the Royal
Astronomical Society, and late Fellow of St. John's College, Cambridge.
8vo. 1s. 6d. [*Ready*.

The Redeemer : a Series of Sermons on Certain Aspects of the
Person and Work of our Lord Jesus Christ. By W. R. Clark, M.A.,
Vicar of Taunton. Fcap. 8vo. 5s. [*Ready*.

The Fulness of the Manifestation of Jesus Christ : being a Course
of Epiphany Lectures. By Hilkiah Bedford Hall, B.C.L. Afternoon
Lecturer of the Parish Church, Halifax, Author of " A Companion to the
Authorised Version of the New Testament." Fcap. 8vo. 2s. [*Ready*.

The Argument of St. Paul's Epistles to the Churches in Rome
Traced and Illustrated : being Twenty-six Sermons with Appendices.
By the Rev. C. P. Shepherd, M.A., Magdalen College, Cambridge. Part
I, containing Chapters I. to VIII. 8vo. 10s. [*Ready*.

The Bishop of Worcester's Primary Charge, August, 1862.
8vo. 2s. [*Ready*.

A Commentary on the Gospels for the Sundays and other Holy
Days of the Christian Year. By the Rev. W. Denton, A.M., Worcester
College, Oxford ; and Incumbent of St. Bartholomew's Cripplegate.
Vol. III. [*Preparing*.

The Book of Psalms; a New Translation, with Introductions
and Notes, Critical and Explanatory. By the Rev. J. J. Stewart
Perowne, B.D., Fellow of C. C. College, Cambridge, and Examining
Chaplain to the Lord Bishop of Norwich. 8vo. [*In the Press*.

The Cotton, Flax, and other Chief Fibre-yielding Plants of India ;
with a coloured Map of the Country, several original Illustrations of the
Native Fibrous Plants, and many important Statistical Tables. By J.
Forbes Watson, A.M., M.D., Reporter to the Indian Government on the
Products of India. Royal 8vo. [*Immediately*.

New Books. 3

Flax and its Products in Ireland. By William Charley, J. P., Juror and Reporter Class XIV, Great Exhibition 1851; also appointed in 1862 for Class XIX. With a Frontispiece. Crown 8vo. 5s. [Ready.

Katie; or the Simple Heart. By D. Richmond, Author of "Annie Maitland." Illustrated by M. I. Booth. Crown 8vo. 6s. [Ready.

Glimpses into Petland. By the Rev. J. G. Wood, M.A., with Frontispiece by Crane. Fcap. 8vo. 3s. 6d. [Immediately.

The Franklyns. By the Author of "Aggesden Vicarage." Fcap. 8vo. [In the press.

The Leadbeater Papers: a Selection from the MSS. and Correspondence of Mary Leadbeater, containing her Annals of Ballitore, with a Memoir of the Author; Unpublished Letters of Edmund Burke; and the Correspondence of Mrs. R. Trench and Rev. G. Crabbe. *Second Edition.* 2 vols. crown 8vo. 14s. [Ready.

Servia and the Servians. By the Rev. W. Denton, M.A. With Illustrations. Crown 8vo. 9s. 6d. [Ready.

Domestic Life in Palestine. By M. E. Rogers. *Second Edition, revised.* Crown 8vo. 10s. 6d. [Ready.

An Old Man's Thoughts about Many Things. Being Essays on Schools, Riches, Statues, Books, Place and Power, The Final Cause, &c. Crown 8vo. 7s. 6d. [Ready.

Hints for Pedestrians, Practical and Medical. By G. C. Watson, M.D. *Third Edition, enlarged.* 2s. 6d. [Ready.

Frederick Lucas. A Biography. By C. J. Riethmüller, author of "Teuton," a Poem. Crown 8vo. 4s. 6d. [Ready.

Church Stories. Edited by the Rev. J. E. Clarke. Crown 8vo. 2s. 6d. [Ready.

Aunt Judy's Letters. By Mrs. Alfred Gatty, Author of "Aunt Judy's Tales," "Parables from Nature," &c. Illustrated by C. S. Lane. Fcap. 8vo. 3s. 6d. [Ready.

Melchior's Dream, and other Tales. By J. H. G. Edited by Mrs. Gatty. Illustrated. Fcap. 8vo. 3s. 6d. [Ready.

Karl and the Six Little Dwarfs. By Julia Goddard. Illustrated. 16mo. 2s. 6d. [Ready.

The Thoughts of the Emperor M. Aurelius Antoninus. Translated by George Long. Fcap. 8vo. 6s. [Ready.

The Schole Master. By Roger Ascham. Edited by the Rev. J. E. B. Mayor, M.A. Fcap. 8vo. 6s. [Ready.

Charades, Enigmas, and Riddles. Collected by a Cantab. *Fourth Edition, enlarged.* Illustrated. Fcap. 8vo. 2s. 6d. [Ready.

Engravings of Unedited or Rare Greek Coins. With Descriptions. By General C. R. Fox. 4to. Part I, Europe. 7s. 6d. Part II, Asia and Africa. [Ready.

Dalzel's Analecta Graeca Minora. Newly edited, with Additions, Notes, and a Vocabulary, by the Rev. C. P. Frost. [Shortly.

Dual Arithmetic. By Oliver Byrne. 8vo. [In the press.

Bell and Daldy's POCKET VOLUMES. A Series of Select Works of Favourite Authors, adapted for general reading, moderate in price, compact and elegant in form, and executed in a style fitting them to be permanently preserved. Imperial 32mo.

Now Ready.

The Sketch-Book. By Washington Irving. 3s.
White's Natural History of Selborne. 3s.
Coleridge's Poems. 2s. 6d.
The Robin Hood Ballads. 2s. 6d.
The Midshipman.—Autobiographical Sketches of his own early Career, by Capt. Basil Hall, R.N., F.R.S. From his "Fragments of Voyages and Travels." 3s.
The Lieutenant and Commander. By the same Author. 3s.
Southey's Life of Nelson. 2s. 6d.
George Herbert's Poems. 2s.
George Herbert's Works. 3s.
Longfellow's Poems. 2s. 6d.
Lamb's Tales from Shakspeare. 2s. 6d.
Milton's Paradise Lost. 2s. 6d.
Milton's Paradise Regained and other Poems. 2s. 6d.

Preparing.

Sea Songs and Ballads. By Charles Dibdin and others.
Burns's Poems.
Burns's Songs.
Walton's Complete Angler. Illustrated.
The Conquest of India. By Capt. Basil Hall, R.N.
Walton's Lives of Donne, Wotton, Hooker, &c.
Gray's Poems.
Goldsmith's Poems.
Goldsmith's Vicar of Wakefield.
Henry Vaughan's Poems.
And others.

In cloth, top edge gilt, at 6d. per volume extra; in half morocco, Roxburgh style, at 1s. extra; in antique or best plain morocco (Hayday) at 4s. extra.

R. RICHARDSON'S New Dictionary of the English Language. Combining Explanation with Etymology, and copiously illustrated by Quotations from the best authorities. *New Edition*, with a Supplement containing additional Words and further Illustrations. In Two Vols. 4to. 4l. 14s. 6d. Half bound in russia, 5l. 15s. 6d. Russia, 6l. 12s.

The WORDS—with those of the same Family—are traced to their Origin.

The EXPLANATIONS are deduced from the Primitive Meaning through the various Usages.

The QUOTATIONS are arranged Chronologically, from the Earliest Period to the Present Time.

⁎ The Supplement separately, 4to. 12s.

AN 8VO. EDITION, without the Quotations, 15s. Half-russia, 20s. Russia, 24s.

"It is an admirable addition to our Lexicography, supplying a great desideratum, as exhibiting the biography of each word—its birth, parentage and education, the changes that have befallen it, the company it has kept, and the connexions it has formed—by rich series of quotations, all in chronological order. This is such a Dictionary as perhaps no other language could ever boast."—*Quarterly Review.*

Dr. Richardson on the Study of Language: an Exposition of Horne Tooke's Diversions of Purley. Fcap. 8vo. 4s. 6d.

New and Standard Publications.

The Library of English Worthies.

A Series of reprints of the best Authors carefully edited and collated with the Early Copies, and handsomely printed by Whittingham in Octavo.

GOWER'S Confessio Amantis, with Life by Dr. Pauli, and a Glossary. 3 vols. 2*l.* 2*s.* Antique calf, 3*l.* 6*s.* Only a limited number of Copies printed.
This important work is so scarce that it can seldom be met with even in large libraries. It is wanting in nearly every collection of English Poetry.

Spenser's Complete Works; with Life, Notes, and Glossary, by John Payne Collier, Esq., F.S.A. 5 vols. 8vo. 3*l.* 15*s.* Antique calf, 6*l.* 6*s.*

Bishop Butler's Analogy of Religion; with Analytical Index, by the Rev. Edward Steere, LL.D. 8vo. 12*s.* Antique calf, 1*l.* 1*s.*
"The present edition has been furnished with an Index of the Texts of Scripture quoted, and an Index of Words and Things considerably fuller than any hitherto published."—*Editor's Preface.*

Bishop Jeremy Taylor's Rule and Exercises of Holy Living and Dying. 2 vols. 8vo. 1*l.* 1*s.* Morocco, antique calf or morocco, 2*l.* 2*s.*

Herbert's Poems and Remains; with S. T. Coleridge's Notes, and Life by Izaak Walton. Revised, with additional Notes, by Mr. J. Yeowell. 2 vols. 8vo. 1*l.* 1*s.* Morocco, antique calf or morocco, 2*l.* 2*s.*

Uniform with the above.

The Physical Theory of Another Life. By Isaac Taylor, Esq. Author of "Logic in Theology," "Ultimate Civilization," &c." *New Edition.* 10*s.* 6*d.* Antique calf, 21*s.*

MR. S. W. Singer's New Edition of Shakespeare's Dramatic Works. The Text carefully revised, with Notes. The Life of the Poet and a Critical Essay on each Play by W. W. Lloyd, Esq. 10 vols. 6*s.* each. Calf, 5*l.* 5*s.* Morocco, 6*l.* 6*s.*
Large Paper Edition, crown 8vo., 4*l.* 10*s.* Calf, 6*l.* 16*s.* 6*d.* Morocco, 8*l.* 8*s.*

"Mr. Singer has produced a text, the accuracy of which cannot be surpassed in the present state of antiquarian and philological knowledge."—*Daily News.*

The Aldine Edition of the British Poets.

The Publishers have been induced, by the scarcity and increasing value of this admired Series of the Poets, to prepare a New Edition, very carefully corrected, and improved by such additions as recent literary research has placed within their reach.

The general principle of Editing which has been adopted is *to give the entire Poems of each author in strict conformity with the Edition which received his final revision, to prefix a Memoir, and to add such notes as may be necessary to elucidate the sense of obsolete words or explain obscure allusions.* Each author will be placed in the hands of a competent editor specially acquainted with the literature and bibliography of the period.

Externally this new edition will resemble the former, but with some improvements. It will be elegantly printed by Whittingham, on toned paper manufactured expressly for it; and a highly-finished portrait of each author will be given.

The *Aldine Edition of the British Poets* has hitherto been the favourite Series with the admirers of choice books, and every effort will be made to increase its claims as a comprehensive and faithful mirror of the poetic genius of the nation.

AKENSIDE'S Poetical Works, with Memoir by the Rev. A. Dyce, and additional Letters, carefully revised. 5s. Morocco, or antique morocco, 10s. 6d.

Collins's Poems, with Memoir and Notes by W. Moy Thomas, Esq. 3s. 6d. Morocco, or antique morocco, 8s. 6d.

Gray's Poetical Works, with Notes and Memoir by the Rev. John Mitford. 5s. Morocco, or antique morocco, 10s. 6d.

Kirke White's Poems, with Memoir by Sir H. Nicolas, and additional notes. Carefully revised. 5s. Morocco, or antique morocco, 10s. 6d.

Shakespeare's Poems, with Memoir by the Rev. A. Dyce. 5s. Morocco, or antique morocco, 10s. 6d.

Young's Poems, with Memoir by the Rev. John Mitford, and additional Poems. 2 vols. 10s. Morocco, or antique morocco, 1l. 1s.

Thomson's Poems, with Memoir by Sir H. Nicolas, annotated by Peter Cunningham, Esq., F.S.A., and additional Poems, carefully revised. 2 vols. 10s. Morocco, or antique morocco, 1l. 1s.

Thomson's Seasons, and Castle of Indolence, with Memoir. 6s. Morocco, or antique morocco, 11s. 6d.

Dryden's Poetical Works, with Memoir by the Rev. R. Hooper. F.S.A. Carefully revised. [*In the Press.*

Cowper's Poetical Works, including his Translations. Edited, with Memoir, by John Bruce, Esq., F.S.A. [*In the Press.*

Uniform with the Aldine Edition of the Poets.

The Works of Gray, edited by the Rev. John Mitford. With his Correspondence with Mr. Chute and others, Journal kept at Rome, Criticism on the Sculptures, &c. *New Edition.* 5 vols. 1*l.* 5*s.*

The Temple and other Poems. By George Herbert, with Coleridge's Notes. *New Edition.* Fcap. 8vo. 5*s.* Morocco, antique calf or morocco, 10*s.* 6*d.*

Vaughan's Sacred Poems and Pious Ejaculations, with Memoir by the Rev. H. F. Lyte. *New Edition.* Fcap. 8vo. 5*s.* Antique calf or morocco, 10*s.* 6*d. Large Paper,* 7*s.* 6*d.* Antique calf, 14*s.* Antique morocco, 15*s.*

" Preserving all the piety of George Herbert, they have less of his quaint and fantastic turns, with a much larger infusion of poetic feeling and expression."—*Lyte.*

Bishop Jeremy Taylor's Rule and Exercises of Holy Living and Holy Dying. 2 vols. 2*s.* 6*d.* each. Morocco, antique calf or morocco, 7*s.* 6*d.* each. In one volume, 5*s.* Morocco, antique calf or morocco, 10*s.* 6*d.*

Bishop Butler's Analogy of Religion; with Analytical Introduction and copious Index, by the Rev. Dr. Steere. 6*s.* Antique calf, 11*s.* 6*d.*

Bishop Butler's Sermons and Remains; with Memoir, by the Rev. E. Steere, LL.D. 6*s.*

*** This volume contains some additional remains, which are copyright, and render it the most complete edition extant.

Bishop Butler's Complete Works; with Memoir by the Rev. Dr. Steere. 2 vols. 12*s.*

Bacon's Advancement of Learning. Edited, with short Notes, by the Rev. G. W. Kitchin, M.A., Christ Church, Oxford. 6*s.*; antique calf, 11*s.* 6*d.*

Bacon's Essays; or, Counsels Civil and Moral, with the Wisdom of the Ancients. With References and Notes by S. W. Singer, F.S.A. 5*s.* Morocco, or antique calf, 10*s.* 6*d.*

Bacon's Novum Organum. Newly translated, with short Notes, by the Rev. Andrew Johnson, M.A. 6*s.* Antique calf, 11*s.* 6*d.*

Locke on the Conduct of the Human Understanding; edited by Bolton Corney, Esq., M. R. S. L. 3*s.* 6*d.* Antique calf, 8*s.* 6*d.*

" I cannot think any parent or instructor justified in neglecting to put this little treatise into the hands of a boy about the time when the reasoning faculties become developed."—*Hallam.*

Ultimate Civilization. By Isaac Taylor, Esq. 6*s.*

Logic in Theology, and other Essays. By Isaac Taylor, Esq. 6*s.*

The Physical Theory of Another Life. By Isaac Taylor, Esq., Author of the " Natural History of Enthusiasm," " Restoration of Belief," &c. *New Edition.* 6*s.* Antique calf, 11*s.* 6*d.*

DOMESTIC Life in Palestine. By M. E. Rogers. Post 8vo. *Second Edition.* 10s. 6d.

By-Roads and Battle Fields in Picardy: with Incidents and Gatherings by the Way between Ambleteuse and Ham; including Agincourt and Crécy. By G. M. Musgrave, M.A., Author of "A Pilgrimage into Dauphiné, &c. Illustrated. Super-royal 8vo. 16s.

The Boat and the Caravan. A Family Tour through Egypt and Syria. *New and cheaper Edition.* Fcap. 8vo. 5s. 6d.

Fragments of Voyages and Travels. By Captain Basil Hall, R.N., F.R.S. 1st, 2nd, and 3rd Series in 1 vol. complete. *New Edition.* Royal 8vo. 10s. 6d.

Adventures of Baron Wenceslas Wratislaw of Mitrowitz; what he saw in the Turkish Metropolis, Constantinople, experienced in his Captivity, and, after his happy return to his country, committed to writing, in the year of our Lord, 1599. Literally translated from the original Bohemian by A. H. Wratislaw, M.A., Head Master of the Grammar School, Bury St. Edmunds, and formerly Fellow and Tutor of Christ's College, Cambridge. Crown 8vo. 6s. 6d.

The Gem of Thorney Island; or, The Historical Associations of Westminster Abbey. By the Rev. J. Ridgway, M.A. Crown 8vo. 7s. 6d.

Gifts and Graces. A new Tale, by the Author of "The Rose and the Lotus." Post 8vo. 7s. 6d.

Childhood and Youth. By Count Nicola Tolstoi. Translated from the Russian by Malwida von Meysenbug. Post 8vo. 8s. 6d.

Baronscliffe; or, the Deed of other Days. By Mrs. P. M. Latham, Author of "The Wayfarers." Crown 8vo. 6s.

The Wayfarers: or, Toil and Rest. By Mrs. Latham. Fcap. 5s.

The Manse of Mastland. Sketches: Serious and Humorous, in the Life of a Village Pastor in the Netherlands. Translated from the Dutch by Thomas Keightley, M.A. Post 8vo. 9s.

The Home Life of English Ladies in the Seventeenth Century. By the Author of "Magdalen Stafford." *Second Edition, enlarged.* Fcap. 8vo. 6s. Calf, 9s. 6d.

The Romance and its Hero. By the Author of "Magdalen Stafford." 2 vols. Fcap. 8vo. 12s.

Magdalen Stafford. A Tale. Fcap. 8vo. 5s.

Claude de Vesci; or, the Lost Inheritance. 2 vols. Fcap. 8vo. 9s.

BY THE LATE MRS. WOODROOFFE.

COTTAGE Dialogues. *New Edition.* 12mo. 4s. 6d.

Shades of Character; or, the Infant Pilgrim. *7th Edition.* 2 vols. 12mo. 12s.

Michael Kemp, the Happy Farmer's Lad. *8th Edition.* 12mo. 4s.

A Sequel to Michael Kemp. *New Edition.* 12mo. 6s. 6d.

New and Standard Publications.

MRS. ALFRED GATTY'S POPULAR WORKS.

" We should not be doing justice to the highest class of juvenile fiction, were we to omit, as particularly worthy of attention at this season, the whole series of Mrs. Gatty's admirable books. They are quite *sui generis*, and deserve the widest possible circulation."—*Literary Churchman.*

ARABLES from Nature; with Notes on the Natural History. Illustrated by W. Holman Hunt, Otto Speckter, C. W. Cope, R. A., E. Warren, W. Millais, G. Thomas, and H. Calderon. 8vo. Ornamental cloth, 10s. 6d. Antique morocco elegant, 1l. 1s.

Parables from Nature. 16mo. with Illustrations. *Tenth Edition.* 3s. 6d. Separately: First Series, 1s. 6d.; Second Series, 2s.

Red Snow, and other Parables from Nature. Third Series with Illustrations. *Second Edition.* 16mo. 2s.

Worlds not Realized. 16mo. *Third Edition.* 2s.

Proverbs Illustrated. 16mo. with Illustrations. *3rd Edition.* 2s.

*** *These little works have been found useful for Sunday reading in the family circle, and instructive and interesting to school children.*

The Human Face Divine, and other Tales. With Illustrations by C. S. Lane. Fcap. 8vo. 3s. 6d.

The Fairy Godmothers and other Tales. *Third Edition.* Fcap. 8vo. with Frontispiece. 2s. 6d.

Legendary Tales. With Illustrations by Phiz. Fcap. 8vo. 5s.

The Poor Incumbent. Fcap. 8vo. Sewed, 1s. Cloth, 1s. 6d.

The Old Folks from Home; or, a Holiday in Ireland in 1861. *Second Edition.* Post 8vo. 7s. 6d.

Aunt Judy's Tales. Illustrated by Clara S. Lane. Fcap. 8vo. *Third Edition.* 3s. 6d.

Aunt Judy's Letters. Illustrated by Clara S. Lane. Fcap. 8vo. 3s. 6d.

Melchior's Dream, and other Tales. By J. H. G. Edited by Mrs. Gatty. Illustrated. Fcap. 8vo. 3s. 6d.

HE Life and Adventures of Robinson Crusoe. By Daniel Defoe. With 100 Illustrations by E. H. Wehnert. Uniform with "Andersen's Tales." Small 8vo. Cloth, gilt edges, 7s. 6d.

Andersen's Tales for Children. Translated by A. Wehnert. With 105 Illustrations by E. H. Wehnert, W. Thomas, and others. Small 8vo. Cloth, gilt edges, 7s. 6d.

Among the Tartar Tents; or, the Lost Fathers. A Tale By Anne Bowman, Author of " Esperanza," " The Boy Voyagers," &c. With Illustrations. Crown 8vo. 5s.

Little Maggie and her Brother. By Mrs. G. Hooper, Author of " Recollections of Mrs. Anderson's School," " Arbell," &c. With a Frontispiece. Fcap. 8vo. 2s. 6d.

A 2

Guessing Stories; or, the Surprising Adventures of the Man with the Extra Pair of Eyes. A Book for Young People. By a Country Parson. Imperial 16mo. Cloth, gilt edges, 3s.

Cavaliers and Round Heads. By J. G. Edgar, Author of "Sea Kings and Naval Heroes." Illustrated by Amy Butts. Fcap. 8vo. 5s.

Sea-Kings and Naval Heroes. A Book for Boys. By J. G. Edgar. With Illustrations by C. K. Johnson and C. Keene. Fcap. 8vo. 5s.

The Life of Christopher Columbus, in Short Words. By Sarah Crompton. Crown 8vo. 2s. 6d. Also an Edition for Schools, 1s.

The Life of Martin Luther, in Short Words. By the same Author. Crown 8vo. 1s. 6d. Stiff cover, 1s.

Nursery Tales. By Mrs. Motherly. With Illustrations by C. S. Lane. Imperial 16mo. 2s. 6d. Coloured, gilt edges, 3s. 6d.

Nursery Poetry. By Mrs. Motherly. With Eight Illustrations by C. S. Lane. Imperial 16mo. 2s. 6d. Coloured, gilt edges, 3s. 6d.

Nursery Carols. Illustrated with 120 Pictures. By Ludwig Riether and Oscar Pletsch. Imperial 16mo. Ornamental Binding. 3s. 6d. coloured, 6s.

Poetry for Play-Hours. By Gerda Fay. With Eight large Illustrations. Imperial 16mo. 3s. 6d. Coloured, gilt edges, 4s. 6d.

Very Little Tales for Very Little Children In single Syllables of *Four* and *Five* letters. *New Edition.* Illustrated. 2 vols. 16mo. 1s. 6d. each, or in 1 vol. 3s.

Progressive Tales for Little Children. In words of *One* and *Two* Syllables. Forming the sequel to "Very Little Tales." *New Edition.* Illustrated. 2 vols. 16mo. 1s. 6d. each, or in 1 vol. 3s.

The White Lady and Undine, translated from the German by the Hon. C. L. Lyttelton. With numerous Illustrations. Fcap. 8vo. 5s. Or, separately, 2s. 6d. each.

The Lights of the Will o' the Wisp. Translated by Lady Maxwell Wallace. With a coloured Frontispiece. Imperial 16mo. Cloth, gilt edges, 5s.

Voices from the Greenwood. Adapted from the Original. By Lady Maxwell Wallace. With Illustrations. Imperial 16mo. 2s. 6d.

Princess Ilse: a Legend, translated from the German. By Lady Maxwell Wallace. With Illustrations. Imperial 16mo. 2s. 6d.

A Poetry Book for Children. Illustrated with Thirty-seven highly-finished Engravings, by C. W. Cope, R. A., Helmsley, Palmer, Skill, Thomas, and H. Weir. *New Edition.* Crown 8vo. 2s. 6d.

The Children's Picture Book Series.
Written expressly for Young People, super-royal 16mo.

Cloth, gilt edges, price 5s. each.

BIBLE Picture Book. Eighty Illustrations. (Coloured, 9s.)

Scripture Parables and Bible Miracles. Thirty-two Illustrations. (Coloured, 7s. 6d.)

English History. Sixty Illustrations. (Coloured, 9s.)

Good and Great Men. Fifty Illustrations. (Coloured, 9s.)

Useful Knowledge. One Hundred and Thirty Figures.

Cloth, red edges, price 2s. 6d. each. (*Coloured, gilt edges,* 3s. 6d.)

Scripture Parables. By Rev. J. E. Clarke. 16 Illustrations.

Bible Miracles. By Rev. J. E. Clarke, M.A. 16 Illustrations.

The Life of Joseph. Sixteen Illustrations.

Bunyan's Pilgrim's Progress. Sixteen Illustrations.

CLARK'S Introduction to Heraldry.—Containing Rules for Blazoning and Marshalling Coats of Armour—Dictionary of Terms—Orders of Knighthood explained—Degrees of the Nobility and Gentry—Tables of Precedency; 48 Engravings, including upwards of 1,000 Examples, and the Arms of numerous Families. *Sixteenth Edition improved.* Small 8vo. 7s. 6d. Coloured, 18s.

Book of Family Crests and Mottoes, with *Four Thousand Engravings* of the Crests of the Peers, Baronets, and Gentry of England and Wales, and Scotland and Ireland. A Dictionary of Mottos, &c. *Tenth Edition, enlarged.* 2 vols. small 8vo. 1l. 4s.

" Perhaps the best recommendation to its utility and correctness (in the main) is, that it has been used as a work of reference in the Heralds' College. No wonder it sells."—*Spectator.*

A Handbook of Mottoes borne by the Nobility, Gentry, Cities, Public Companies, &c. Translated and Illustrated, with Notes and Quotations, by C. N. Elvin, M.A. Small 8vo. 6s.

Gothic Ornaments; being a Series of Examples of enriched Details and Accessories of the Architecture of Great Britain. Drawn from existing Authorities. By J. K. Colling, Architect. Royal 4to. Vol. I. 3l. 13s. 6d. Vol. II. 3l. 16s. 6d.

Details of Gothic Architecture, Measured and Drawn from existing Examples. By J. K. Colling, Architect. Royal 4to. 2 vols. 5l. 5s.

The Architectural History of Chichester Cathedral, with an Introductory Essay on the Fall of the Tower and Spire. By the Rev. R. Willis, M.A., F.R.S., &c., Jacksonian Professor in the University of Cambridge.—Of Boxgrove Priory, by the Rev. J. L. Petit, M.A., F.S.A. —And of Shoreham Collegiate Church, together with the Collective Architectural History of the foregoing buildings, as indicated by their mouldings, by Edmund Sharpe, M.A., F.R.I B.A. Illustrated by one hundred Plates, Diagrams, Plans and Woodcuts. Super-royal 4to. 1*l*. 10*s*.

Architectural Studies in France. By the Rev. J. L. Petit, M.A., F.S.A. With Illustrations from Drawings by the Author and P. H. Delamotte. Imp. 8vo. 2*l*. 2*s*.

Remarks on Church Architecture. With Illustrations. By the Rev. J. L. Petit, M.A. 2 vols. 8vo. 1*l*. 1*s*.

A Few Notes on the Temple Organ. By Edmund Macrory, M.A. *Second Edition*. Super-royal 16mo. Half morocco, Roxburgh, 3*s*. 6*d*.

Scudamore Organs, or Practical Hints respecting Organs for Village Churches and small Chancels, on improved principles. By the Rev. John Baron, M.A., Rector of Upton Scudamore, Wilts. With Designs by George Edmund Street, F.S.A. *Second Edition, revised and enlarged*. 8vo. 6*s*.

The Bell; its Origin, History, and Uses. By Rev. A. Gatty. 3*s*.

Practical Remarks on Belfries and Ringers. By the Rev. H. T. Ellacombe, M.A., F.A.S., Rector of Clyst St. George, Devonshire. *Second Edition*, with an Appendix on Chiming. Illustrated. 8vo. 3*s*.

Proceedings of the Archæological Institute at Newcastle, in 1853. With Numerous Engravings. 2 vols. 8vo. 2*l*. 2*s*.

History of the Parish of Ecclesfield, in the County of York. By the Rev. J. Eastwood, M.A., Incumbent of Hope, Staffordshire, formerly Curate of Ecclesfield. 8vo. 16*s*.

A Handbook for Visitors to Cambridge. By Norris Deck. Illustrated by 8 Steel Engravings, 97 Woodcuts, and a Map. Crown 8vo. 5*s*.

Canterbury in the Olden Time: from the Municipal Archives and other Sources. By John Brent, F.S.A. With Illustrations. 5*s*.

Whirlwinds and Dust-Storms of India. With numerous Illustrations drawn from Nature, bound separately; and an Addendum on Sanitary Measures required for European Soldiers in India. By P. F H. Baddeley, Surgeon, Bengal Army, Retired List. Large 8vo. With Illustrations, 8*s*. 6*d*.; without Illustrations, 3*s*.

Two Transparent Wind Cards in Horn, adapted to the Northern and Southern Hemispheres, for the use of Sailors. 2*s*.

The Addresses of the Hungarian Diet of 1861, to H. I. M. the Emperor of Austria, with the Imperial Rescript and other Documents. Translated for presentation to Members of both Houses of the British Parliament. By J. Horne Payne, Esq., M.A., Lond., of the Inner Temple. Royal 8vo. 2*s*. 6*d*.

EBSTER'S Complete Dictionary of the English Language. *New Edition*, revised and greatly enlarged, by CHAUNCEY A. GOODRICH, Professor in Yale College. 4to. (1624 pp.) 1*l*. 11*s*. 6*d*.; half calf, 2*l*.; calf, or half russia, 2*l*. 2*s*.; russia, 2*l*. 10*s*.

Though the circulation of Dr. Webster's celebrated Dictionary, in its various forms, in the United States, in England, and in every country where the English Language is spoken, may be counted by hundreds of thousands, it is believed that there are many persons to whom the book is yet unknown, and who, if seeking for a Dictionary which should supply all reasonable wants, would be at a loss to select one from the numerous competitors in the field.

In announcing this New Edition, the Proprietors desire to call attention to the features which distinguish it, and to put before those who are in want of such a book, the points in which it excels all other Dictionaries, and which render it the best that has as yet been issued for the practical purposes of daily use:—

1. Accuracy of Definition. 2. Pronunciation intelligibly marked. 3. Completeness. 4. Etymology. 5. Obsolete Words. 6. Uniformity in the Mode of Spelling. 7. Quotations. 8. Cheapness.

With the determination that the superiority of the work shall be fully maintained, and that it shall keep pace with the requirements of the age and the universal increase of education, the Proprietors have added to this New Edition, under the editorship of Professor Goodrich,—

A Table of Synonyms. An Appendix of New Words. Table of Quotations, Words, Phrases, &c.

Tables of Interest, enlarged and Improved; calculated at Five per Cent.; Showing at one view the Interest of any Sum, from £1 to £365: they are also carried on by hundreds to £1,000, and by thousands to £10,000, from one day to 365 days. To which are added, Tables of Interest, from one to 12 months, and from two to 13 years. Also Tables for calculating Commission on Sales of Goods or Banking Accounts, from ¼ to 5 per Cent., with several useful observations, among which are Tables for calculating Interest on large sums for 1 day, at the several rates of 4 and 5 per Cent. to £100,000,000. By Joseph King, of Liverpool. 24*th Edition*. With a Table showing the number of days from any one day to any other day in the Year. 8vo. 1*l*. 1*s*.

The Housekeeping Book, or Family Ledger; on an Improved Principle. By which an exact Account can be kept of Income and Expenditure; suitable for any Year, and may be begun at any time. With Hints on Household Management, Receipts, &c. By Mrs. Hamilton. 8vo. Cloth, 1*s*. 6*d*. sewed, 1*s*.

The Executor's Account Book, with short Practical Instructions for the guidance of Executors. By a Solicitor. Folio. 4*s*.

EGENDS and Lyrics, by Adelaide Anne Procter. 6*th Edition*. Fcap. 5*s*. Antique or best plain morocco, 10*s*. 6*d*

—— *Second Series*. *Second Edition*. Fcap. 8vo. 5*s*.; antique or best plain morocco, 10*s*. 6*d*.

The Legend of the Golden Prayers, and other Poems. By C. F. Alexander, Author of "Moral Songs," &c. Fcap. 8vo. 5*s*.; antique or best plain morocco, 10*s*. 6*d*.

Verses for Holy Seasons. By the Same Author. Edited by the Very Rev. W. F. Hook, D.D. 4*th Edition*. Fcap. 3*s*. 6*d*.; morocco, antique calf or morocco, 8*s*. 6*d*.

Nightingale Valley ; a Collection of Choice Lyrics and Short
Poems. From the time of Shakespeare to the present day. Edited by
William Allingham. Fcap. 8vo. 5s.; mor., antique calf or mor., 10s.6d.

Latin Translations of English Hymns. By Charles Buchanan
Pearson, M. A., Prebendary of Sarum, and Rector of Knebworth. Fcap.
8vo. 5s.

The Frithiof Saga. A Poem. Translated from the Norwegian.
By the Rev. R. Mucklestone, M.A., Rector of Dinedor, Herefordshire;
late Fellow and Tutor of Worcester Coll. Oxford. Cr. 8vo. 7s. 6d.

Saul, a Dramatic Poem ; Elizabeth, an Historical Ode; and other
Poems. By William Fulford, M.A. Fcap. 8vo. 5s.

Lays and Poems on Italy. By F. A. Mackay. Fcap. 8vo. 5s.

Poems from the German. By Richard Garnett, Author of "Io
in Egypt, and other Poems." Fcap. 8vo. 3s. 6d.

Io in Egypt, and other Poems. By R. Garnett. Fcap. 8vo. 5s.

The Monks of Kilcrea, and other Poems. *Third Edition.* Post 8vo.
7s. 6d.

Christopheros, and other Poems. By the Ven. W. B. Mant,
Archdeacon of Down. Crown 8vo. 6s.

Teuton. A Poem. By C. J. Riethmüller. Crown 8vo. 7s. 6d.

Dryope, and other Poems. By T. Ashe. Fcap. 8vo. 6s.

Wild Thyme. By E. M. Mitchell. Fcap. 8vo. 5s.

Lyrics and Idylls. By Gerda Fay. Fcap. 8vo. 4s.

The Defence of Guenevere, and other Poems. By W. Morris. 5s.

David Mallet's Poems. With Notes and Illustrations by F. Dinsdale, LL.D., F.S.A. *New Edition.* Post 8vo. 10s. 6d.

Ballads and Songs of Yorkshire. Transcribed from private MSS.,
rare Broadsides, and scarce Publications; with Notes and a Glossary.
By C. J. D. Ingledew, M.A., Ph.D., F.G.H.S., author of "The History
of North Allerton." Fcap. 8vo. 6s.

Percy's Reliques of Ancient English Poetry. 3 vols. sm. 8vo. 15s.
Half-bound, 18s. Antique calf, or morocco, 1l. 11s. 6d.

Ellis's Specimens of Early English Poetry. 3 vols. sm. 8vo. 15s.
Half-bound, 18s. Antique calf, or morocco, 1l. 11s. 6d.

The Book of Ancient Ballad Poetry of Great Britain, Historical,
Traditional and Romantic: with Modern Imitations, Translations, Notes
and Glossary, &c. Edited by J. S. Moore. *New and Improved Edition*,
8vo. Half-bound, 14s. Antique morocco, 21s.

The Promises of Jesus Christ. Illuminated by Albert H. Warren,
Second Edition. Ornamental cloth, 15s. Antique morocco elegant, 21s.

Christmas with the Poets : a Collection of English Poetry
relating to the Festival of Christmas. Illustrated by Birket Foster, and
with numerous initial letters and borders beautifully printed in gold and
colours by Edmund Evans. *New and improved Edition.* Super royal 8vo.
Ornamental binding, 21s. Antique morocco, 31s. 6d.

ATHENÆ Cantabrigienses. By C. H. Cooper, F.S.A., and Thompson Cooper. Volume I. 1500—1585. 8vo. 18s. Vol. II. 1586—1609. 8vo. 18s.

This work, in illustration of the biography of notable and eminent men who have been members of the University of Cambridge, comprehends notices of:—1. Authors. 2. Cardinals, archbishops, bishops, abbots, heads of religious houses and other church dignitaries. 3. Statesmen, diplomatists, military and naval commanders. 4. Judges and eminent practitioners of the civil or common law. 5. Sufferers for religious or political opinions. 6. Persons distinguished for success in tuition. 7. Eminent physicians and medical practitioners. 8. Artists, musicians, and heralds. 9. Heads of colleges, professors, and principal officers of the university. 10. Benefactors to the university and colleges, or to the public at large.

The Early and Middle Ages of England. By C. H. Pearson, M.A., Fellow of Oriel College, Oxford, and Professor of Modern History, King's College, London. 8vo. 12s.

History of England, from the Invasion of Julius Cæsar to the End of the Reign of George II., by Hume and Smollett. With the Continuation, to the Accession of Queen Victoria, by the Rev. T. S. Hughes, B.D. late Canon of Peterborough. *New Edition*, containing Historical Illustrations, Autographs, and Portraits, copious Notes, and the Author's last Corrections and Improvements. In 18 vols. crown 8vo. 4s. each.

Vols. I. to VI. (Hume's portion), 1l. 4s.
Vols. VII. to X. (Smollett's ditto), 16s.
Vols. XI. to XVIII. (Hughes's ditto), 1l. 12s.

History of England, from the Accession of George III. to the Accession of Queen Victoria. By the Rev. T. S. Hughes, B.D. *New Edition*, almost entirely re-written. In 7 vols. 8vo. 3l. 13s. 6d.

Choice Notes from "Notes and Queries," by the Editor. Fcap. 8vo. 5s. each.
VOL. I.—HISTORY. VOL. II.—FOLK LORE.

Master Wace's Chronicle of the Conquest of England. Translated from the Norman by Sir Alexander Malet, Bart., H.B.M. Plenipotentiary, Frankfort. With Photograph Illustrations of the Bayeaux Tapestry. Medium 4to. Half-morocco, Roxburgh, 2l. 2s.

The Prince Consort's Addresses on Different Public Occasions. Beautifully printed by Whittingham. 4to. 10s. 6d.

Life and Books; or, Records of Thought and Reading. By J. F. Boyes, M.A. Fcap. 8vo. 5s.; calf, 8s. 6d.

Life's Problems. By Sir Rutherford Alcock, K.C.B. *Second Edition*, revised and enlarged. Fcap. 5s.

Parliamentary Short-Hand (Official System). By Thompson Cooper. Fcap. 8vo. 2s. 6d.

This is the system *universally practised by the Government Official Reporters*. It has many advantages over the system ordinarily adopted, and has hitherto been inaccessible, except in a high-priced volume.

English Retraced; or, Remarks, Critical and Philological, founded on a Comparison of the Breeches Bible with the English of the present day. Crown 8vo. 5s.

16   *Messrs. Bell and Daldy's*

The Pleasures of Literature. By R. Aris Willmott, Incumbent of Bear-Wood. *Fifth Edition*, enlarged. Fcap. 8vo. 5s. Morocco, 10s. 6d.

Hints and Helps for Youths leaving School. By the Rev. J. S. Gilderdale, M.A. Fcap. 8vo. 5s. Calf, 8s. 6d.

Hints to Maid Servants in Small Households, on Manners, Dress, and Duties. By Mrs. Motherly. Fcap. 8vo. 1s. 6d.

A Wife's Home Duties; containing Hints to inexperienced Housekeepers. Fcap. 8vo. 2s. 6d.

Geology in the Garden: or, The Fossils in the Flint Pebbles. With 106 Illustrations. By the Rev. Henry Eley, M.A. Fcap. 8vo. 6s.

Halcyon: or Rod-Fishing in Clear Waters. By Henry Wade, Secretary to the Weardale Angling Association. With Coloured representations of the principal Flies, and other Illustrations. Cr. 8vo. 7s. 6d.

A Handy Book of the Chemistry of Soils: Explanatory of their Composition, and the Influence of Manures in ameliorating them, with Outlines of the various Processes of Agricultural Analysis. By John Scoffern, M.B. Crown 8vo. 4s. 6d.

SERMONS.

PARISH SERMONS. By the Rev. M. F. Sadler, M.A., Vicar of Bridgwater. Author of the " Sacrament of Responsibility," and " TheSecond Adam and the New Birth." Fcap. 8vo. Vol. I, Advent to Trinity; Vol. II, Trinity to Advent. 7s. 6d. each.

Twenty-four Sermons on Christian Doctrine and Practice, and on the Church, By C. J. Blomfield, D.D., late Lord Bishop of London. (*Hitherto unpublished.*) 8vo. 10s. 6d.

King's College Sermons. By the Rev. E. H. Plumptre, M.A., Divinity Professor. Fcap. 8vo. 2s. 6d.

Sermons preached in Westminster. By the Rev. C. F. Secretan, M.A., Incumbent of Holy Trinity, Vauxhall-Bridge Road. Fcap. 8vo. 6s.

Sermons. By the Rev. A. Gatty, D.D., Vicar of Ecclesfield. 12mo. 8s.

Twenty Plain Sermons for Country Congregations and Family Reading. By the Rev. A. Gatty, D.D., Vicar of Ecclesfield. Fcap. 5s.

Sermons to a Country Congregation—Advent to Trinity. By the Rev. Hastings Gordon, M.A. 12mo. 6s.

Sermons on Popular Subjects, preached in the Collegiate Church, Wolverhampton. By the Rev. Julius Lloyd, M.A. 8vo. 4s. 6d.

Gospel Truths in Parochial Sermons for the Great Festivals. By the Rev. J. Townson, M.A. Fcap. 8vo. 2s. 6d.

Four Sermons on the "Comfortable Words" in the Office for the Holy Communion. By Alexander Goalen, B.A. Fcap. 8vo. 2s.

The Prodigal Son. Sermons by W. R. Clark, M.A., Vicar of Taunton, S. Mary Magdalene. Fcap. 8vo. 2s. 6d.

The Redeemer: a Series of Sermons on Certain Aspects of the Person and Work of our Lord Jesus Christ. By W. R. Clark, M.A., Vicar of Taunton. Fcap. 8vo. 5s.

New and Standard Publications. 17

The Fulness of the Manifestation of Jesus Christ; being a Course
of Epiphany Lectures. By Hilkiah Bedford Hall, B.C.L., Afternoon
Lecturer of the Parish Church, Halifax, Author of " A Companion to the
Authorized Version of the New Testament. Fcap. 8vo. 2s.

Parochial Sermons. By the Rev. D. G. Stacy, Vicar of Hornchurch, Essex. Fcap. 8vo. 5s.

Sermons Suggested by the Miracles of our Lord and Saviour Jesus Christ. By the Very Rev. Dean Hook. 2 vols. Fcap. 8vo. 12s.

Five Sermons Preached before the University of Oxford. By the
Very Rev. W. F. Hook, D.D., Dean of Chichester. *Third Edition.* 3s.

Plain Parochial Sermons. By the Rev. C. F. C. Pigott, B.A.,
late Curate of St. Michael's, Handsworth. Fcap. 8vo. 6s.

Our Privileges, Responsibilities, and Trials. By the Rev. E.
Phillips, M.A. Fcap. 8vo. 5s.

Sermons, chiefly Practical. By the Rev. T. Nunns, M.A. Edited
by the Very Rev. W. F. Hook, D.D., Dean of Chichester. Fcap. 8vo. 6s.

Sermons, Preached in the Parish Church of Godalming, Surrey,
by the Rev. E. J. Boyce, M.A., Vicar. *Second Edition.* Fcap. 8vo. 6s.

Life in Christ. By the Rev. J. Llewellyn Davies, M.A., Rector
of Christ Church, Marylebone. Fcap. 8vo. 5s.

The Church of England; its Constitution, Mission, and Trials.
By the Rt. Rev. Bishop Broughton. Edited, with a Prefatory Memoir, by
the Ven. Archdeacon Harrison. 8vo. 10s. 6d.

Plain Sermons, Addressed to a Country Congregation. By the
late E. Bleucowe, M.A. 1st and 3rd Series, fcap. 8vo. 7s. 6d. each.

Occasional Sermons. By a Member of the Church of England.
Fcap. 8vo. 2s. 6d.

Missionary Sermons preached at Hagley. Fcap. 3s. 6d.

The Sufficiency of Christ. Sermons preached during the Reading
Lenten Mission of 1860. Fcap. 8vo. 2s. 6d.

Westminster Abbey Sermons for the Working Classes. Fcap.
Authorized Edition. 1858. 2s.: 1859. 2s. 6d.

Sermons preached at St. Paul's Cathedral. *Authorized Edition.*
1859. Fcap. 8vo. 2s. 6d.

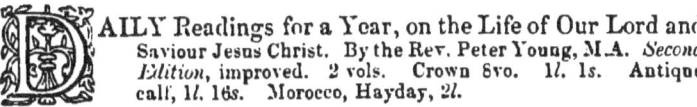

AILY Readings for a Year, on the Life of Our Lord and
Saviour Jesus Christ. By the Rev. Peter Young, M.A. *Second
Edition,* improved. 2 vols. Crown 8vo. 1l. 1s. Antique
calf, 1l. 16s. Morocco, Hayday, 2l.

Short Sunday Evening Readings, Selected and Abridged from
various Authors by the Dowager Countess of Cawdor. In large type.
8vo. 5s.

A Commentary on the Gospels for the Sundays and other Holy Days of the Christian Year. By the Rev. W. Denton, A.M., Worcester College, Oxford, and Incumbent of St. Bartholomew's, Cripplegate. 8vo. Vol. 1. Advent to Easter, 15s. Vol. II. Easter to the Sixteenth Sunday after Trinity, 14s.

Lights of the Morning: or, Meditations for every Day in the Year. From the German of Frederic Arndt. With a Preface by the Rev. W. C. Magee, D.D. Fcap. 8vo. Advent to Whitsuntide, 5s. 6d. Trinity, 5s. 6d.

The Second Adam, and the New Birth; or, the Doctrine of Baptism as contained in Holy Scripture. By the Rev. M. F. Sadler, M.A. Vicar of Bridgewater, Author of "The Sacrament of Responsibility." Third Edition, greatly enlarged. Fcap. 8vo. 4s. 6d.

The Sacrament of Responsibility; or, Testimony of the Scripture to the teaching of the Church on Holy Baptism, with especial reference to the Cases of Infants, and Answers to Objections. Sixth Edition. 6d.

Popular Illustrations of some Remarkable Events recorded in the Old Testament. By the Rev. J. F. Dawson, LL.B., Rector of Toynton. Post 8vo. 8s. 6d.

The Acts and Writings of the Apostles. By C. Pickering Clarke, M.A., late Curate of Teddington. Post 8vo. Vol. I., with Map., 7s. 6d.

The Spirit of the Hebrew Poetry. By Isaac Taylor, Esq., Author of "The Natural History of Enthusiasm," "Ultimate Civilization," &c. 8vo. 10s. 6d.

The Wisdom of the Son of David: an Exposition of the First Nine Chapters of the Book of Proverbs. Fcap. 8vo. 5s.

A Companion to the Authorized Version of the New Testament: being Explanatory Notes, together with Explanatory Observations and an Introduction. By the Rev. H. B. Hall, B.C.L. Second and cheaper Edition, revised and enlarged. Fcap. 8vo. 3s. 6d.

A History of the Church of England from the Accession of James II. to the Rise of the Bangorian Controversy in 1717. By the Rev. T. Debary, M.A. 8vo. 14s.

A Treatise on Metaphysics in Connection with Revealed Religion. By the Rev. J. H. MacMahon. 8vo. 14s.

Aids to Pastoral Visitation, selected and arranged by the Rev. H. B. Browning, M.A., Curate of St. George, Stamford. Second Edition. Fcap. 8vo. 3s. 6d.

Remarks on Certain Offices of the Church of England, popularly termed the Occasional Services. By the Rev. W. J. Dampier. 12mo. 5s.

The Sympathy of Christ. Six Readings for the Sundays in Lent, or for the Days of the Holy Week. By the Rev. W. J. Dampier, M.A., Vicar of Coggeshall. Second Edition. 18mo. 2s. 6d.

New and Standard Publications. 19

Reasons of Faith; or, the Order of the Christian Argument developed and explained. By the Rev. G. S. Drew, M.A. Fcap. 8vo. 4s. 6d.

Charles and Josiah; or, Friendly Conversations between a Churchman and a Quaker. Crown 8vo. 5s.

Papers on Preaching and Public Speaking. By a Wykehamist. Fcap. 8vo. 5s.
This volume is an enlargement and extension, with corrections, of the Papers which appeared in the "Guardian" in 1858-9.

The Speaker at Home. Chapters on Public Speaking and Reading aloud, by the Rev. J. J. Halcombe, M.A., and on the Physiology of Speech, by W. H. Stone, M.A., M.B. *Second Edition.* Fcap. 8vo. 3s. 6d.

The English Churchman's Signal. By the Writer of "A Plain Word to the Wise in Heart." Fcap. 8vo. 2s. 6d.

A Plain Word to the Wise in Heart on our Duties at Church, and on our Prayer Book. *Fourth Edition.* Sewed, 1s. 6d.

Readings on the Morning and Evening Prayer and the Litany. By J. S. Blunt. *Second Edition, enlarged.* Fcap. 8vo. 3s. 6d.

Confirmation. By J. S. Blunt, Author of "Readings on the Morning and Evening Prayer," &c. Fcap. 8vo. 3s. 6d.

Life after Confirmation. By the same Author. 18mo. 1s.

The Book of Psalms (Prayer Book Version). With Short Headings and Explanatory Notes. By the Rev. Ernest Hawkins, B.D., Prebendary of St. Paul's. *Second and cheaper Edition, revised and enlarged,* Fcap. 8vo., cloth limp, red edges, 2s. 6d.

Family Prayers:—containing Psalms, Lessons, and Prayers, for every Morning and Evening in the Week. By the Rev. Ernest Hawkins, B.D., Prebendary of St. Paul's. *Eighth Edition.* Fcap. 8vo. 1s.; sewed, 9d.

Household Prayers on Scriptural Subjects, for Four Weeks. With Forms for various occasions. By a Member of the Church of England. *Second Edition, enlarged.* 8vo. 4s. 6d.

Forms of Prayer adapted to each Day of the Week. For use in Families or Households. By the Rev. John Jebb, D.D., 8vo. 2s. 6d.

Walton's Lives of Donne, Wotton, Hooker, Herbert, and Sanderson. A New Edition, to which is now added a Memoir of Mr. Isaac Walton, by William Dowling, Esq. of the Inner Temple, Barrister-at-Law. With Illustrative Notes, numerous Portraits, and other Engravings, Index, &c. Crown 8vo. 10s. 6d. Calf antique, 15s. Morocco, 18s

The Life of Martin Luther. By H. Worsley, M.A., Rector of Easton, Suffolk. 2 vols. 8vo. 1l. 4s.

Civilization considered as a Science in Relation to its Essence, its Elements, and its End. By George Harris, F.S.A., of the Middle Temple, Barrister at Law, Author of "The Life of Lord Chancellor Hardwicke." 8vo. 12s.

The Church Hymnal, (with or without Psalms.) 12mo. Large Type, 1s. 6d. 18mo. 1s. 32mo. for Parochial Schools, 6d.
This book is now in use in every English Diocese, and is the *Authorized* Book in some of the Colonial Dioceses.

Three Lectures on Archbishop Cranmer. By the Rev. C. J. Burton, M.A., Chancellor of Carlisle. 12mo. 3s.

Church Reading: according to the method advised by Thomas Sheridan. By the Rev. J. J. Halcombe, M.A. 8vo. 3s. 6d.

The Kafir, the Hottentot, and the Frontier Farmer. Passages of Missionary Life from the Journals of the Ven. Archdeacon Merriman. Illustrated. Fcap. 8vo. 3s. 6d.

Lectures on the Tinnevelly Missions. By the Rev. Dr. Caldwell, of Edeyenkoody. Crown 8vo. 2s. 6d.

The " Cruise of the Beacon." A Narrative of a Visit to the Islands in Bass's Straits. By the Right Rev. the Bishop of Tasmania. With Illustrations. Crown 8vo. 5s.

⁎ Messrs. Bell and Daldy are agents for all the other Publications of the Society for the Propagation of the Gospel in Foreign Parts.

Authentic Memoirs of the Christian Church in China. By John Laurence de Mosheim, Chancellor of the University of Göttingen. Translated from the German. Edited, with an Introduction and notes, by Richard Gibbings, B.D., Rector of Tessauran, and Vicar of Ferbane, in the Diocese of Meath. 3s. 6d.

Giles Witherne; or, The Reward of Disobedience. A Village Tale for the Young. By the Rev. J. P. Parkinson, D.C.L. *Sixth Edition.* Illustrated by the Rev. F. W. Mann. Super-royal 16mo.
[*In the press.*

The Disorderly Family; or, the Village of R * * * *. A Tale for Young Persons. In Two Parts. By a Father. 6d.; Cloth, gilt edges, 1s.

The Offertory : the most excellent way of contributing Money for Christian Purposes. By J. H. Markland, D.C.L., F.R.S., S.A. *Second Edition, enlarged,* 2d.

BY THE REV. J. ERSKINE CLARKE, *of Derby*.

EART Music, for the Hearth-Ring; the Street-Walk; the Country Stroll; the Work-Hours; the Rest-Day; the Trouble-Time. *New Edition.* 1s. paper; 1s. 6d. cloth limp.

The Giant's Arrows. A Book for the Children of Working People. 16mo. 6d.; cloth, 1s.

Children at Church. Twelve Simple Sermons. 2 vols. 1s. each; 1s. 6d. cloth, gilt; or together in 1 vol. cloth gilt, 2s. 6d.

Little Lectures for Little Folk. 16mo. 1s.

Plain Papers on the Social Economy of the People. Fcap. 8vo. 2s. 6d.
No. 1. Recreations of the People.—No. 2. Penny Banks.—No. 3. Labourers' Clubs and Working Men's Refreshment Rooms.—No. 4. Children of the People. 6d. each.

New and Standard Publications. 21

The Devotional Library.
Edited by the Very Rev. W. F. HOOK, D.D., Dean of Chichester.

A Series of Works, original or selected from well-known Church of England Divines, published at the lowest price, and suitable, from their practical character and cheapness, for Parochial distribution.

HORT Meditations for Every Day in the Year. 2 vols. (1260 pages,) 32mo. Cloth, 5s.; calf, gilt edges, 9s. Calf antique, 12s.

In Separate Parts.

ADVENT to LENT, cloth, 1s.; limp calf, gilt edges, 2s. 6d.; LENT, cloth, 9d.; calf, 2s. 3d. EASTER, cloth, 9d.; calf, 2s. 3d. TRINITY, Part I. 1s.; calf, 2s. 6d. TRINITY, Part II. 1s.; calf, 2s. 6d.

*** *Large Paper Edition*, 4 vols. fcap. 8vo. large type. 14s. Morocco, 30s.

The Christian taught by the Church's Services. (490 pages), royal 32mo. Cloth, 2s. 6d.; calf, gilt edges, 4s. 6d. Calf antique, 6s.

In Separate Parts.

ADVENT TO TRINITY, cloth, 1s.; limp calf, gilt edges, 2s. 6d. TRINITY, cloth, 8d.; calf, 2s. 2d. MINOR FESTIVALS, 8d.; calf, 2s. 2d.

*** *Large Paper Edition*, Fcap. 8vo. large type. 6s. 6d. Calf antique, or morocco, 11s. 6d.

Devotions for Domestic Use. 32mo. cloth, 2s.; calf, gilt edges, 4s. Calf antique, 5s. 6d. Containing:—

The Common Prayer Book the best Companion in the Family as well as in the Temple. 3d.
Litanies for Domestic Use, 2d.
Family Prayers; or, Morning and Evening Services for every Day in the Week. By the Bishop of Salisbury; cloth, 6d.; calf, 2s.
Bishop Hall's Sacred Aphorisms. Selected and arranged with the Texts to which they refer. By the Rev. R. B. Exton, M.A.; cloth, 9d.

*** These are arranged together as being suitable for Domestic Use; but they may be had separately at the prices affixed.

Aids to a Holy Life. First Series. 32mo. Cloth, 1s. 6d.; calf, gilt edges, 3s. 6d. Calf antique, 5s. Containing:—

Prayers for the Young. By Dr. Hook, ½d.
Pastoral Address to a Young Communicant. By Dr. Hook, ½d.
Helps to Self-Examination. By W. F. Hook, D.D., ½d.
Directions for Spending One Day Well. By Archbishop Synge, ½d.
Rules for the Conduct of Human Life. By Archbishop Synge. 1d.
The Sum of Christianity, wherein a short and plain Account is given of the Christian Faith; Christian's Duty; Christian Prayer; Christian Sacrament. By C. Ellis, 1d.
Ejaculatory Prayer; or, the Duty of Offering up Short Prayers to God on all Occasions. By R. Cook. 2d.
Prayers for a Week. From J. Sorocold, 2d.
Companion to the Altar; being Prayers, Thanksgivings, and Meditations. Edited by Dr. Hook. Cloth, 6d.

*** Any of the above may be had for distribution at the prices affixed; they are arranged together as being suitable for Young Persons and for Private Devotion.

The Devotional Library continued.

Aids to a Holy Life. Second Series. 32mo. Cloth, 2s.; calf, gilt edges, 4s. Calf antique, 5s. 6d. Containing:—
Holy Thoughts and Prayers, arranged for Daily Use on each Day in the Week, 3d.
The Retired Christian exercised on Divine Thoughts and Heavenly Meditations. By Bishop Ken. 3d.
Penitential Reflections for the Holy Season of Lent, and other Days of Fasting and Abstinence during the Year. 6d.
The Crucified Jesus; a Devotional Commentary on the XXII and XXIII Chapters of St. Luke. By A. Horneck, D.D. 3d.
Short Reflections for every Morning and Evening during the Week. By N. Spinckes, 2d.
The Sick Man Visited; or, Meditations and Prayers for the Sick Room. By N. Spinckes, 3d.

⁎ These are arranged together as being suitable for Private Meditation and Prayer: they may be had separately at the prices affixed.

Helps to Daily Devotion. 32mo. Cloth, 8d. Containing:—
The Sum of Christianity, 1d.
Directions for spending One Day Well, ½d.
Helps to Self-Examination, ½d.
Short Reflections for Morning and Evening, 2d.
Prayers for a Week, 2d.

The History of our Lord and Saviour Jesus Christ; in Three Parts, with suitable Meditations and Prayers. By W. Reading, M.A. 32mo. Cloth, 2s.; calf, gilt edges, 4s. Calf antique, 5s. 6d.

Hall's Sacred Aphorisms. Selected and arranged with the Texts to which they refer, by the Rev. R. B. Exton, M.A. 32mo. cloth, 9d.; limp calf, gilt edges, 2s. 3d.

Devout Musings on the Book of Psalms. 2 vols. 32mo. Cloth, 5s.; calf, gilt edges, 9s.; calf antique, 12s. Or, in four parts, price 1s. each; limp calf, gilt edges, 2s. 6d.

The Church Sunday School Hymn Book. 32mo. cloth, 8d.; calf, gilt edges, 2s. 6d.

⁎ A *Large Paper Edition* for Prizes, &c. 1s. 6d.; calf, gilt edges, 3s. 6d.

HORT Meditations for Every Day in the Year. Edited by the Very Rev. W. F. Hook, D. D. *New Edition.* 4 vols. fcap. 8vo., large type, 14s.; morocco, 30s.

The Christian taught by the Church's Services. Edited by the Very Rev. W. F. Hook, D. D. *New Edition*, fcap. 8vo. large type. 6s. 6d. Antique calf, or morocco, 11s. 6d.

Holy Thoughts and Prayers, arranged for Daily Use on each Day of the Week, according to the stated Hours of Prayer. *Fifth Edition,* with additions. 16mo. Cloth, red edges, 2s.; calf, gilt edges, 3s.

A Companion to the Altar. Being Prayers, Thanksgivings, and Meditations, and the Office of the Holy Communion. Edited by the Very Rev. W. F. Hook, D.D. *Second Edition.* Handsomely printed in red and black. 32mo. Cloth, red edges, 2s. Morocco, 3s. 6d.

The Church Sunday School Hymn Book. Edited by W. F. Hook, D.D. *Large paper.* Cloth, 1s. 6d.; calf, gilt edges, 3s. 6d.

⁎ For cheap editions of the above Five Books, see List of the Devotional Library.

EDUCATIONAL BOOKS.

Bibliotheca Classica.

A Series of Greek and Latin Authors. With English Notes. 8vo. Edited by various Scholars, under the direction of G Long, Esq., M.A., Classical Lecturer of Brighton College: and the late Rev. A. J. Macleane, M.A., Head Master of King Edward's School, Bath.

ESCHYLUS. By F. A. Paley, M.A. 18s.

Cicero's Orations. Edited by G. Long, M.A. 4 vols.
Vol. I. 16s.; Vol. II. 14s; Vol. III. 16s.; Vol. IV. 18s.

Demosthenes. By R. Whiston, M.A., Head Master of Rochester Grammar School. Vol. I. 16s. Vol. II. *preparing.*

Euripides. By F. A. Paley, M.A. 3 vols. 16s. each.

Herodotus. By J. W. Blakesley, B.D., late Fellow and Tutor of Trinity College, Cambridge. 2 vols. 32s.

Hesiod. By F. A. Paley, M. A. 10s. 6d.

Homer. By F. A. Paley, M. A. Vol. I. [*Preparing.*]

Horace. By A. J. Macleane, M.A. 18s.

Juvenal and Persius. By A. J. Macleane, M.A. 14s.

Plato. By W. H. Thompson, M.A. Vol. I. [*Preparing.*]

Sophocles. By F. H. Blaydes, M.A. Vol. I. 18s. Vol. II. *preparing.*

Terence. By E. St. J. Parry, M.A., Balliol College, Oxford. 18s.

Virgil. By J. Conington, M.A., Professor of Latin at Oxford.
Vol. I. containing the Bucolics and Georgics. 12s. Vol. II. *nearly ready.*

Grammar-School Classics.

A Series of Greek and Latin Authors. Newly Edited, with English Notes for Schools. Fcap. 8vo.

CAESARIS Commentarii de Bello Gallico. *Second Edition.* By G. Long, M.A. 5s. 6d.

Caesar de Bello Gallico, Books 1 to 3. With English Notes for Junior Classes. By G. Long, M.A. 2s. 6d.

M. Tullii Ciceronis Cato Major, Sive de Senectute, Laelius, Sive de Amicitia, et Epistolae Selectae. By G. Long, M.A. 4s. 6d.

Quinti Horatii Flacci Opera Omnia. By A. J. Macleane, 6s. 6d.

Juvenalis Satirae XVI. By H. Prior, M.A. (Expurgated Edition). 4s. 6d.

Grammar-School Classics continued.

P. Ovidii Nasonis Fastorum Libri Sex. By F. A. Paley. 5s.

C. Sallustii Crispi Catilina et Jugurtha. By G. Long, M.A. 5s.

Taciti Germania et Agricola. By P. Frost, M.A. 3s. 6d.

Xenophontis Anabasis, with Introduction; Geographical and other Notes, Itinerary, and Three Maps compiled from recent surveys. By J. F. Macmichael, B.A. *New Edition.* 5s.

Xenophontis Cyropaedia. By G. M. Gorham, M.A., late Fellow of Trinity College, Cambridge. 6s.

Uniform with the above.

The New Testament in Greek. With English Notes and Prefaces by J. F. Macmichael, B.A. 730 pages. 7s. 6d.

Cambridge Greek and Latin Texts.

THIS series is intended to supply for the use of Schools and Students cheap and accurate editions of the Classics, which shall be superior in mechanical execution to the small German editions now current in this country, and more convenient in form.

The texts of the *Bibliotheca Classica* and *Grammar School Classics*, so far as they have been published, will be adopted. These editions have taken their place amongst scholars as valuable contributions to the Classical Literature of this country, and are admitted to be good examples of the judicious and practical nature of English scholarship; and as the editors have formed their texts from a careful examination of the best editions extant, it is believed that no texts better for general use can be found.

The volumes will be well printed at the Cambridge University Press, in a 16mo. size, and will be issued at short intervals.

AESCHYLUS, ex novissima recensione F. A. Paley. 3s.

Caesar de Bello Gallico, recensuit G. Long, A.M. 2s.

Cicero de Senectute et de Amicitia et Epistolae Selectae, recensuit G. Long, A.M. 1s. 6d.

Euripides, ex recensione F. A. Paley, A. M. 3 vols. 3s. 6d. each.

Herodotus, recensuit J. W. Blakesley, S.T.B. 2 vols. 7s.

Horatius, ex recensione A. J. Macleane, A.M. 2s. 6d.

Lucretius, recognovit H. A. J. Munro, A.M. 2s. 6d.

Sallusti Crispi Catilina et Jugurtha, recognovit G. Long, A.M. 1s. 6d.

Thucydides, recensuit J. G. Donaldson, S.T.P. 2 vols. 7s.

Vergilius, ex recensione J. Conington, A.M. 3s. 6d.

Xenophontis Anabasis recensuit J. F. Macmichael, A.B. 2s. 6d.

Novum Testamentum Graecum Textus Stephanici, 1550. Accedunt variae Lectiones editionum Bezae, Elzeviri, Lachmanni, Tischendorfii, Tregellesii, curante F. H. Scrivener, A.M. 4s. 6d.

Also, on 4to. writing paper, for MSS. notes. Half bound, gilt top, 21s.

Foreign Classics.

With English Notes for Schools. Uniform with the GRAMMAR SCHOOL CLASSICS. Fcap. 8vo.

AVENTURES de Télémaque, par Fénelon. Edited by C. J. Delille. *Second Edition, revised.* 4s. 6d.

Histoire de Charles XII. par Voltaire. Edited by L. Direy. *Second Edition, revised.* 3s. 6d.

Select Fables of La Fontaine. *Third Edition, revised.* Edited by F. Gasc, M.A. 3s.

"None need now be afraid to introduce this eminently French author, either on account of the difficulty of translating him, or the occasional licence of thought and expression in which he indulges. The renderings of idiomatic passages are unusually good, and the purity of English perfect."—*Athenæum*.

Picciola, by X. B. Saintine. Edited by Dr. Dubuc. 3s. 6d.

This interesting story has been selected with the intention of providing for schools and young persons a good specimen of contemporary French literature, free from the solecisms which are frequently met with in writers of a past age.

Schiller's Wallenstein, complete Text. With Notes, &c. by Dr. A. Buchheim. 6s 6d.

Classical Tables. 8vo.

NOTABILIA Quædam: or, the principal tenses of such Irregular Greek Verbs and such elementary Greek, Latin, and French Constructions as are of constant occurrence. 1s. 6d.

Greek Accidence. By the Rev. P. Frost, M. A. 1s.

Latin Accidence. By the Rev. P. Frost, M. A. 1s.

Latin Versification. 1s.

The Principles of Latin Syntax. 1s.

Homeric Dialect: its leading Forms and Peculiarities. By J. S. Baird, T.C.D. 1s. 6d.

A Catalogue of Greek Verbs, Irregular and Defective; their leading formations, tenses in use, and dialectic inflexions; with a copious Appendix, containing Paradigms for conjugation, Rules for formation of tenses, &c. &c. By J. S. Baird, T.C.D. *New Edition, revised.* 3s. 6d.

Richmond Rules to form the Ovidian Distich, &c. By J. Tate, M.A. *New Edition, revised.* 1s. 6d.

AN Atlas of Classical Geography, containing 24 Maps; constructed by W. Hughes, and edited by G. Long. *New Edition*, with coloured outlines, and an Index of Places. 12s. 6d.

A Grammar School Atlas of Classical Geography. The Maps constructed by W. Hughes, and edited by G. Long. Imp. 8vo. 5s.

First Classical Maps, with Chronological Tables of Grecian and Roman History, Tables of Jewish Chronology, and a Map of Palestine. By the Rev. J. Tate, M.A. *Third Edition.* Imp. 8vo. 7s. 6d.

The Choephorae of Æschylus and its Scholia. Revised and interpreted by J. F. Davies, Esq., B.A., Trin. Coll., Dublin. 8vo. 7s. 6d.

Homer and English Metre. An Essay on the Translating of the Iliad and Odyssey. With a Literal Rendering in the Spenserian Stanza of the First Book of the Odyssey, and Specimens of the Iliad. William G. T. Barter, Esq., Author of " A Literal Translation, in Spenserian Stanza, of the Iliad of Homer." Crown 8vo. 6s. 6d.

Auxilia Graeca: containing Forms of Parsing and Greek Trees, the Greek Prepositions, Rules of Accentuation, Greek Idioms, &c. &c. By the Rev. H. Fowler, M.A. 12mo. 3s. 6d.

A Latin Grammar. By T. Hewitt Key, M.A., F.R.S., Professor of Comparative Grammar, and Head Master of the Junior School, in University College. Third Edition, revised. Post 8vo. 8s.

A Short Latin Grammar, for Schools. By T. H. Key, M.A., F.R.S. Third Edition. Post 8vo. 3s. 6d.

Latin Accidence. Consisting of the Forms, and intended to prepare boys for Key's Short Latin Grammar. Post 8vo. 2s.

A First Cheque Book for Latin Verse Makers. By the Rev. F. Gretton, Stamford Free Grammar School. 1s. 6d. Key, 2s. 6d.

Reddenda; or Passages with Parallel Hints for translation into Latin Prose and Verse. By the Rev. F. E. Gretton. Crown 8vo. 4s. 6d.

Rules for the Genders of Latin Nouns, and the Perfects and Supines of Verbs; with hints on Construing, &c. By H. Haines, M.A. 1s. 6d.

Latin Prose Lessons. By the Rev. A. Church, M.A., one of the Masters of Merchant Taylors' School. Fcap. 8vo. 2s. 6d.

Materials for Latin Prose Composition. By the Rev. P. Frost, M.A., St. John's College, Cambridge. Second Edition. 12mo. 2s. 6d. Key, 4s.

Materials for Greek Prose Composition. By the Rev. P. Frost, M.A. Fcap. 8vo. 3s. 6d. Key to ditto. 5s.

The Works of Virgil, closely rendered into English Rhythm, and illustrated from British Poets of the 16th, 17th, and 18th Centuries. By the Rev. R. C. Singleton, M.A. 2 vols. post 8vo. 18s.

Quintus Horatius Flaccus. Illustrated with 50 Engravings from the Antique. Fcap. 8vo. 5s. Morocco, 9s.

Selections from Ovid: Amores, Tristia, Heroides, Metamorphoses. With English Notes, by the Rev. A. J. Macleane, M.A. Fcap. 8vo. 3s. 6d.

Sabrinae Corolla in hortulis Regiae Scholae Salopiensis contexuerunt tres viri floribus legendis. *Editio Altera.* 8vo. 12s. Morocco, 21s.

Rudimentary Art Instruction for Artisans and others, and for Schools. FREEHAND OUTLINE. Part I. OUTLINE FROM OUTLINE, or from the Flat. 3s. Part II. OUTLINE FROM OBJECTS, or from the Round. 4s. By John Bell, Sculptor. Oblong 4to.

A Graduated Series of Exercises in Elementary Algebra, with an Appendix containing Papers of Miscellaneous Examples. Designed for the Use of Schools. By the Rev. G. F. Wright, M.A., Mathematical Master at Wellington College. Crown 8vo. 3s. 6d.

The Elements of Euclid. Books I.—VI. XI. 1—21; XII. 1, 2; a new text, based on that of Simson, with Exercises. Edited by H. J Hose, late Mathematical Master of Westminster School. Fcap. 4s. 6d.

Educational Books. 27

A Graduated Series of Exercises on the Elements of Euclid:
Books I.—VI.; XI. 1—21; XII. 1, 2. Selected and arranged by Henry
J. Hose, M.A. 12mo. 1s.

The Enunciations and Figures belonging to the Propositions in
the First Six and part of the Eleventh Books of Euclid's Elements,
(usually read in the Universities,) prepared for Students in Geometry
By the Rev. J. Brasse, D.D. *New Edition.* Fcap. 8vo. 1s. On cards,
in case, 5s. 6d.; without the Figures, 6d.

A Compendium of Facts and Formulæ in Pure and Mixed
Mathematics. For the use of Mathematical Students. By G. R.
Smalley, B.A., F.R.A.S. Fcap. 8vo. 3s. 6d.

A Table of Anti-Logarithms; containing to seven places of decimals, natural numbers, answering to all Logarithms from ·00001 to ·99999;
and an improved table of Gauss' Logarithms, by which may be found the
Logarithm of the sum or difference of two quantities. With an Appendix,
containing a Table of Annuities for three Joint Lives at 3 per cent. Carlisle. By H. E. Filipowski. *Third Edition.* 8vo. 15s.

Handbook of the Slide Rule: showing its applicability to Arithmetic, including Interest and Annuities; Mensuration, including Land
Surveying. With numerous Examples and useful Tables. By W. H.
Bayley, H. M. East India Civil Service. 12mo. 6s.

The Mechanics of Construction; including the Theories on the
Strength of Materials, Roofs, Arches, and Suspension Bridges. With
numerous Examples. By Stephen Fenwick, Esq., of the Royal Military
Academy, Woolwich. 8vo. 12s.

A NEW FRENCH COURSE, BY MONS. F. E. A. GASC, M.A.
French Master at Brighton College.

LE Petit Compagnon: a French Talk-book for Little
Children. With 52 Illustrations. 16mo. 2s. 6d.

First French Book; being a New, Practical, and Easy
Method of Learning the Elements of the French Language.
New Edition. Fcap. 8vo. 1s. 6d.

French Fables, for Beginners, in Prose, with an Index of all the
words at the end of the work. Fcap. 8vo. 2s.

Second French Book; being a Grammar and Exercise Book, on
a new and practical plan, exhibiting the chief peculiarities of the French
Language, as compared with the English, and intended as a sequel to the
"First French Book." Fcap. 8vo. 2s. 6d.

A Key to the First and Second French Books. Fcap. 8vo. 3s. 6d.

Histoires Amusantes et Instructives; or, Selections of Complete
Stories from the best French Authors, who have written for the Young.
With English Notes. *New Edition.* Fcap. 8vo. 2s. 6d.

Practical Guide to Modern French Conversation: containing:—
I. The most current and useful Phrases in Every-Day Talk; II. Everybody's Necessary Questions and Answers in Travel-Talk. Fcap. 2s. 6d.

French Poetry for the Young. With English Notes, and preceded by a few plain Rules of French Prosody. Fcap. 8vo. 2s.

Materials for French Prose Composition; or, Selections from the
best English Prose Writers. With copious Foot Notes, and Hints for
Idiomatic Renderings. *New Edition.* Fcap. 8vo. 4s. 6d. Key, 6s.

THE French Drama; being a Selection of the best Tragedies and Comedies of Molière, Racine, P. Corneille, T. Corneille, and Voltaire. With Arguments in English at the head of each scene, and Notes, Critical and Explanatory, by A. Gombert. 18mo. Sold separately at 1s. each. Half-bound, 1s. 6d. each.

COMEDIES BY MOLIERE.

Le Misanthrope.
L'Avare.
Le Bourgeois Gentilhomme.
Le Tartuffe.
Le Malade Imaginaire.
Les Femmes Savantes.
Les Fourberies de Scapin.

Les Précieuses Ridicules.
L'Ecole des Femmes.
L'Ecole des Maris.
Le Médecin Malgré Lui.
M. de Pourceaugnac.
Amphitryon.

TRAGEDIES, &c. BY RACINE.

La Thébaïde, ou les Frères Ennemis.
Alexandre le Grand.
Andromaque.
Les Plaideurs, (*Com.*)
Britannicus.
Bérénice.

Bajazet.
Mithridate.
Iphigénie.
Phédre.
Esther.
Athalie.

TRAGEDIES, &c. BY P. CORNEILLE.

Le Cid.
Horace.
Cinna.
Polyeucte.

Pompée.

BY T. CORNEILLE.

Ariane.

PLAYS BY VOLTAIRE.

Brutus.
Zaire.
Alzire.
Oreste.

Le Fanatisme.
Mérope.
La Mort de César.
Semiramis.

Le Nouveau Trésor : or, French Student's Companion : designed to facilitate the Translation of English into French at Sight. *Thirteenth Edition,* with Additions. By M. E*** S*****. 12mo. Roan, 3s. 6d.

A Test-Book for Students: Examination Papers for Students preparing for the Universities or for Appointments in the Army and Civil Service, and arranged for General Use in Schools. By the Rev. Thomas Stantial, M.A., Head Master of the Grammar School, Bridgwater. Part I.—History and Geography. 2s. 6d. Part II.—Language and Literature. 2s. 6d. Part III.—Mathematical Science. 2s. 6d. Part IV.—Physical Science. 1s. 6d. Or in 1 vol., Crown 8vo., 7s. 6d.

Tables of Comparative Chronology, illustrating the division of Universal History into Ancient, Mediæval, and Modern History; and containing a System of Combinations, distinguished by a particular type, to assist the Memory in retaining Dates. By W. E. Bickmore and the Rev. C. Bickmore, M.A. *Third Edition.* 4to. 5s.

A Course of Historical and Chronological Instruction. By W. E. Bickmore. 2 Parts. 12mo. 3s. 6d. each.

A Practical Synopsis of English History : or, A General Summary of Dates and Events for the use of Schools, and Candidates for Public Examinations. By Arthur Bowes. *Third Edition,* enlarged. 8vo. 2s.

Educational Books.

The 1862 Edition of Under Government: an Official Key to the Civil Service, and Guide for Candidates seeking Appointments under the Crown. By J. C. Parkinson, Inland Revenue, Somerset House. *New Edition.* Cr. 8vo. 3s. 6d.

Government Examinations; being a Companion to "Under Government," and a Guide to the Civil Service Examinations. By J. C. Parkinson. Crown 8vo. 2s. 6d.

The Student's Text-Book of English and General History, from B. C. 100 to the present time. With Genealogical Tables, and a Sketch of the English Constitution. By D. Beale. *Sixth Edition.* Post 8vo. Sewed, 2s. Cloth, 2s. 6d.

"This is very much in advance of most works we have seen devoted to similar purposes. We can award very high praise to a volume which may prove invaluable to teachers and taught."—*Athenæum.*

The Elements of the English Language for Schools and Colleges. By Ernest Adams, Ph. D. University College School. *New Edition, enlarged, and improved.* Crown 8vo. 4s. 6d.

The Geographical Text-Book; a Practical Geography, calculated to facilitate the study of that useful science, by a constant reference to the Blank Maps. By M. E... S..... 12mo. 2s.
II. The Blank Maps done up separately. 4to. 2s. coloured.

The Manual of Book-keeping; by an Experienced Clerk. 12mo. *Eighth Edition.* 4s.

Double Entry Elucidated. By B. W. Foster. 4to. 8s. 6d.

Penmanship, Theoretical and Practical, Illustrated and Explained By B. F. Foster. 12mo. *New Edition.* 2s. 6d.

Goldsmith's (J.) Copy Books: five sorts, large, text, round, small, and mixed. Post 4to. on fine paper. 6s. per dozen.

The Young Ladies' School Record: or, Register of Studies and conduct. 12mo. 6d.

Welchman on the Thirty-nine Articles of the Church of England, with Scriptural Proofs, &c. 18mo. 2s. or interleaved for Students, 3s.

Bishop Jewel's Apology for the Church of England, with his famous Epistle on the Council of Trent, and a Memoir. 32mo. 2s.

A Short Explanation of the Epistles and Gospels of the Christian Year, with Questions for Schools. Royal 32mo. 2s. 6d.; calf, 4s. 6d.

Manual of Astronomy: a Popular Treatise on Descriptive, Physical, and Practical Astronomy. By John Drew, F.R.A.S. *Second Edition.* Fcap. 8vo. 5s.

The First Book of Botany. Being a Plain and Brief Introduction to that Science for Schools and Young Persons. By Mrs. Loudon. Illustrated with 36 Wood Engravings. *Second Edition.* 18mo. 1s.

English Poetry for Classical Schools; or, Florilegium Poeticum Anglicanum. 12mo. 1s. 6d.

BELL AND DALDY'S ILLUSTRATED SCHOOL BOOKS.
Royal 16mo.

CHOOL Primer. 6d.
School Reader. 1s. [*Shortly*.
Poetry Book for Schools. 1s.

COURSE OF INSTRUCTION FOR THE YOUNG, BY HORACE GRANT.

XERCISES for the Improvement of the Senses; for Young Children. 18mo. 1s. 6d.
Geography for Young Children. *New Edition*. 18mo. 2s.
Arithmetic for Young Children. *New Edition*. 18mo. 1s. 6d.
Arithmetic. Second Stage. *New Edition*. 18mo. 3s.

PERIODICALS.

OTES and Queries: a Medium of Intercommunication for Literary Men, Artists, Antiquaries, Genealogists, &c. Published every Saturday. 4to. 4d., stamped, 5d. Vols. I. to XII. Second Series now ready, 10s. 6d. each.
 *** General Index to the First Series, 5s.
———— Second Series. Sewed 5s.; cloth 5s. 6d.

The Monthly Medley for Happy Homes. A New Miscellany for Children. Conducted by the Rev. J. Erskine Clarke. Price 1d. Volumes for 1860 and 1861, 1s. 6d. each.

The Parish Magazine. Edited by J. Erskine Clarke, M.A., Derby. Monthly, price 1d. Volumes for 1859, 1860, and 1861, 1s. 6d. and 2s. each.

The Mission Field: a Monthly Record of the Proceedings of the Society for the Propagation of the Gospel. Vols. II. to VI. post 8vo. 3s. each. (Vol. I. is out of print.) Continued in Numbers, 2d. each.

The Gospel Missionary. Published for the Society for the Propagation of the Gospel in Foreign Parts, Monthly at ½d. Vols. II. to XI. in cloth, 1s. each. (Vol. I. is out of print.)

Missions to the Heathen; being Records of the Progress of the Efforts made by the Society for the Propagation of the Gospel in Foreign Parts for the Conversion of the Heathen. Published occasionally in a cheap form for distribution, at prices varying from 1d. to 1s. 6d. each. Nos. 1 to 43 are already published.

Church in the Colonies, consisting chiefly of Journals by the Colonial Bishops of their Progress and Special Visitations. Published occasionally at prices varying from 2d. to 1s. 6d. each. Nos. 1 to 37 are already published.

CLARKE'S COMMERCIAL COPY-BOOKS.
Price 4d. A liberal allowance to Schools and Colleges.

The FIRST COPY-BOOK contains *elementary turns*, with a broad mark like a T, which divides a well-formed turn into two equal parts. This exercise enables the learner to judge of *form, distance, and proportion*.

The SECOND contains *large-hand letters*, and the means by which such letters may be properly combined; the joinings in writing being probably as difficult to learn as the form of each character. This book also gives the whole alphabet, not in separate letters, but rather as one *word;* and, at the end of the alphabet, the difficult letters are repeated so as to render the writing of the pupil more thorough and *uniform*.

The THIRD contains additional *large-hand practice*.

The FOURTH contains *large-hand words*, commencing with *unflourished* capitals; and the words being short, the capitals in question receive the attention they demand. As Large, and Extra Large-text, to which the fingers of the learner are not equal, have been dispensed with in this series, the popular objection of having *too many Copy-books* for the pupil to drudge through, is now fairly met. When letters are very large, the scholar cannot compass them without stopping to change the position of his hand, which *destroys* the *freedom* which such writing is intended to promote.

The FIFTH contains the essentials of a useful kind of *small-hand*. There are first, as in large-hand, five easy letters of the alphabet, forming four copies, which of course are repeated. Then follows the remainder of the alphabet, with the difficult characters alluded to. The letters in this hand, especially the *a, c, d, g, o*, and *q*, are so formed that when the learner will have to correspond, his writing will not appear stiff. The copies in this book are not *mere Large-hand reduced*.

The SIXTH contains *small-hand copies*, with instructions as to the manner in which the pupil should hold his pen, so that when he leaves school he may not merely have some facility in copying, but really possess the information on the subject of writing which he may need at any future time.

The SEVENTH contains the foundation for a style of *small-hand*, adapted to females, *moderately pointed*.

The EIGHTH contains copies for females; and the holding of the pen is, of course, the subject to which they specially relate.

This Series is specially adapted for those who are preparing for a commercial life. It is generally found when a boy leaves school that his writing is of such a character that it is some months before it is available for book-keeping or accounts. The special object of this Series of Copy-Books is to form his writing in such a style that he may be put to the work of a counting-house at once. By following this course from the first the writing is kept free and legible, whilst it avoids unnecessary flourishing.

Specimens of hand-writing after a short course may be seen on application to the Publishers.

BELL AND DALDY'S

POCKET VOLUMES.
A SERIES OF SELECT WORKS OF FAVOURITE AUTHORS.

THE intention of the Publishers is to produce a Series of Volumes adapted for general reading, moderate in price, compact and elegant in form, and executed in a style fitting them to be permanently preserved.

They do not profess to compete with the so-called cheap volumes. They believe that a cheapness which is attained by the use of inferior type and paper, and absence of editorial care, and which results in volumes that no one cares to keep, is a false cheapness. They desire rather to produce books superior in quality, and relatively as cheap.

Each volume will be carefully revised by a competent editor, and printed at the Chiswick Press, on fine paper, with new type and ornaments and initial letters specially designed for the series.

The *Pocket Volumes* will include all classes of Literature, both copyright and non-copyright;—Biography, History, Voyages, Travels, Poetry, sacred and secular, Books of Adventure and Fiction. They will include Translations of Foreign Books, and also such American Literature as may be considered worthy of adoption.

The Publishers desire to respect the moral claims of authors who cannot secure legal copyright in this country, and to remunerate equitably those whose works they may reprint.

The books will be issued at short intervals, in paper covers, at various prices, from 1s. to 3s. 6d., and in cloth, top edge gilt, at 6d. per volume extra, in half morocco, Roxburgh style, at 1s. extra, in antique or best plain morocco (Hayday), at 4s. extra.

Now Ready.
The Sketch-Book. By Washington Irving. 3s.
White's Natural History of Selborne. 3s.
Coleridge's Poems. 2s. 6d.
The Robin Hood Ballads. 2s. 6d.
The Midshipman. By Capt. Basil Hall, R.N. 3s.
The Lieutenant and Commander. By the same Author. 3s.
Southey's Life of Nelson. 2s. 6d.
George Herbert's Poems. 2s.
George Herbert's Works. 3s.
Longfellow's Poems. 2s. 6d.
Lamb's Tales from Shakspeare. 2s. 6d.
Milton's Paradise Lost. 2s. 6d.
Milton's Paradise Regained and other Poems. 2s. 6d.

Preparing.
Sea Songs and Ballads. By Charles Dibdin, and others.
Burns's Poems.
Burns's Songs.
Walton's Complete Angler. Illustrated.
The Conquest of India. By Capt. Basil Hall, R.N.
Walton's Lives of Donne, Wotton, Hooker, &c.
Gray's Poems.
Goldsmith's Poems.
Goldsmith's Vicar of Wakefield.
Henry Vaughan's Poems.
And others.

CHISWICK PRESS:—PRINTED BY WHITTINGHAM AND WILKINS, TOOKS COURT, CHANCERY LANE.

www.ingramcontent.com/pod-product-compliance
Lightning Source LLC
Chambersburg PA
CBHW021953220426
43663CB00007B/802